Metaprogramming GPUs
with Sh

Metaprogramming GPUs
with Sh

Michael McCool

Stefanus Du Toit

University of Waterloo, Ontario, Canada

CRC Press
Taylor & Francis Group
Boca Raton London New York

CRC Press is an imprint of the
Taylor & Francis Group, an **informa** business

AN A K PETERS BOOK

CRC Press
Taylor & Francis Group
6000 Broken Sound Parkway NW, Suite 300
Boca Raton, FL 33487-2742

First issued in hardback 2019

© 2004 by Taylor & Francis Group, LLC
CRC Press is an imprint of Taylor & Francis Group, an Informa business

No claim to original U.S. Government works

ISBN-13: 978-1-56881-229-8 (pbk)
ISBN-13: 978-1-138-42809-6 (hbk)

Visit the Taylor & Francis Web site at
http://www.taylorandfrancis.com

and the CRC Press Web site at
http://www.crcpress.com

Library of Congress Cataloging-in-Publication Data

Congress Control Number is 2004053399.

Contents

List of Tables

List of Listings

Preface

What is Sh, anyway? Is it a language, or an API? It's both: an API for a powerful metaprogramming system that is indistinguishable from a purpose-built language. Sh is as expressive as a special-purpose GPU shading or programming language. In addition, its close integration with C++ and capacity for dynamic, program-driven generation of optimized code makes many advanced programming techniques not only possible, but straightforward.

Sh allows you to program both your application and the GPU simultaneously in one language: C++. Sh programs act like extensions of the host application. No annoying "glue code" is required; binding is handled automatically and transparently. All of the abstraction and modularity capabilities of C++ are also available for use in Sh programs. Sh manages textures and uniform parameters as well as shader code, so you can encapsulate data representations as well as programs, and employ a modular, object-oriented approach to GPU programming. Want a special compressed texture representation? No problem. Pack the data into a supported Sh texture type, wrap the decompression shader code in a class supporting the same interface as other Sh texture objects, and you can use your new texture representation anywhere a regular Sh texture can be used. Want to create an abstract object-oriented encapsulation of arbitrary reflectance models, and hide the parameters of those models when they are used in shaders? No problem; in fact, we use this as an example.

There's more. Because Sh programs are defined and optimized at runtime, you can easily generate and manipulate code on the fly. Sh has operators for manipulating programs as first-class objects, so large programs can be built out of small, modular pieces under the application's control, and complex shaders can be specialized. Sh can even generate code for the host CPU on the fly, enabling (for instance), dynamically tuned inner loops or the implementation of complex algorithms using a generator program.

Although Sh is powerful, we have tried to make it easy to learn and understand. Sh programs look and act like functions, and Sh parameters act like external variables that are bound to Sh programs by the usual scope rules of C++. This illusion, however, is a conscious choice supported by a powerful and non-trivial runtime system—which we describe in detail in this book.

The Sh system was developed over a number of years in the Computer Graphics Lab at the University of Waterloo and has gone through several iterations. It started out as part of a system called SMASH, which was split into two projects: a GPU simulator project called Sm (which is still ongoing) and the subject of this book, a high-level metaprogramming interface called Sh.

Zheng Qin implemented the initial prototype of Sh, which was the subject of her M.Math thesis and a paper at Graphics Hardware in 2002. The current implementation was reengineered by Stefanus Du Toit to be robust enough for use in practical applications. It took the best ideas from the prototype but also took a different approach to some tasks to resolve certain issues. In particular, the new implementation builds an intermediate representation of a program object directly as a sequence of instructions rather than first building an explicit parse tree as the prototype did. We depend on our own optimizer to remove redundant statements generated by constructors, rather than trying to do this optimization directly in C++. While, in general, we tried to keep the new implementation simple, we also exploited code generation and selective use of templates (where necessary) to reduce redundancy. This greatly reduced complexity; at the same level of capability, the new system was one-fourth the size of the prototype.

Within two months, the new implementation was producing code for the Sm simulator at the same level as the previous implementation. We have since added a modular backend system to target different GPUs, a backend to generate code for the CPU, a buffer management system for textures, a stream abstraction and shader algebra, a collection of shader kernels, and many other extensions. We are currently adding many more capabilities and optimizations, such as a pass scheduler and multipass virtualization. The stream programming and buffer management support in Sh is under rapid evolution (tracking the evolution of GPUs themselves) and a more powerful optimizer is under development. However, we have decided that the core system is stable enough to document it and release it for others to use.

Besides Zheng Qin and Stefanus Du Toit, several other people have contributed to the development of Sh. Kevin Moule implemented the just-in-time gcc backend. Tiberiu Popa is working on a multipass scheduler and implemented the Julia set shader showcased in this book. Bryan Chan implemented the shader kernel library, the shader algebra demos, noise functions (in particular the non-trivial Worley noise functions), and many other utility functions. He also provided proofreading and feedback on the documentation. Gabriel Renaud implemented the initial version of the matrix library. Jack Wang improved the matrix library and implemented a quaternion library. Gabriel Moreno-Fortuny implemented some stream processing test cases and is currently working on a path tracer. Zaid Mian did a lot of testing and implemented subsurface scattering as part of a course project. Ju-Lian Kwan did more testing and implemented some tone mapping operators. Sylvain Vasseur has implemented various shaders, Edwin Vane has implemented cloud volume rendering using Sh, and Filip Špaček has done a large amount of testing as well as implementing matrix light transport. He has also helped with proofreading the documentation. Generally, the members of the Computer Graphics Lab at the University of Waterloo are to be thanked for supporting this project. Finally, we would like to thank Alice Peters and Klaus Peters for agreeing to take on this complex book project and for being patient with authors who were trying to simultaneously write code and words.

The development of Sh was funded by a generous grant from Communications and Information Technology Ontario (CITO) and ATI, as well as hardware donations from both ATI and NVIDIA, grants from the National Science and Engineering Research Council of Canada (NSERC), and a grant from the Canadian Foundation for Innovation (CFI). The Computer Graphics Lab at the University of Waterloo is also funded by the Bell University Labs initiative.

This book is a tutorial, a user guide, a reference manual, and a guide to the technology behind Sh. We hope you will find it and Sh useful.

Michael McCool
Stefanus Du Toit

May 15, 2004

Part I

Introduction

Chapter 1

Overview

Any sufficiently advanced technology
is indistinguishable from magic.

Arthur C. Clarke

Sh is a high-level embedded programming language capable of dynamically generating optimized GPU and CPU programs. It is a real-time graphics shading language whose parser is implemented using C++ operator overloading. It is also an advanced C++ toolkit for (meta)-programming GPUs and CPUs for general-purpose applications using the stream processing computational model. Soon, and without significant change to the base language, we plan to make it an object-oriented high-level graphics programming interface and a parallel programming language, too.

Although this sounds exotic and complex, the real problem is with English, not Sh. Sh is something new; there just isn't a word yet for what it is, exactly, so we will interchangeably use the terms "language," "system," and "toolkit." However, we hope to demonstrate in this book that Sh is easy and straightforward to use and provides a simple interface to surprisingly powerful functionality. Sh provides a clean and common interface to shader programming on GPUs, general-purpose CPU and GPU stream programming, and dynamic CPU and GPU metaprogramming (generative programming, to be more precise: the ability of one program to build another).

Writing a shader or stream function in Sh is not much more difficult than writing a C++ function or class definition. Sh *looks* simple because it automates many tasks, such as buffer management and parameter binding, that have made it difficult and complex to perform GPU programming in the past. We tried very hard to provide a conceptual model that is as close as possible to what C++ programmers expect and to integrate Sh well with C++ scope rules, in particular. Sh also (very selectively) incorporates some powerful ideas from

3

functional programming to provide a stream computing model, but provides at its core a comfortable imperative programming model. A language is a user interface, and we have tried to build the simplest and cleanest user interface to GPU programming and metaprogramming that we could.

The surface simplicity of the Sh system is an intentional design choice, based on a specific conceptual model of encapsulated remote procedure calls. The implementation of the conceptual programming model in Sh is transparently supported by an extensive runtime bookkeeping system. This system automatically tracks and manages the web of dependencies between buffers, textures, parameters, shader code, and even CPU computation. Our ultimate goal is to address the *whole* problem of programming GPUs and exploiting their power and to eventually extend the *same* programming model to other targets as well, such as parallel machines.

Sh looks at first like a standard graphics library, with matrices, points, and vectors, and you can use it that way if you want. We call this "immediate mode." But you can also capture sequences of operations in a "retained mode," much like a display list (if you are a graphics person) or a dynamic function definition (if you are not). Sh can then compile these operations for later execution on a GPU or CPU. This generates an optimized program object that can either be loaded into a GPU shading unit for use with real-time graphics applications or can be applied as a parallel computation to streams of data for high-performance, general-purpose applications.

The Sh compilation engine has its own optimizer and supports a loosely bound, modular backend system. The runtime engine tries to make best use of the available hardware and graphics API features but without burdening the programmer with low-level details. Since Sh manages buffers and textures as well as programs, Sh makes it much more convenient to program multipass algorithms and to encapsulate data representations than is possible with other approaches. For general-purpose numerical or scientific applications, it is also possible to use Sh to express and execute a computation without making any graphics API calls.

Sh programs, which are dynamically generated and optimized, can run on the GPU or CPU but act like extensions of the host application. In particular, Sh programs mimic C++ functions and Sh textures mimic arrays. Uniform parameters to Sh programs are just variables defined external to program definitions, and textures are just an array-valued parameter type. The C++ scope rules control which parameters and textures get bound to which programs, while the Sh runtime system manages updates of uniform parameters, buffers, and binding of texture units. Because Sh bindings follow C++ scope rules, C++ modularity constructs can be used to organize Sh programs: namespaces, templates, and classes can be used to organize and parameterize Sh shaders and programs; you can define your own types and operators; and you can define libraries of functions and shaders. C++ control constructs can also be used to manipulate and construct Sh programs on the fly. Such metaprogramming can be used to adapt implementation complexity and performance to the target platform, to generate variants of shaders for different levels of detail, to generate shaders from data files read in at runtime, or to specify complex operations using a higher-level metaprogram. As an additional benefit of our binding mechanism, very little glue code is needed between application code and Sh programs.

Sh can be used for single shaders, to implement complex multipass algorithms, or for general-purpose metaprogrammed stream computation on both GPUs and CPUs. For general-purpose computation, compiled Sh program objects can be applied as functions to streams of data. These programs can be executed on a GPU without it ever being necessary for the user to make a graphics API call. The same programs can be compiled (on the fly, using just-in-time compilation, and with full support for metaprogramming) to the host CPU as well, so the decision to execute an algorithm on the CPU or GPU can be deferred—to runtime if necessary, or after profiling multiple implementations and seeing which one is faster, or after load-balancing the entire system. Program objects can also be manipulated as first-order objects in various ways: specialization, conversion of uniform variables to inputs, conversion of inputs to uniform variables, conversion of inputs to texture lookups, partial evaluation, functional composition, concatenation, and other operations are available. Introspection on program objects is also supported.

Sh comes with an extensive standard library that includes complex numbers, quaternions, matrix and geometry functions, lighting models, noise functions (including cellnoise, Perlin noise, turbulence, and Worley noise functions), advanced texture representations, standard shader kernels, and other functionality.

Sh programs are usually compiled to GPUs, but can also be dynamically compiled to the host CPU, enabling a form of metaprogramming suitable for scientific applications. Sh also treats such CPU programs as first-class objects and can manipulate them to create new, modified programs on the fly. Therefore, in addition to being a powerful way to program GPUs, Sh can also be used for dynamic CPU metaprogramming, while the Sh compiler will efficiently exploit the ability of modern CPUs to operate on tuples of floating-point values. Of course, GPU programs can also be dynamically generated. Whatever the target, metaprogramming can be a powerful programming technique, permitting the generation of simpler, more efficient, and more adaptable programs in many situations.

Figure 1.1. Some example shaders. See Plate 1 on page 111.

There are some disadvantages to Sh. First, it runs inside C++, so you have to know C++ to use it. Second, this also means that you can't use it in web applications: you don't want to download and run an arbitrary C++ program. Eventually we hope to bind it to a sandboxed scripting language, which would address this issue while maintaining the metaprogramming capability of the system, but the language design is currently quite tied to C++. Third, Sh must be integrated with a host application, so you do not *automatically* have a clean separation of shader code and host application code. You can, however, use appropriate C++ frameworks to enforce your own rules for modularity. Finally, general Sh programs do not always fit into the model of "assets" as shaders are currently conceptualized by artists. You can *restrict* an Sh program to function-ality that would fit this model, but again, it is not automatic and you might lose the benefits that Sh gains by tracking dependencies between elements like uni-form parameters, shaders, and buffers. We are working on a system for exter-nalizing this web of dependencies. Essentially, the internal bookkeeping that Sh supports *is* an asset management system; it can even track user-defined meta-data. One idea is simply to cache this data in an external database or archive file. However, this functionality is still on the drawing board, since we want to do it in a way that is transparent and compatible with metaprogramming.

Sh is under heavy development at the moment, as it tracks the evolving fea-ture set of GPUs. We have not yet converged to the final state of the system,

although certain aspects of Sh (such as the core shader programming functionality) are stable and unlikely to change; hence our current effort at documentation (this book). Areas of Sh most likely to see elaboration in the future are in the
area of stream processing and certain features, such as asset management, that
are primarily of interest to commercial and advanced users. Of course, we will
also be working on improving the performance and optimization capability of
the system over time, but this will not change the interface.

Sh is open-source and free, and the core system is given a liberal license that
permits commercial use and extension. All the examples used in this book, and
many more, are available from the Sh web site:

```
http://libsh.sourceforge.net/
```

This book is divided into three parts. Part I, which includes this chapter, is
an introductory user's guide and tutorial and presents the features of Sh via a
sequence of simple examples. We use these examples to demonstrate the modularity and metaprogramming capabilities of the system. Users interested in
using Sh for writing shaders should be able to get started right away by downloading the system from the web site and modifying the examples provided.
Part II is a reference manual and language specification and methodically and
exhaustively presents details of the various features of Sh. It also includes a
guide to the Sh library, which includes a large set of useful utility functions.
This part of the book is meant to be referred to as needed, in a nonlinear order.
Finally, Part III is a guide to the engineering of Sh. It walks through the source
code of the public distribution of Sh and is meant as a guide for developers
wishing to extend or modify Sh, or for users who want a deeper understanding
of how Sh implements various features.

This chapter is a high-level overview of Sh and its relationship to other real-
time shading and GPU programming languages. Section 1.1 describes in more
detail the features of modern programmable GPUs and the abstraction of their
computational model that Sh uses. Section 1.2 surveys existing and past shading languages and compares them with Sh. Section 1.3 discusses the stream
processing computational model and other programming systems that support
it. Section 1.4 provides some background on metaprogramming in general and
how Sh relates to other forms of metaprogramming. Section 1.5 gives some
short examples of Sh programs and demonstrates how C++ constructs can be
used to organize Sh code. Section 1.6 presents notational conventions used
throughout the book. Section 1.7 describes the history of Sh, its license, and
how to obtain a copy. Finally, in Section 1.8, we talk about the current state of
Sh and our plans for its future development.

1.1   Programmable GPUs

A GPU, or graphics processing unit, is the core chip of the graphics and video subsystem in a modern personal computer. Due to economies of scale, these chips are now also used in graphics supercomputers as well, such as the SGI Onyx 4 or cluster machines. In a supercomputer, multiple GPUs can be used and their digital video (DVI) outputs combined using special-purpose compositing hardware. Clusters are just collections of PC workstations, and so can each host a graphics accelerator with a GPU. In the near future, GPUs will be available that use the PCI Express interface, and it will be theoretically possible to put multiple GPUs into a single machine. Such machines should be capable of truly astonishing computational performance at an excellent cost/performance ratio.

Although it is possible to build a system with parallel GPUs, internally GPUs are also parallel processors [39]. From the beginning, the internal architecture of graphics accelerators has exploited both task (pipeline) and data parallelism to improve performance and custom hardware to accelerate key algorithms such as polygon and line rasterization [142, 5, 119, 4, 55, 73]. Although in the 1980s and 1990s graphics accelerators were mostly fixed-function, internally they often used microcode to program certain operations. Earlier systems had exposed this functionality [41], but the focus in commercial systems was on the performance of a fixed-function graphics pipeline until the mid to late 1990s. The PixelPlanes and PixelFlow project at UNC was an ambitious research project to investigate high-performance and eventually programmable graphics acceleration [77, 79, 96, 97, 47, 48, 103, 105], and a version of the RenderMan shading language, pfMan, was developed that could be compiled to an array of parallel SIMD processors.

In a SIMD processor, a single instruction stream is applied in parallel to many data elements. Increased efficiency can be obtained since only one control unit is required and synchronization is not an issue, but data-dependent control flow is not possible, and conditional execution can only be simulated with conditional assignment. Conditional assignment throws away results on some processors, but those results are still computed (although in parallel).

NVIDIA was the first to expose a more general programming model for GPUs, starting with the vertex unit [81]. The vertex shader programming model exposed previously hidden microcoded functionality and provided both a SIMD mode of execution (multiple vertices might be processed in parallel) and a SWAR model of execution on a single vertex (SIMD Within a Register: shader instructions that act on 4-tuples). The fragment unit, which processed individual pixels, was also gradually made programmable, first with multitexturing, then with register combiners, then with floating-point texture shaders, and finally with a full programming model very similar to that initially supported on the vertex unit. A healthy competition between ATI and NVIDIA has also been driving the area forward technologically. For the last couple of years, new models have been introduced on a frequent basis by either ATI or NVIDIA with significantly improved capabilities. Most recently, models have been announced by NVIDIA and 3DLabs that support data-dependent branching.

The new data-dependent branching capabilities of these GPUs *probably* imply a departure from the SIMD processing model, perhaps using multithreading. Unfortunately, internal details are closely guarded secrets, as the whole area is highly competitive, and it is not yet clear if the performance of shaders with branches will compare with that of SIMD shaders.

Modern GPUs have now evolved into systems capable of high-performance general-purpose programmable floating point computation at both the vertex and fragment levels. Unlike CPUs, GPUs are optimized for a streaming mode of execution, where a relatively complex operation is applied to a long stream of homogeneously structured input records. GPUs exploit parallelism among applications of their operation to multiple input records. The regular access patterns of streaming data and the predictable synchronization of the SIMD execution model are key ingredients in the enhanced performance of GPUs. This means they are better than CPUs at some tasks and worse than them at others. However, many scientific applications, as well as (of course) graphics applications, perform well under this execution model. GPUs have been shown to be up to five times faster on some applications than CPUs; this gap is expected to grow, since the streaming model of execution makes better use of limited memory bandwidth, which is what limits the performance of modern CPUs. At the same time, there are some annoying historical limitations in GPUs that are preventing them from reaching their full potential. For instance, drivers may enforce a "type" system that separates vertex and pixel data. However, it would be very useful to be able to feed pixel data back through the vertex unit, since (among other things), this would permit use of the rasterizer to write this data to other arbitrary pixels (this is called a scatter operation). In general, some relatively small architectural and driver changes in GPUs would make them even more powerful computational engines, and now that the trend is set towards general-purpose computation, these changes are expected.

General computation on GPUs has been studied by many researchers. In recent years many graphics, vision, simulation, and numerical applications have been (often laboriously) implemented on GPUs [143, 62, 18, 74]. Implementing these systems is extremely challenging since graphics APIs are not designed with general-purpose computation in mind. Crucial features are often lacking, or exist on some cards and driver versions, and not others. If the necessary features for some specific algorithm do exist, if the drivers that support them are recently released these features may be broken, incomplete, incompatible with some other crucial feature, or good ways to crash the machine in interesting and exciting ways if not used in just the "right" sequence. Pioneers in this area are often criticized for "just" porting an algorithm to a GPU. However, these pioneers have identified several crucial missing features in GPUs and have developed many interesting and non-obvious programming techniques. Readers interested in this topic should visit the GPGPU website at `http://www.gpgpu.org/`, organized by Mark Harris, for up-to-date information.

As the more basic issues with implementing general-purpose computation on GPUs get ironed out, there has been interest in developing high-level languages to make it easier to implement more sophisticated algorithms on GPUs. However, this is a non-trivial task. Several interesting applications, such as distance transformations [63] and photon mapping [121], make use of the rasterizer or compositor as well as the shading units, and these are harder to encapsulate in shading languages or stream processing models of computation. Implementing a language is also a harder task than implementing a particular algorithm, since *all* programs have to work, not just one particular carefully debugged application. When developing a single application at a low level, you can carefully avoid the bugs in the driver (both those known and the ones you discover experimentally), and then once it works, leave it alone. A compiler has to automate the process and has to have an explicit and robust representation of the system; it can't afford to try out things and see if they work or not! As support for the new features in GPUs are more robustly supported and various issues are ironed out, however, several high-level GPU programming systems have emerged.

1.2   Shading Languages

A shading language is a domain-specific programming language for specifying shading computations in graphics. In a shading language, a program is specified for computing the color of each pixel as a function of light direction, surface position, orientation, and other parameters made available by a rendering system. Typically shading languages are focused on color computation, but some shading systems also support limited modelling capabilities, such as support for displacement mapping.

Specialized shading languages and other forms of user programmability have been exploited for a long time in offline CPU-based renderers, most prominently in RenderMan. The RenderMan shading language dominates the use of shading languages in offline rendering [54, 147, 10, 50, 51, 116] and has strongly influenced other shading languages, particularly with its concept of uniform and varying computational frequencies. The RenderMan standard was also originally intended as a hardware API, and, in fact, is explicitly designed to permit SIMD execution.

The original idea for programming shaders is often attributed to Cook. He used shade trees [24] to capture expressions used to compute pixels so if the parameters of the lighting model changed in a raytracer, an image could be quickly recomputed without redoing intersection calculations. Peachey and Perlin [110, 113] developed the idea of procedural textures and lighting and also experimented with noise functions.

Visual and dataflow languages have also been explored as alternative approaches for specifying shading computations. Block shaders used a network of configurable modules [2] described using either a visual or a textual language. Explicit control was provided over the order of execution of modules so that side effects could be used for global communications. In their textual language, a netlist was used to specify the connections between modules. Dataflow languages (visual and otherwise) have also been used for procedural modeling [57] and lighting networks [138].

The CONDOR system, for instance, was a constraint-based dataflow language [67], which compiled a visual language to C++ code. The compiler was written in Lisp and Mathematica, and included support for symbolic derivatives and interval analysis. CONDOR was applied to both shading and geometric modeling, as well as numerical optimization—a suite of applications similar to the problems being tackled by modern GPUs. Operator-based systems such as GENMOD have also been developed for procedural geometry [140, 139].

Recently, real-time graphics accelerators have been targeted with shading language compilers [84, 112, 120], new techniques have been found to implement sophisticated lighting models using a relatively small number of programmable operations [59, 60, 68, 69, 88], and vendors have begun to implement and expose explicitly programmable components [12, 81] in their accelerators.

The original programming model exposed in the APIs for these programmable components was at the level of assembly language [12, 93, 102]. However, OpenGL 2.0 [1, 71, 128] specifies a high-level shading language as an integral part of the API. Microsoft supports similar functionality with their High-Level Shading Language for DirectX 9, although the actual driver interface is in the form of assembly language [94].

Most shading languages and shading APIs place the shader program in a string or file and then implement a relatively traditional assembler or compiler to convert this specification to a machine language representation. Using a separate language has some advantages—a "little language" can be more tightly focused [54, 70], shaders can be managed as "assets"—but using a custom language has problems too.

First, although the shader programs themselves can be simple, binding them to the application program can be a nuisance. Many of the extensions to OpenGL required to support shaders in UNC's PixelFlow system, for instance, were concerned with named parameter declaration and management [77, 79, 105, 103]. Second, due to limitations on the implementation effort that can reasonably be expended, custom shading languages usually will not be as powerful as full programming languages. They often may be missing important features such as modularity and typing constructs useful for organizing complex multipart algorithms or for creating data abstractions. Additional useful features, such as specialization [52] or interfaces between multiple components [83], have to be explicitly provided for by the language and shader compiler.

The RenderMan shading language in its current form is not compatible with existing graphics APIs, so new GPU shading languages have been developed. However, there is still a strong interest in mapping RenderMan shaders to GPUs, since there is a large set of developers and artists familiar with them. It was actually shown relatively early that the RenderMan shading language's computational model could be mapped to graphics accelerators even without programmable shading units if a certain small set of operations were added, and if floating point support were available for all operations [112].

Shading languages developed specifically for programmable GPUs include the OpenGL Shading Language (GLSL) [71, 128], the Stanford Real-Time Shading Language (RTSL) [120, 84], Microsoft's High-Level Shading Language (HLSL) [111], and NVIDIA's Cg [83]. Of these languages, HLSL is DirectX-specific, GLSL is OpenGL-specific, Cg is multiplatform and API neutral, but developed by NVIDIA (and so not well supported by ATI), and RTSL is no longer under active development (having evolved into Cg, basically). There is definitely still an open niche for a vendor and API-independent shading language.

The existing GPU shading languages are all very similar semantically, differing mostly in minor syntactic issues. For instance, the OpenGL shading language binds to OpenGL state using a number of predefined (and OpenGL-specific) variables and uses a vec$n$ datatype for n-tuples, rather than Cg and HLSL's float$n$. Also, Cg and HLSL specify bindings to attributes using structure declarations, while GLSL uses a function declaration syntax. However, all existing shading languages use the C language syntax, support operations on n-tuples, and support some concept of computational frequency.

While useful for implementing shaders specifically, these languages do not address the implementation of multipass algorithms involving several shaders, and the binding of these languages to the host application is loose and requires the use of API glue code. NIVDIA's CgFX and Microsoft's Direct3D Effects system provide mechanisms for specifying multipass combinations of shaders and GPU state for each pass, but provide only limited control mechanisms. The SGI Interactive Shading Language [112] compiles shaders described in a relatively high-level language to a multipass implementation [33, 32, 34], but does not generate complex kernels for programmable GPUs, only primitive passes for the traditional OpenGL fixed-function pipeline.

1.3   Stream Processing

Recently, researchers at Stanford have developed what they call a stream processing architecture [66, 127, 72, 65, 86, 30]. Stream processing is based on the application of SIMD programs (kernels) to ordered buffers (streams) of homogeneous data records. Stream processors are distinguished from vector processors [136] by the fact that on-chip temporary registers are available, so it is possible to perform a significant amount of arithmetic on each stream record before the result needs to be written back to memory. In fact, the *Imagine* stream processor has an even deeper memory hierarchy than that and supports two forms of on-chip memory: local registers and a stream register file. The latter is similar to a managed cache optimized for sequential access to data.

The *Imagine* stream processor is capable of general-purpose computations and non-trivial applications have been implemented on it, including implementations of both the OpenGL and Reyes graphics architectures [108, 107, 109]. However, without a hardware rasterizer, these researchers found that the performance of their system could not match that of a more specialized GPU.

GPUs are not designed as stream processors but have similar capabilities. Both the vertex unit and the fragment unit operate on streams (of vertices and fragments) and have local registers, and so can execute non-trivial kernels. However, there are differences, too. GPUs are designed to operate on arrays of pixels, and if we try to simulate stream reads with textures in the fragment units, the texture caches cannot necessarily take advantage of the sequential access. Still, it is interesting to consider using a common programming model for both GPUs and stream processors.

A language called Brook [21, 22] has been developed to target both stream processors and GPUs. Brook is defined as an extension of ANSI C. It is implemented as a preprocessor that maps Brook programs to a C++ and Cg implementation and is supported by a runtime engine. Kernel bodies in Brook are essentially specified using Cg syntax.

Sh also supports a stream processing model, but Brook's data abstraction capabilities are (currently) more limited. Also, Sh targets both graphics and scientific computation, while Brook is focused on scientific computation. On the other hand, Brook supports at present a more complete set of stream functionality than Sh (although we hope to address this, given time).

Extensions to the typical graphics pipeline have been proposed to support multipass virtualization of limited resources such as the number of registers and texture units available in a single SIMD pass [85, 23]. The F-buffer, which recirculates fragments in rasterization order through the fragment shader, bears a strong similarity to stream processing, without, however, the ability to execute conditionals efficiently. Similar techniques can be used to virtualize resource limits such as number of texture lookups, instructions, and registers. Virtualization is an important concern for high-level shading language portability and usability.

Architectures other than stream processing can potentially be used to achieve high performance in a graphics accelerator while supporting data-dependent control constructs and general memory access patterns. A possibility worth comparing stream processing with is multithreading [7, 146, 136]. Multithreading comes in several flavors. In the simplest flavor, an "interleaved" multithreaded processor acts as a virtual SIMD machine by issuing each instruction multiple times on different data elements. This can be used to hide memory access and functional unit latency but, like a SIMD processor, an interleaved multithreaded processor cannot efficiently support data-dependent loops or iteration. Still, some of the performance properties of the GeForceFX 5000 series imply that this is how they operate internally (specifically, the fact that the fragment shader slows down as more registers are used. This implies a shared register file and a multithreaded mode of execution). If separate program counters are supplied to each thread, then data-dependent operations can be performed efficiently. However, if ordering is to be maintained, some mechanism (such as stalling or a reorder buffer) is needed to deal with threads that complete out-of-order. Also, in the independent thread variant of multithreading, multiple accesses to the instruction memory are needed, one for each thread.

We have recently developed techniques to map data-dependent control constructs to GPUs using multipass stream routing. This is currently still (highly) experimental, but we hope to officially support this capability in Sh in the near future. This approach also tends to reorder data when data-dependent control constructs are used. We argue that the simplest solution in both cases is to write algorithms that can tolerate out-of-order completion in exchange for efficient iteration and conditionals. Therefore, if multithreading is used for data-dependent conditionals, and if true packed stream output is supported, a mode that writes data to streams out of order (in exchange for improved efficiency) should be considered.

Simultaneous multithreading [146] is a combination of superscalar processing and multithreading: instructions are fetched from multiple threads in parallel and scheduled together. This can achieve high performance and utilization of functional units, but is complex, requires multiple instruction caches and/or memory ports, and can require a lot of state to be maintained in the processor (multiple register files and program counters). However, it is possible to convert a program with data-dependent branches to a control graph for a stream processor and vice-versa by basic-block analysis; a multithreaded processor could also be a target of the stream programming abstraction—and this appears to be similar to the hyperthreading execution model used by the latest Pentium processors.

A vector processor [136] is like a stream processor in that it operates on sequentially ordered data. However, vector operations are simpler than stream processing kernels; a vector processor puts a heavier load on the memory system. A stream processor executes a small SIMD program (kernel) on every element of a stream and can take advantage of high memory bandwidth to a local register file when executing these kernels. We say that a stream processor has a higher *arithmetic intensity* than a vector processor, i.e., more computation is (potentially) performed per memory access. However, conceptually, a vector processor can be considered a stream processor that only supports very simple kernels and so could also be a target of a compiler supporting a multipass stream processing model of computation.

Finally, independent processors can also support a stream processing model by simply operating in parallel on different parts of the stream and/or by using a dataflow execution approach and routing streams of data through a pipeline. In the context of Sh, this is interesting because the Playstation 3, according to the latest rumors, will probably be a distributed memory parallel machine with vector processors at each node. This is called a cellular architecture by Sony and IBM, who are co-developing the processor. These companies have also announced their intention to make this processor available on workstations. If we develop a stream processing model for GPUs, we may be able to extend it to such an architecture in the future. Of course, clusters of workstations and parallel supercomputers also have a similar distributed processing architecture.

In summary, the stream processing computational model maps to a large number of different high-performance processing models; multithreaded, pipelined SIMD, distributed and shared memory parallel architectures. It is therefore an interesting model to study for the design of programming languages that need to map common descriptions of algorithms to all these targets.

1.4 Metaprogramming

Metaprogramming is the use of one program to generate or manipulate another; it is a fundamental capability of modern computer systems. The standard stored-program computer architecture is built upon the idea that programs can and should be represented as data that can be manipulated by other programs. Operating systems, compilers, assemblers, linkers, and loaders are all programs that manipulate and transform other programs.

Despite the fundamental capacity of modern computers for metaprogramming and its potential power, dynamic metaprogramming support is rare in mainstream programming languages. Although it is powerful, it is also potentially very confusing and dangerous if not supported with careful language and system design. However, metaprogramming has been shown to be a useful mechanism for implementing domain-specific embedded languages and binding them to a host application [40, 36, 29], and this is exactly what Sh does.

> By calling Sh a "domain-specific embedded language," we do not mean to imply that Sh is limited to only expressing shaders. It has broader applicability than that, but Sh does support an intentionally more limited computational model than general C++ programs. In particular, Sh program kernels cannot have side effects. Therefore, even though they are imperative "on the inside," they are functional "on the outside," and we can apply functional programming concepts to the application of kernels to streams. Sh is also domain-specific in the sense that certain optimizations are targeted at graphics applications since these are, after all, the major application area of GPUs. General-purpose applications would not benefit from these optimizations, but they won't hurt such applications, either.

Template metaprogramming [148, 78, 31] has become a popular method for reorganizing C++ code by using template rewriting rules as a functional language at compile time. However, template rewriting is a very inefficient way to implement a functional language; the syntax of templates used this way is (to put it mildly) baroque, and it is hard to specify complex operations using it since data structures must be expressed as type expressions. We should emphasize that Sh is *not* a template metaprogramming library, although we do use templates in a more straightforward fashion to help implement the type system in Sh.

At any rate, template metaprogramming takes place at the wrong time. Template metaprogramming generates C++ code for the host, not for a GPU. Templates perform metaprogramming *before* compilation of the host program. We want to do metaprogramming at a later stage, driven by the *execution* of the host program. Sh is actually a "staged compiler". We do most type analysis and parsing at C++ compile time, but defer some compilation and optimization until later and, in particular, perform code generation under the control of the application at run time. Our approach makes it straightforward and efficient to implement an optimizer library using standard compiler techniques that can support (among other things) shader specialization [52].

"Generative programming," or code generation via textual substitution [61] is now a standard software engineering tool. It can be used to embed a domain-specific language (such as an SQL query) into a host program and generate appropriate boilerplate binding code. Languages such as Ruby, Perl, Tcl, or Python can be used to specify textual transformations on code. However, the embedded code is still in a different language, integration with the host language may be incomplete unless a very sophisticated preprocessor is implemented, and the build process becomes more complex. Compiling such code now also depends on a tool which also has to be maintained. For instance, if the input is C++ plus some extensions, we need to maintain a parser that tracks the latest version of C++. Also, like template metaprogramming, this is applying metaprogramming at the application program compile time, whereas Sh applies it at the host application's run time.

The implementation approach of Sh is closest to that of Tick CC [117], which defined special types and operators for representing and combining program fragments. However, rather than extending C, we use the standard abstraction capabilities of C++ to define interfaces to our new operations. We then operate on our own internal representation of shaders to support program combination and to perform optimizations.

All the real-time shading languages mentioned so far place the program in a string or file and then implement a relatively traditional assembler or compiler to convert this specification to a machine language representation, or in the case of Brook, a C++/Cg implementation. As we mentioned earlier, custom languages may lack useful features that more general languages have, and the interface between the host program and the shaders it uses may involve a lot of "glue code."

Instead, Sh uses the features of standard C++ to define a high-level shading language directly in the API, without having to resort to the use of string manipulation. Basically, sequences of calls into an API can interpreted as a sequence of words in a "language." Consider the X11 protocol supporting the use of OpenGL across a network: it is basically a one-to-one mapping from API calls to a sequence of data values and tokens. Parsing of the API token sequence may be necessary, however, to support the expressions and structured control constructs used in modern high-level languages. Fortunately, with appropriate syntactic sugaring provided by operator overloading, the ordinary semantics of C++ can be use to automatically parse Sh arithmetic expressions during application program compilation. Since the Sh parser does not need to deal with expressions, the remaining parsing job is simplified. In Sh, preprocessor macros are also defined so "keywords" can be used to specify control constructs. These macros generate API calls that insert appropriate tokens into the command stream. Sh parses these explicitly at run time using a recursive-descent parser.

The result of this approach to parsing is a high-level embedded language which is nearly indistinguishable from a custom programming language. Since this language is embedded in the application language, more direct interaction with the specification of textures, attributes, and parameters is possible, and programs can be dynamically manipulated. Implementing a shading language this way is not difficult, and, in fact, is in some respects simpler than the traditional approach: in addition to parsing expressions, the C++ compiler can be persuaded to take care of most type checking, scoping, and modularity issues.

With a metaprogramming API, precompiled shader programs could still be used in the traditional manner simply by compiling and running a C++ program that defines an appropriate shader and dumps a compiled binary representation of it to a file. This approach could be used to invoke shaders when using an application language other than C++, such as Java or Fortran. A C++ compiler and some wrapper code would simply replace the specialized separate shader compiler. However, parameter naming and binding are simplified if the application program and the shader program are compiled together, since objects defining named parameters and textures can be accessed by the shader definition directly. Compilation of shader programs can be very fast, even with optimization, and compiling at runtime lets the program adapt to variable hardware support (important in a plug-and-play context). In the following, therefore, we will assume that the application program is also written in C++ and that shader compilation happens on the fly.

Metaprogramming has been used extensively in the functional and logic programming language community to build specialized embedded languages [40]. Metaprogramming has also been used to dynamically specify programs for practical programmable embedded systems, in particular, for programming protocol handlers in network systems [42]. Specialized C compilers have been implemented that explicitly support an operator algebra for metaprogramming [117]. Our approach does not require specialized extensions to the compiler, just exploitation of standard C++ features and an appropriate library, but we do support a similar algebra for manipulating Sh program objects.

Partial evaluation, or the partial specification of the parameters of a function generating a new function with fewer parameters, is a fundamental capability in many functional languages. It is usually implemented using deferred execution but can also be implemented using dynamic incremental compilation of specialized functions [78]. This leads to more efficient execution if the partially evaluated function is used often enough to amortize the cost of compilation. One nice thing about this form of metaprogramming is that the syntax and the semantics of the original program can remain unchanged. Metaprogramming is just an alternative implementation technique for partial evaluation or "currying." The resulting programs are therefore as easy to read as the originals.

The Sh library supports partial evaluation via currying and program specialization for both the CPU and the GPU. When Sh targets the CPU, it is in fact generating and optimizing CPU code that is linked dynamically. Host-side metaprogramming is a structured application of "self-modifying code," and, in some applications, can have major performance benefits (with a suitable optimizing backend) for graphics and multimedia applications [36]. For instance, suppose the inner loop of your application requires many branches to support various options. This is common, for instance, in software implementations of OpenGL. With metaprogramming, once the options are set, you could generate a specialized version of the inner loop that eliminates the branches. In essence, you can generate a custom "fast path" for each invocation of your program.

Although we do not consider it further here, a metaprogramming API approach could be used to program other embedded processors, for instance, the DSP engines on sound cards or printer and display engines. In fact, when you output a PostScript file and send it to the printer, one might say that you are metaprogramming the printer, since PostScript is a programming language.

1.5   The Sh Metaprogramming Toolkit

Sh is based around a set of C++ types for representing small n-tuples and matrices upon which appropriate operators have been defined. In this section, we give a series of short examples meant to impart the flavor of Sh programming. More detailed examples are given in later chapters.

1.5.1   Immediate Mode

We can declare and initialize a three-dimensional point and a three-dimensional vector as follows:

```
ShPoint3f a(0.4,0.5,2.3);
ShVector3f b(0.2,0.6,0.8);
```

Small matrices can be declared similarly:

```
ShMatrix3x4f M;
```

Here "*Point*," "*Vector*," and "*Matrix*" gives the meaning (semantics) of the type, the number of components is given with a numerical designation, and the storage type used to actually represent the components of the tuple is given with a suffix, in this case, *f* for single-precision floating-point numbers.

We can operate on these values using operators and library functions. For instance, suppose we wish to compute the point c which is 5 units away from point a in the direction of vector b, then transform the resulting point by the matrix M. In Sh, this can be expressed as

```
ShPoint3f c = M | (a + 5.0 * normalize(b));
```

Listing 1.1. Displacement computation.

Here the normalize function normalizes the vector b to unit length (since we are interested only in the direction) and "5.0 *" computes a scalar/vector product. We then add the result of this expression to the point a to get the translated point, and finally perform a matrix-point product (with automatic inferral of the homogeneous coordinate 1) with the "|" operator.

When we create instances of Sh types, such as those above, and operate on them using normal C++ program sequencing, we say we are operating in *immediate mode*. In immediate mode, the indicated operations take place when they are specified (i.e., immediately), and Sh operates like a standard graphics matrix/vector utility library, executing its operations on the host.

1.5.2   Stream Programming

Sequences of Sh operations can be "recorded" using a retained-mode mechanism, then compiled for a number of targets. In other words, we can define functions that encapsulate a number of operations for later reuse. Sh tries to make such definitions behave as much as possible like C++ functions, so that they fit in naturally with the modularity and scope constructs of C++. Sh functions differ from native C++ functions, though, because Sh function definitions can be retargetted to another processor and compilation happens dynamically, at runtime, so C++ can be used to assemble programs via metaprogramming. Compiled Sh functions are optimized and transformed to run as efficiently as possible while maintaining common semantics for all target platforms.

Usually for graphics applications we will target the GPU, although we can also target other platforms, including other shading languages and the host CPU, via a modular backend system. Sh has its own optimizer that handles dead-code elimination, forward substitution and copy propagation (among other transformations). Sh also provides a runtime engine that transparently manages buffers and textures.

As a simple example, suppose we wanted to apply the transformation given in Listing 1.1 to a sequence of vertices. We want to apply the same matrix to all vertices in the sequence, but want to use a different scale factor and translation vector for each vertex. Such a function might be used to implement displacement mapping.

First, we will create a program object that records the desired computation in an **ShProgram** object.

```
ShProgram displace = SH_BEGIN_PROGRAM("gpu:stream") {
  ShInputPoint3f a;
  ShInputVector3f b;
  ShInputAttrib1f s;
  ShOutputPoint3f c = M | (a + s * normalize(b));
} SH_END;
```

Listing 1.2. Displacement stream function.

We reference the previously declared Sh matrix object M, but the other three values a, b, and s are declared as inputs. Sh uses the semantic type **Attrib** for generic tuples, including (in this case) scalars.

Now, we declare a container for the data using **ShStream** and **ShChannel** classes. For the purposes of this introduction, an **ShChannel** is equivalent to a std::vector template (a 1D array of a given element type) and an **ShStream** object is just a container that organizes (by reference, not by copying) a collection of channels.

```
ShChannel<ShPoint3f> p;
ShChannel<ShVector3f> v;
ShChannel<ShAttrib1f> t;
ShStream data = (p & v & t);
```

We use the "&" operator to combine channels into streams. Now we can apply the program object displace to the stream, generating an output stream. Formally, program objects map streams to streams and operate on each element separately (and conceptually in parallel). However, for convenience, we can also use a channel object as a single-channel stream, which we do here for the output stream:

```
ShChannel<ShPoint3f> q;
q = displace << data;
```

Here "<<" is the apply operator and is used to feed the data stream into the displace stream function, generating the single-channel output stream which is then stored in channel q.

Various alternative syntaxes are supported, and streams can be built from channels using inline expressions. The following statements are all equivalent given the above definitions:

```
q = displace << data;
q = displace << (p & v & t);
q = displace << p << (v & t);
q = displace << p << v << t;
q = displace(p) << v << t;
q = displace(p,v) << t;
q = displace(p,v,t);
q = displace(p & v & t);
q = displace(data);
```

The "<<" apply operator supports partial evaluation via *currying*. You do not have to provide all the arguments to a stream program at once—you can apply them one at a time. When a program gets applied to an argument with k channels of data, it returns another program object requiring k fewer arguments. Programs with no arguments left to consume are ready to run, and execution is triggered by assignment to a stream or channel.

As shown ealier, function application can also be indicated with "()" and this makes Sh program objects look a lot like normal C++ functions, even though the computation (in this case) runs on the GPU. You can also apply Sh programs to single tuples rather than streams, although this is not a very efficient use of the GPU. If we wanted to use short streams, or if the data were on the CPU already, or if we just wanted to see if the CPU or GPU would be faster for a given algorithm, we might want to run the computation on the CPU instead.

This can be done by changing the compilation target to "cpu:stream", which generates, compiles, optimizes, and links in host machine language on the fly.

What if we want to change the value of M? No problem, just assign a new value to it. The next time the stream programs that use it are run, they will use the new value. Externally declared tuples like this are called *parameters*, and behave like you would expect global variables to behave. This behavior is an intentional illusion maintained by Sh, regardless of compilation target. It actually requires a fair amount of behind-the-scenes bookkeeping to implement for some targets. Sh also provides facilities for pulling out inputs like a and b and binding them to global parameters instead, or vice-versa, and for combining program objects in various ways, such as functional composition.

Stream expressions can be used on the left-hand side, and stream programs can have multiple outputs (whether or not the target supports it directly: Sh transforms the code as appropriate to maintain the same computational model regardless of the compilation target, a process called *virtualization*). For instance, we can define another stream program offset that displaces the input point stream in two opposite directions and outputs two displaced vertex streams.

```
ShProgram offset = SH_BEGIN_PROGRAM("gpu:stream") {
  ShInputPoint3f a;
  ShInputVector3f b;
  ShInputAttrib1f s;
  a = M | a;
  b = M | (s * normalize(b));
  ShOutputPoint3f c1 = a + b;
  ShOutputPoint3f c2 = a - b;
} SH_END;
```

The offset program assigns new values to some of its inputs. Inputs are conceptually passed by value, so these assignments change only the internal copy. You may be aware that some GPUs do not permit writes to input registers or reads from output registers. The Sh conceptual model supports both these operations and automatically transforms programs as appropriate so they will work on such machines. Sh also initializes temporaries inside program objects with zeros if they are not given a value before their first use.

Now we can apply the offset stream program to the original data stream and can generate an output stream with two channels:

```
ShChannel<ShPoint3f> q1, q2;
(q1 & q2) = offset << data;
```

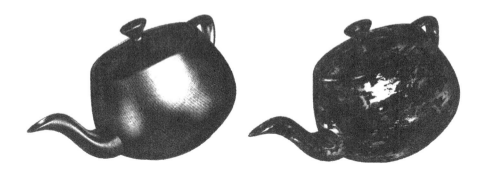

Figure 1.2. Examples of the textured Blinn-Phong shader.

1.5.3   Shader Programming

Sh can also be used for programming both vertex and fragment shaders, as you might expect. As an example, we will define a pair of vertex and fragment shaders to compute a modified version of the Blinn-Phong lighting model, with texture mapping of both the diffuse and specular terms [14]. Some sample renderings generated by this shader are given in Figure 1.2. The vertex shader will also transform vertices and normals from model space to view space for lighting and vertices to device space for rasterization.   First, we declare a set of *parameters*: kd, ks, $spec\_exp$, $light\_position$, and $light\_color$. This pair of shaders also depends on the $modelview$ model space to view space transfor-

```
ShMatrix3x4f modelview;       // MCS to VCS transformation
ShMatrix4x4f projection;      // VCS to DCS transformation
ShMatrix3x3f n_modelview;     // MCS to VCS normal transformation

ShMatrix2x3f texture_xform;   // texture coordinate transformation matrix

ShTexture2D<ShColor3f> kd;    // diffuse color texture
ShTexture2D<ShColor3f> ks;    // specular color texture
ShAttrib1f spec_exp;          // specular exponent

ShPoint3f light_position;     // VCS light position
ShColor3f light_color;        // light source color
```

Listing 1.3. Blinn-Phong lighting model parameters.

mation matrix, the *projection* view space to device space transformation matrix, the *n_modelview* model space to view space normal transformation matrix, and a texture coordinate transformation matrix *texture_xform*. These matrices are defined only for this example; in the rest of the book, we use an alternative set of global definitions; see Section 1.6.4.

Note that the *kd* and *ks* parameters are texture maps. Textures in Sh are represented using templated types with the element type (which must be an Sh type) as a template argument. Textures act like arrays in both immediate mode and inside shader programs. Inside programs they are read-only, like other parameters. All parameters, including texture maps, are declared outside of a shader definition; they can be acted upon in immediate mode on the host using whatever operators are defined for their types. To use shader terminology, parameters are equivalent to *uniform* variables in RenderMan.

We then construct two shader program objects, *vert* and *frag*. We are assuming here that these definitions are inside some C++ function, since Sh definitions are in fact executable C++ code, not C++ definitions.

First, we define the vertex shader:

```
ShProgram vert = SH_BEGIN_PROGRAM("gpu:vertex") {
  // Declare inputs
  ShInputNormal3f nm;          // input MCS normal vector
  ShInputTexCoord2f ui;        // input texture coordinate
  ShInputPosition3f pm;        // input MCS vertex position

  // Declare outputs
  ShOutputPoint3f pv;          // output VCS position
  ShOutputVector3f lv;         // output VCS light-vector
  ShOutputNormal3f nv;         // output VCS normal
  ShOutputColor3f ec;          // output irradiance
  ShOutputTexCoord2f uo;       // output texture coordinate
  ShOutputPosition4f pd;       // output DCS position

  // Perform computations
  uo = texture_xform | ui;     // xform texture coords
  pv = modelview | pm;         // xform vertex position from MCS to VCS
  pd = projection | pv;        // xform vertex position from VCS to DCS
  lv = normalize(light_position - pv);   // compute light vector
  nv = normalize(n_modelview | nm);      // xform normal from MCS to VCS
  ec = light_color * max(0.0,nv|lv);     // compute irradiance
} SH_END;
```

Listing 1.4. Blinn-Phong vertex shader.

The corresponding fragment shader is given in Listing 1.5.

```
ShProgram frag = SH_BEGIN_PROGRAM("gpu:fragment") {
    ShInputPoint3f pv;          // input position (VCS)
    ShInputVector3f lv;         // input light-vector (VCS)
    ShInputNormal3f nv;         // input normal (VCS)
    ShInputColor3f ec;          // input irradiance
    ShInputTexCoord2f u;        // input texture coordinate

    ShOutputColor3f fc;         // output fragment color

    nv = normalize(nv);                     // normalize VCS normal
    ShVector3f vv = normalize(-pv);         // compute VCS view vector
    ShVector3f hv = normalize(lv + vv);     // compute VCS half vector

    // compute the (modified) Blinn-Phong lighting model
    fc = kd(u)*ec + ks(u)*pow(max(0.0,hv|nv),spec_exp);
} SH_END;
```

Listing 1.5. Blinn-Phong fragment shader.

Shaders use the same types as we used for parameters, but with some of the declarations marked with Input and Output qualifiers, as with stream programs. Local temporaries internal to a shader are declared without such qualifiers. Parameters and local temporaries use the same types and are distinguished only by their location of definition: inside or outside a shader.

Input and output *attributes* are bound to the input and output data channels of the shaders using a set of rules that depend on their order of declaration and their type. To find out how to set up your graphics API to generate data for a shader, however, you can just ask a program object what it needs using an introspection method.

Input attributes act like varying variables in RenderMan (roughly, in that they are different for each invocation of a shader). Note the distinction between *parameters* and *attributes*: this terminology is used extensively later and is meant to be compatible with the terminology in OpenGL.

As with stream functions, shaders can refer to parameters previously declared outside the shader definition, but cannot assign to them. When a shader is loaded into the appropriate GPU unit, copies of the values of the necessary parameters are loaded into constant registers (or bound to texture units; Sh considers textures to be a kind of array-valued parameter). If in immediate mode a new value is assigned to a parameter that is in use by a bound shader, the copy in the GPU is automatically updated. The net effect is that parameters act like external variables relative to the definition of the shader, and C++ scope rules can be used to manage the binding of parameters to shaders.

1.6 Conventions and Notation

In this section, we document some important conventions used throughout the book to make our examples more concise.

1.6.1 Typesetting and Stylistic Conventions

Listings will be given both inline and as numbered figures. Listings are numbered separately from figures and tables and a list of all numbered listings appears at the front of the book. An example inline listing follows:

```
ShProgram p = SH_BEGIN_PROGRAM("cpu:stream") {
   ShInputAttrib1f a;
   ShOutputAttrib1f b;
   ShAttrib1f c = sqrt(a) + a;
   b = c*c;      // this is a comment
} SH_END;
```

A special font is used in this book to distinguish listings from the main text. Sh types such as *ShProgram* and *ShAttrib1f* are also highlighted everywhere they appear. All Sh types begin with the prefix "*Sh.*" User-defined types are not highlighted this way, but all class and struct types normally use a mixed case convention for their name.

Macros and compile-time constants use a mixture of uppercase and underscores for their names: MAX_LIGHTS. In addition, Sh "keywords," such as *SH_END* are also highlighted and use an *SH_* prefix. Normal C++ macros and defines are not highlighted in this manner, only macros specific to Sh.

Functions that manipulate the Sh system, or are necessary for it to interact with graphics APIs, use a convention like shUpdate: mixed case, but with an initial lower-case sh. Nibbles and kernels (functions in the standard library which generate Sh program objects) also use this naming convention to distinguish them from library functions. For instance, shAbs is a templated function that creates and returns an Sh program object that reads a value from an input attribute, takes the absolute value of its components, and outputs it again as an output attribute (the term *attribute* has a special meaning in Sh, as was explained earlier).

Library functions and member functions in Sh are in lower-case with underscores separating words. Library functions do not have an initial prefix, but are still in the SH namespace. It is assumed that they will be used in shader definition contexts, and that it will be desirable to simply globally activate the SH namespace in files that define shaders.

Methods on objects can be divided into actions and properties. Actions are generally given names that are verbs. Properties are values that can be set and retrieved and are given names that are nouns. For properties, the same method name is used for both set and retrieve. If a property member function takes an argument, it sets the value of the associated property. If it doesn't take an argument, it retrieves the value of the associated property.

Finally, comments are typeset in a different, proportional font to make them more compact and easier to read and to distinguish them from program code.

1.6.2   Coordinate Systems

Our examples will make use of five standard coordinate systems: model space (MCS), world space (WCS), view space (VCS), device space (DCS), and surface space (SCS).

The modeling coordinate system will be given the abbreviated name MCS; it is unique to each individual model in a scene. It is the coordinate system in which the actual vertices in the definition of any given model are defined.

The world coordinate system, given the abbreviation WCS, is the common coordinate system for a scene; it is independent of both the modeling coordinate systems and the view. Very often we do not need to compute coordinates in the WCS, but it is occasionally useful for computations of such things as reflection vectors indexing into environment maps.

The viewing coordinate system, or VCS, is a camera-relative coordinate system with the camera at the origin and looking down the negative z-axis. It is a right-handed coordinate system, with x going to the right, y going up and z coming towards the viewer.

The device coordinate space is a normalized coordinate system for the current viewport, with minimum x and y mapped to -1 and maximum x and y mapped to 1. Values of z at the near plane are mapped to 0, those close to the far plane are mapped to 1. This follows OpenGL conventions [133, 135]. We use both homogeneous and non-homogeneous coordinates for the DCS. Normally the vertex shader generates homogeneous device coordinates, and these are normalized by the rasterizer by dividing out the homogeneous coordinate. We will say that homogeneous coordinates are in the HDCS space and normalized coordinates are in DCS.

The final space is the surface coordinate system (SCS). A surface coordinate system is defined at every non-degenerate point of a surface by a normal and two non-parallel tangents. Points and vectors can be defined relative to this frame, and often are for the purposes of evaluating reflectance models. We will say that a vector or point defined by a linear combination of these normals and tangents is expressed relative to the surface coordinate system.

The transformations relating the MCS and the WCS are normally affine, but the transformations relating the WCS and VCS are normally Euclidean (rigid-body: length and angle preserving). We will assume this in our shaders. We will not write shaders assuming the MCS to WCS transformation is Euclidean; we will assume that general affine transformations are possible. Therefore, some simplifications to our shaders our possible in the (common) case that the MCS to WCS transformations do not include non-uniform scales and shears. Our examples will not be guaranteed to work if either of these transformations is projective. The surface frame is not always orthonormal. In particular, the normal is always perpendicular to the two tangents in the frame, but the tangents are not always perpendicular to each other. Despite this, we usually define lighting models relative to the local surface frame as if it were a Euclidean frame.

1.6.3 Standard Vectors and Variable Names

Our example shaders will be written with all vectors pointing *away* from the surface point being shaded. We will also use the letters and symbols given in Table 1.1 for common vectors, and the suffixes and symbols defined in Table 1.2 to indicate in which coordinate system these objects are defined, or, when an input and output have the same name (and are not distinguished by coordinate system), to give them a unique name.

For example, in code, the view vector relative to the surface coordinate system will be expressed as vs, the vertex position relative to the modeling coordinate system will be given as pm, the reflected view vector in the world coordinate system will be given as rw, and a light direction vector in the modeling coordinate system will be lm. An input texture coordinate will be called ui, while an output texture coordinate will be called uo. If there is more than one of some attribute type, numbers will be used to distinguish them. We will not depend on these names alone to define the meaning of attributes, but hopefully they will help to clarify code examples. We will mention exceptions to these rules when they occur.

In mathematics, we will use the related symbols also given in Table 1.1 and superscripts indicating the coordinate systems given in Table 1.2 when necessary. For instance, a generic light vector will be indicated by $\hat{l}$, while one expressed specifically in the SCS will be indicated by $\hat{l}^s$. In addition, the notation $\hat{l}$ will be used to indicate a vector that has been normalized to unit length, $\vec{l}$ a vector of arbitrary length, and $\ell = |\vec{l}|$ will be equivalent to the Euclidean length of $\vec{l}$. Components will generally be indicated where necessary using

v	$\hat{\mathbf{v}}$	$=$	(v_x, v_y, v_z)	The view vector: the normalized
		$=$	(v_0, v_1, v_2)	vector directed towards the position
				of the eye
l	$\hat{\mathbf{l}}$	$=$	(ℓ_x, ℓ_y, ℓ_z)	The light vector: the normalized
				vector directed towards the position
				of the light source
p	$\underline{\mathbf{p}}$	$=$	(p_x, p_y, p_z)	The surface position:
		$=$	(p_0, p_1, p_2)	vertex or fragment position,
		$=$	(x, y, z)	depending on context
h	$\hat{\mathbf{h}}$	$=$	(h_x, h_y, h_z)	The half vector: the normalized
		$=$	(h_0, h_1, h_2)	vector halfway between the view and
				light vectors
r	$\hat{\mathbf{r}}$	$=$	(r_x, r_y, r_z)	The reflected view vecto:
			(r_0, r_1, r_2)	mirrored vector in the same plane as
				the normal and the view vector
f	$\hat{\mathbf{f}}$	$=$	(f_x, f_y, f_z)	The refracted view vector
			(f_0, f_1, f_2)	
t	$\hat{\mathbf{t}}$	$=$	(t_x, t_y, t_z)	The primary surface tangent
			(t_0, t_1, t_2)	
s	$\hat{\mathbf{s}}$	$=$	(s_x, s_y, s_z)	The secondary surface tangent
			(s_0, s_1, s_2)	
n	$\hat{\mathbf{n}}$	$=$	(n_x, n_y, n_z)	The surface normal
			(n_0, n_1, n_2)	
u	$\underline{\mathbf{u}}$	$=$	(u, v)	Texture coordinates
			(u_0, u_1)	

Table 1.1. Standard vectors and points.

m	$\mathcal{M}$	The modeling coordinate system (MCS)
w	$\mathcal{W}$	The world coordinate system (WCS)
v	$\mathcal{V}$	The view coordinate system (VCS)
d	$\mathcal{D}$	The device coordinate system (DCS)
s	$\mathcal{S}$	The surface coordinate system (SCS)
i		Input (if not otherwise distinguished)
o		Output (if not otherwise distinguished)
c		Color (usually final color of shader)

Table 1.2. Standard attribute suffixes.

either (ℓ_x, ℓ_y, ℓ_z) or (ℓ_0, ℓ_1, ℓ_2). Normalization of a vector to unit length is a common operation in graphics, but there is no standard notation for it. We will use $\hat{a} = \text{norm}(\vec{a}) = a^{-1}\vec{a}$. In particular, the normalized half vector $\hat{h}$ is defined as

$$\hat{h} = \text{norm}\left(\hat{l} + \hat{v}\right).$$

We will drop the accents when we just want to treat a vector or point as a (column) tuple of coordinates and not a geometric object. For instance, the coordinate tuple representing $\hat{n}$ is n, and $\vec{a} \cdot \vec{b} = a^T b$ in a Cartesian (orthonormal) coordinate system.

The vectors $\hat{t}$, $\hat{s}$, and the normal $\hat{n}$, in that order, give a basis for a right-handed surface coordinate frame rooted at the surface point $\underline{p}$. A vector can be expressed relative to the surface using a linear combination of these vectors; for instance, we can convert some vector $\vec{a}$ expressed in the surface frame to the view frame using

$$
\begin{aligned}
\vec{a}^{\mathcal{V}} &= a_x^{\mathcal{S}}\hat{t}^{\mathcal{V}} + a_y^{\mathcal{S}}\hat{s}^{\mathcal{V}} + a_z^{\mathcal{S}}\hat{n}^{\mathcal{V}} \\
&= a_0^{\mathcal{S}}\hat{t}^{\mathcal{V}} + a_1^{\mathcal{S}}\hat{s}^{\mathcal{V}} + a_2^{\mathcal{S}}\hat{n}^{\mathcal{V}} \\
&= \begin{bmatrix} \hat{t}^{\mathcal{V}} & \hat{s}^{\mathcal{V}} & \hat{n}^{\mathcal{V}} \end{bmatrix} \begin{bmatrix} a_0^{\mathcal{S}} \\ a_1^{\mathcal{S}} \\ a_2^{\mathcal{S}} \end{bmatrix} \\
&= S\vec{a}^{\mathcal{S}}.
\end{aligned}
$$

In Sh code, this can be expressed as

```
av = as[0]*tv + as[1]*sv + as[2]*nv;
```

Alternative formulations of this computation in Sh include use of a matrix constructor to build a change of basis matrix:

```
av = colmat(tv,sv,nv) | as;
```

We intentionally use the terminology "secondary surface tangent" for $\hat{s}$ rather than "binormal" since the binormal in the Frenet frame, which is defined for curves (not surfaces), points in the wrong direction and would give us a left-handed coordinate system [106].

When a function or shader is expressed in such a way that the computation is coordinate-system independent, the suffixes will be dropped. For instance, the reflection vector $\vec{r}$ of an incident vector $\vec{v}$ can be computed in a coordinate-free fashion as a function of $\vec{v}$ and $\hat{n}$ as follows:

$$\vec{r} = 2(\vec{v} \cdot \hat{n})\hat{n} - \vec{v}.$$

An Sh function for this computation can be expressed as

```
ShVector3f
reflect (ShVector3f v, ShNormal3f n) {
  n = normalize(n);   // ensure precondition
  ShVector3f r = 2*(v|n)*n - v;
  return r;
}
```

Listing 1.6. Reflection function.

Some standard angles are also defined and used in various places. We give these in terms of dot products of standard vectors:

$$
\begin{aligned}
\cos \alpha &= \hat{\mathbf{l}} \cdot \hat{\mathbf{n}}, \\
\cos \beta &= \hat{\mathbf{v}} \cdot \hat{\mathbf{n}}, \\
\cos \delta &= \hat{\mathbf{h}} \cdot \hat{\mathbf{n}}, \\
\cos \gamma &= \hat{\mathbf{h}} \cdot \hat{\mathbf{v}} \\
&= \hat{\mathbf{h}} \cdot \hat{\mathbf{l}}.
\end{aligned}
$$

In particular, $\cos \gamma$ will sometimes be used to emphasize the fact that $\hat{\mathbf{h}} \cdot \hat{\mathbf{v}}$ and $\hat{\mathbf{h}} \cdot \hat{\mathbf{l}}$ are always equal and, therefore, interchangeable.

Finally, we often need to clamp a value to 0 if it is negative, such as these very dot products. In graphics, many interesting quantities such as power and reflectance must be physically positive. Likewise, colors in graphics are often stored in datatypes that can only represent a maximum value of 1. We make and use the following definitions:

$$
\begin{aligned}
\mathrm{pos}(x) &= \max(0, x), \\
\mathrm{sat}(x) &= \min(1, x).
\end{aligned}
$$

1.6.4   Global Parameters

The examples in this book make use of some predefined global types, parameters, and constants. These are defined in Table 1.3. The names are short to keep the lengths of listings from getting out of control. The names of matrices are capitalized to distinguish them from tuples (although otherwise, we only capitalize macros).

These global parameters are *not* part of the Sh language definition. Sh permits the definition of arbitrary sets of global parameters. These parameters are, however, encapsulated in a class framework distributed with Sh, as described in Chapter 3. We also use these parameters, as simple global variables, in a GLUT-based test application within which all code given in this book will work.

Global Constants and Parameters	
Definition	Represents
// for multiple light source shaders	
struct Light {	
ShPoint3f pm;	Light position (in MCS)
ShVector3f lm;	Light direction (in MCS)
ShPoint3f pv;	Light position (in VCS)
ShVector3f lv;	Light direction (in VCS)
ShColor3f c;	Light color (in RGB)
};	
Light *lights*[NLIGHTS];	Many lights
Light& *light* = *lights*[0];	One light
// forward transformations	
ShMatrix4x4f MW;	MCS to WCS transformation
ShMatrix4x4f MV;	MCS to VCS transformation
ShMatrix4x4f MD;	MCS to DCS transformation
ShMatrix4x4f WV;	WCS to VCS transformation
ShMatrix4x4f WD;	WCS to DCS transformation
ShMatrix4x4f VD;	VCS to DCS transformation
// inverse transformations	
ShMatrix4x4f WM;	WCS to MCS transformation
ShMatrix4x4f VM;	VCS to MCS transformation
ShMatrix4x4f DM;	DCS to MCS transformation
ShMatrix4x4f VW;	VCS to WCS transformation
ShMatrix4x4f DW;	DCS to WCS transformation
ShMatrix4x4f DV;	DCS to VCS transformation

Table 1.3. Global constants and parameters. These definitions will often be assumed in our examples, highlighted as shown.

Note the convention used for the names of transformation matrices: we state the source space first and the destination space second. So the MW matrix is the transformation from the modeling coordinate system $\mathcal{M}$ to the world coordinate system $\mathcal{W}$, *not* the product of two matrices "M" and "W." Matrices are set up so that points and vectors are transformed as column vectors on the right of the matrix, and normals and plane equations are transformed as row vectors on the left of the inverse matrix.

All matrices are 4×4. This means that after a transformation, the result will always be a 4-tuple. If you want to store a result to a 3-tuple, a swizzle or cast must be used to discard the homogeneous coordinate. However, the

homogeneous coordinate is automatically filled in with either a 0 or 1 (based on
the type) if a 3-tuple is used as input with a 4×4 matrix.

Transformations of normals and planes specify the normals as row vectors
on the left and use the inverse transformation. This is equivalent to the rule
that normals (when represented with column vectors) are transformed by the
inverse transpose. Normals are really *covectors*, which are dual to vectors, and
are defined by the fact that they must always be perpendicular to the tangent
plane.

Suppose we are given a tangent $\hat{t}$ and a transformation matrix A. Then, for
any normal $\hat{n}$, we must have $\hat{n} \cdot \hat{t} = 0$, and we want $\hat{n}' \cdot \hat{t}' = 0$ for transformed
normal $\hat{n}'$ and transformed tangent $\hat{t}'$. We know that $\hat{t}' = A\hat{t}$. We can derive
the transformation of normal $\hat{n}$ as follows:

$$
\begin{aligned}
\hat{n} \cdot \hat{t} &= \mathbf{n}^T \mathbf{t} \\
&= \mathbf{n}^T A^{-1} A \mathbf{t} \\
&= (\mathbf{n}^T A^{-1})(A\mathbf{t}) \\
&= ((A^{-1})^T \mathbf{n})^T (A\mathbf{t}) \\
&= \hat{n}' \cdot \hat{t}'.
\end{aligned}
$$

Representing normals as row vectors is equivalent to transposing the inverse
matrix and representing normals as column vectors. In our examples, we choose
to represent normals as row vectors.

Putting this all together, to transform a point pm stored as a 3-tuple given in
the MCS to the VCS and store the result in a 3-tuple pw, (assuming the transformation is affine), use

```
pv = (MV | pm)(0,1,2);
```

where "|" is the matrix-tuple product, and tuples appearing on the left of this
operator are interpreted as columns. The "(0,1,2)" is a swizzle to extract the
first three components of the result.

To transform and normalize a normal from the MCS to the VCS, with input
and output both represented using 3-tuples, generally one should use

```
nv = normalize((nm | VM)(0,1,2));
```

This is really only required for normals if the transformation *VM* is non-Euclidean
(contains shears or non-uniform scales), and is equivalent to

```
nw = normalize((transpose(inverse(MV)) | nm)(0,1,2));
```

If it is known that the transformation is Euclidean, then the same rule (and matrix) as that used for points and vectors can be used. In fact, in this case the normalization also can be avoided when the input normals are unit length. We are working on tracking this sort of thing in a future release of Sh via more sophisticated transformation classes, metainformation declarations, and domain-specific optimizations. In the meantime, for all the examples used in this book, we use the most generally correct idiom.

1.7 License, History, and Access

Sh is a free Open Source project, distributed under a license which reads as follows:

> *Permission is granted to anyone to use this software for any purpose, including commercial applications, and to alter it and redistribute it freely, subject to the following restrictions:*
>
> 1. *The origin of this software must not be misrepresented; you must not claim that you wrote the original software. If you use this software in a product, an acknowledgment in the product documentation would be appreciated but is not required.*
>
> 2. *Altered source versions must be plainly marked as such, and must not be misrepresented as being the original software.*
>
> 3. *This notice may not be removed or altered from any source distribution.*

Sh was developed in the Computer Graphics Lab at the School of Computer Science at the University of Waterloo. The SMASH API [87, 104] was a conceptual predecessor to Sh, but targeted a simulated GPU, since no GPUs were available at the time that supported the necessary features. This system has since been factored into two projects: a GPU simulator component called Sm (which Sh can still target, but which it does not depend on) and a high-level programmable API/language component called Sh. The prototype of the current design of Sh was implemented as part of Zheng Qin's M.Math thesis [122]. The current version of Sh was significantly reengineered by Stefanus Du Toit, now a graduate student at the University of Waterloo. Other contributors include Kevin Moule (just-in-time CPU backend), Tiberiu Popa (multipass scheduler, Julia set shader), Bryan Chan (kernel library, shader algebra demos, noise functions, many many other utility functions, proofreading and feedback on documentation), Jack Wang (matrix and quaternion library), Gabriel Moreno-Fortuny (stream processing test cases), Gabriel Renaud (matrix library), Zaid Mian (testing: subsurface scattering), Ju-Lian Kwan (testing: tone mapping), Sylvain Vasseur (various shaders), Edwin Vane (testing: cloud volume rendering), and Filip Špaček (testing: matrix light transport, demos, proofreading and feedback on documentation). Michael McCool is the team leader and is responsible for the overall design of the language. (He even occasionally gets to write some code.)

Sh is under active development and as of April 2004 is in an alpha state. The core of the language is stable, but we are working on improving performance and standard library support. We plan a beta release in August 2004 with a complete standard library and more powerful optimizer.

Sh will continue to improve in performance and capabilities, but it is the intent of the developers that all further extensions to the language will be backward compatible with the beta version, and that the core of the implementation will always be platform and graphics API independent, vendor neutral, and available under an Open Source license. Sh requires a floating-point capable GPU such as an NVIDIA GeForceFX 5200 (or better) or an ATI Radeon 9600 (or better).

The most recent version of Sh may be downloaded from

```
http://libsh.sourceforge.net/
```

Mailing lists for news related to Sh, code from this book, applications using Sh, many sample shaders, and other documentation may also be accessed at this site. Additional online documentation includes an up-to-date HTML version of the reference manual (including documentation on functions and kernels possibly added since this book was published), links to papers on Sh [90, 91], errata on this book (hopefully not too many), internal documentation generated from structured comments via `doxygen`, and various other propaganda.

1.8   Status and Future Development

We are documenting the intended state of the beta release in this book. At the time the book was submitted, some of the features documented in this manual are not yet functional. For readers using a preliminary version of Sh, in this section we document how the "current" Sh differs from the "documented" Sh discussed in the rest of this book. Online documentation at the Sh web site will provide updates on the differences between what is documented here and what is actually available, if necessary. We have also documented some features that require expected, but not yet available, hardware features in GPUs, or that we have implemented but that are still experimental. This includes, for instance, data-dependent control flow. Where features are unlikely to be available for the August 2004 beta release due to factors beyond our control, we have noted that in the text.

Section 1.8.1 discusses features that are not fully functional at the time of submission of this book, but should be in the beta release. Section 1.8.2 mentions some slightly more ambitious features that we intend to implement, which will likely not be ready by August 2004, but should be available before the end of 2004. Finally, in Section 1.8.3, we discuss some future plans for Sh that are really research projects at this point and are *not* described in detail elsewhere.

1.8.1   Beta Release Features

These features should be functional by August 2004, but currently are not in the released version.

Complete Support for the Standard Library. Not all the functions documented here for the standard library are implemented in the alpha release, or they are implemented but have not yet been merged into the standard library, or differ in some small details (such as the name) from what is documented here. All functions documented here will definitely be included in the standard library in the beta release, and the details will match this documentation as closely as possible. The exceptions (which we hope will be a small number) will be noted in an errata page available from the Sh web site.

Conditional Assignment Blocks. The *SH_WHEN* conditional assignment control construct is not yet implemented, but should be available in the beta release. The cond function is already implemented and supports the same functionality. Implementation of *SH_WHEN* just requires a syntactic transformation of the code (inserting conditional outputs on all basic blocks guarded by such a clause).

Until a true *SH_IF* is implemented, *SH_IF* will use the same implementation as *SH_WHEN*.

Better Optimizations. Certain optimizations, such as common subexpression elimination and some domain-specific algebraic simplifications (such as normalization eliminations) are not yet implemented, but are a high priority for completion by the beta release since some parts of the design of the standard library depend on them. In particular, modularity is hard to take seriously if it leads to less efficient code than flattening and hand-optimization. Most hand optimizations that would break modularity can be made unnecessary by the above two automatic optimizations.

Storage Types. Integer storage types are not yet supported, only floating point.

Texture Mode Simulation. Some combinations of texture modes and storage types, such as interpolation on floating-point textures, floating-point MIP mapping, and floating-point cube maps, have not yet been implemented, but are in progress.

Derivatives. We plan to support derivatives on NVIDIA platforms. Current ATI platforms are more difficult, since a multipass implementation will be required (and so may only be available after the beta release, once we implement a native Sh rendering interface; see below). Basically, to implement derivatives on current ATI platforms, we would need to render textures containing all values for which we need the basic partials and then read them back with differencing in a later pass.

1.8.2   Year-End Features

Data-Dependent Control Constructs. True data-dependent control constructs are currently only reliable for CPU stream processing targets. We have a prototype implementation of control constructs using a multipass implementation on ATI 9700 GPUs, but it is still highly experimental and will likely not be included in the beta release.

Part of the problem is that we decided that pbuffers would be too slow for our multipass implementation due to context switching overhead, so we focused on superbuffers. However, superbuffers are not yet fully supported—and may never be. We have abstracted buffer management in Sh, so the prototype now works both with pbuffers and with some experimental überbuffer support. However, we were unable to implement some features efficiently due to lack of support in the existing APIs and drivers. When better buffer management APIs are available and better supported, we should be able to get our approach to work on GPU stream targets.

Some GPUs may be available by August 2004 that support data-dependent conditionals internally. We will add support for these on both shaders and stream programs as soon as these GPUs are available, and we can get one for testing.

Virtualization of Stream Programs. Currently we only virtualize the number of outputs of stream programs, but not other resources, such as the number of texture reads or instruction length. We hope to complete virtualization of other resources shortly after the beta release.

Virtualization of Shaders. Virtualization of shaders will require Sh to define a rendering API so we can issue multiple passes over the geometry. This is also necessary for derivatives on current ATI platforms.

Direct3D Binding. In theory, this should be easy, and in fact multipass compilation should be more straightforward. However, we have not yet begun it, so it is unlikely it would be stable enough for the beta release. We plan to get a Direct3D binding working in the early fall.

HLSL, GLSL, and Cg Backends. One way to get a Direct3D backend and make Sh "at least as good as" the compilers in existing shading languages would be to target other shading languages as backends. We can't guarantee this functionality by the beta release. However, we already do something similar for the CPU backend, which generates C++ code and compiles it.

TCC Backend and Improved CPU Metaprogramming. The TCC or "Tiny cc" compiler is designed explicitly for use in just-in-time compilation applications, such as the implementation of scripting languages and dynamic code generation. It compiles code an order of magnitude faster than gcc, does a reasonable job of optimization, and supports a library interface so we can avoid the file access overhead of our current gcc-based CPU backend. In addition to improving performance, TCC will also allow us to use Sh in situations where file system access and installation of gcc would be awkward, for instance, on mobile devices and game platforms. TCC [13] is also free and open source (GNU Lesser General Public License). For more information, see

```
http://fabrice.bellard.free.fr/tcc/
```

To better support "small" applications of CPU metaprogramming, we also plan to add support for an alternative statically-typed Sh type for programs, to be called **ShFunction***k*, where k is the number of arguments. An **ShFunction** would be a template type parameterized by the types of its return value and arguments so that it can be statically type checked. This would avoid the current dynamic type-checking overhead in the invocation of **ShProgram** objects. Dynamic type-checking overhead is minor for stream computations but not for computation on tuples. We will also define an inlined overloaded () operator on this new type to invoke a function pointer which can be initialized to point at the dynamically compiled code. The goal is to reduce the cost of invoking a dynamically generated function to that of a single function pointer dereference while supporting a clean and easy-to-use interface. Implementing this may also require a new keyword, **SH_BEGIN_FUNCTION***k* that takes a sequence of types and returns an **ShFunction***k*, and probably some further optimization of the Sh immediate mode.

Shared Uniform Computations. Currently, if a shader specifies a computation that depends only on a parameter, that computation still takes place on the GPU. It should be identified (automatically) as a "uniform" computation and performed on the host. However, then the derived value is dependent on the parameters it references, so code needs to be generated to compute the updated value on the CPU (either compiled just-in-time or interpreted). But then several uniform computations might be shared in different shaders, such as computation of the inverse of the model-view matrix, and we want to defer updates of uniforms until we load a shader that needs them. We plan to implement a system that transparently manages all this—the problem is similar to that of texture update and common subexpression elimination, so this will be part of the general goal of improving the optimizer.

1.8.3   Future Features

These features will probably not be functional by the end of 2004 except as research prototypes, but they are either under development or are under serious consideration.

Rendering Interface. Once we specify a stream-based interface for rendering, users could avoid all the rules for binding Sh shaders to OpenGL or Direct3D applications, and instead implement applications directly in Sh, with Sh managing the bindings directly. This also means we could automate more optimizations and could avoid problems arising from synchronization with another API. However, we plan to continue to support, extend, improve, and document bindings to both OpenGL and Direct3D.

Parallel and Distributed Computation. We can already compile to CPU code. Why not compile to CPUs other than the one on which the host application is running?

We plan to implement backends that will take streaming computations specified by stream algebra expressions or control graphs and map them to parallel machines. This has applications in real-time graphics, since large scientific visualizations use parallel machines and the PlayStation 3 will likely be a parallel distributed-memory machine. Of course, automatic parallelization of Sh code would also be useful for straight numerical applications, especially if the same numerical libraries (written on top of Sh) could be used on GPUs and scalar CPUs as well.

We plan to implement this feature under the framework of our Sm "simulator," which already has a packet-stream architecture suitable for this application. The Sh buffer management system is also already designed to handle distributed storage of streams and textures. Finally, we intend to use CPU metaprogramming to upgrade our Sm "simulator" into a high-performance software renderer supporting shaders.

Campaigns. Since we can specify stream computations with the stream algebra, and this is basically a functional language, it would be useful to capture and compile a sequence of stream computations as a higher-level language in its own right. We plan to call these "campaigns" to distinguish them from "programs," since program objects currently only describe operations in kernels. We might also want to add parallel programming constructs such as *SH_PAR* and *SH_SEQ* to the stream language. Once such a retained-mode, higher-order stream language is defined, it would be interesting to investigate algorithms for optimizing stream computations further. For instance, it might be possible to reorder computations to reduce overhead due to buffer copies and shader rebindings.

Chapter 2

Tuples, Matrices, Operators, and Functions

This chapter presents the basic capabilities available in Sh when it is used in immediate mode. In this mode, operations specified on Sh types execute immediately, and Sh can be used like an object-oriented matrix-vector utility library. To organize and encapsulate code and data, C++ functions and classes can be used in the usual fashion. We discuss several reflectance models and show how they can be given a uniform interface and how they can be encapsulated together with their parameters.

2.1 Tuples

The core types in Sh are n-tuples of numbers. Tuples have a *semantic type* (including **Point**, **Vector**, **Normal**, **Plane**, and **TexCoord**), a length, and a *storage type*. The length must be a compile-time constant, but may otherwise be arbitrary. In particular, tuples in Sh are not limited to length 4, and most library functions are designed to extend to tuples of arbitrary length.

For example, **ShPoint3f** is a three-dimensional point stored as a triple of single-precision floating-point numbers, and **ShColor4ub** is a four-component color whose components are stored as unsigned bytes. Normally in shaders we just use floating-point tuples, but the other storage types are useful for streams and textures. Tuple types are discussed in more detail in Section 7.2 on page 138. Textures will be discussed in Chapter 4 and streams will be discussed in Chapter 5.

Generic tuples are given the semantic type **Attrib**. This semantic type is also the supertype of all other semantic types. The tuple type names presented

43

so far are actually predefined convenience `typedefs` wrapping a more general template mechanism for specifying tuple types. To specify a tuple of a length greater than 4, the template interface must be used. For instance, to declare a generic 9-tuple of floating point values, the declaration **ShAttrib**<9,- **SH_TEMP**,**float**> can be used. Arbitrary-length tuples are useful for many purposes, including high-spectral representations of color and basis function coefficients (for instance, for use with spherical harmonics). The meaning of the **SH_TEMP** *binding type* will be discussed in Chapter 3.

2.2   Operators and Library Functions

Many operators are overloaded on Sh tuple types to provide a simple interface to common functionality. Sh also provides a number of standard library functions that complement the operators.

Arithmetic operators on tuples usually act componentwise, except for multiplication and division on certain semantic types in which an alternative definition makes sense (matrices in particular). As well as addition "+," subtraction/negation "−," multiplication "∗," and division "/," Sh also defines modulo "%," which is equivalent to the mod library function.

Scalar promotion works on most operators. You can multiply a vector by a scalar (and that scalar can be a C++ floating-point value or an Sh 1-tuple). To take the reciprocals of all the elements of a tuple x, the expression 1/x suffices. Most library functions are also defined to act componentwise. For example, the expression sqrt(x) will take the square roots of all the elements of tuple x and return the results in a tuple of the same length. Although we have extended their semantics to tuples, whenever possible, we have defined Sh library functions to use the same names as the C math library and/or other shading languages.

The "|" and "^" operators are used for dot product and cross product respectively, although dot and cross functions are also supported. The cross product only works on 3-tuples, but the dot product works on tuples of arbitrary dimension. To normalize an n-tuple to unit length, the expressions x/sqrt(x|x) or x∗rsqrt(x|x) can be used. However, there is also a library function called normalize that does the same thing. In fact, the normalize library function should be used instead of the above expressions, as the Sh optimizer has special rules for it, taking advantage of the fact that a tuple which is known to be normalized need not be normalized again.

Sh supports a large number of other built-in functions, including both procedural and texture-based noise functions of various kinds (including signed and unsigned cellnoise, Perlin, turbulence, and Worley functions, with summation over octaves or multiple basis functions), tuple sorting (on tuples of arbitrary length), trigonometric, exponential, logarithmic, and geometric operations, smoothed discontinuities, and spline evaluators. All functions in the standard library are designed to compile to targets without data-dependent branches or loops. The available operators and library functions are documented in Chapter 8.

Sh is not overly picky about type checking in the implementation of the standard operators and functions. It does catch common errors like size mismatches, but does not try to enforce strict geometric consistency with the C++ type system. For example, in Sh it is possible to add two points, even though this is geometrically questionable. However, if we made this particular operation illegal, common and geometrically consistent operations such as affine combinations would be annoying to specify.

Most of the standard library functions will silently accept most semantic types and do something useful with them. Even though the type checking in Sh is not very strict, the semantic types provide useful documentation and metainformation, and in some cases control the meaning of operators and functions (multiplication on complex numbers, for instance). They are also relevant to homogeneous promotion, a useful feature discussed in the next section.

The "()" notation is used for *swizzling*, using integers to index components. If c is an **ShColor3f** representing an RGB color, then c(2,1,0) gives that color in BGR order. Swizzles can also change the length of a tuple or repeat elements. If we are given a 2-component LA color b and want to convert it to a 3-component RGB color while ignoring the A component, we could use b(0,0,0). The swizzle notation with one argument can be used to select single elements of a tuple, although the "[]" operator can also be used in this case. A similar notation on the left-hand side of an assignment expression supports *writemasking*, or the selective update and reordering of the elements of a tuple.

Comparison operations return tuples whose components are either 0 or 1, using the same storage types as their inputs. The "&&" and "||" operators are defined to mean min and max respectively, which is consistent with Boolean operations. Negative and zero numbers are false in Sh, while any positive number is true. The any and all operations can be used to reduce Boolean tuples to a single decision and are equivalent to componentwise max (OR) and min (AND), respectively. The cond function supports conditional assignment (unfortunately, "?:" cannot be overloaded in C++) with both Boolean tuples and scalars. When used with Boolean tuples, the conditional assignment is applied componentwise.

2.3   Matrices

Sh supports small fixed-size matrices to represent affine and projective transformations. Matrix types have names like **ShMatrix3x4f** and can be square or rectangular. There is a standard library that supports operations on these matrices; it includes functions to compute the determinant, adjoint, trace, inverse, and transpose, and to build matrices from tuples by row, column, or diagonal. There are also functions to build matrices for standard transformations like rotation, translation, and scale.

Matrices also support swizzling and slicing. If M is a 4 × 4 matrix, then M(2,1,0)(2,1,0) extracts the 3 × 3 upper-left submatrix and transposes it. Both row and column swizzles must be supplied with this notation, but the empty swizzle "()" is the identity. Therefore, the expression M()(3,2,1,0) reverses the columns of M and the expression M(3,2,1,0)() reverses the rows.

Matrices also support the "[]" operator. Application of this operator extracts a tuple representing a row of the matrix. Unlike the case with "()," the result can be interpreted directly as a tuple. A second application of "[]" selects a component of the returned tuple, so M[2] selects row 2 of matrix M as an **ShAttrib4f** and M[2][3] selects the scalar element at row 2, column 3. On the left-hand side of an assignment, these operators can be also used to write selectively to elements of matrices.

Transformations of tuples by matrices is supported by the "*" or "|" operators, which have identical semantics. Both support matrix/tuple and tuple/matrix multiplication. We support "*" for consistency with other shading languages, but prefer the use of "|" to emphasize the distinction between componentwise multiplication and matrix multiplication.

If the matrix M is on the left and the tuple t is on the right of a matrix/tuple product as in M|t, the tuple t is interpreted as a column vector. If the tuple is on the left and the matrix is on the right as in t|M, the tuple is interpreted as a row vector. This rule avoids a lot of transpose operators. For example, a general quadratic form can be expressed directly with t|M|t and is consistent with the use of "|" for the inner (dot) product.

If a tuple is one element too small for the matrix being applied to it, it is automatically extended with a homogeneous coordinate appropriate for its type. For instance, if you try to transform an **ShPoint3f** by an **ShMatrix4x4f**, the point will be automatically extended with a homogeneous coordinate of 1. If an **ShVector3f** is transformed the same way, it will be extended with a homogeneous coordinate of 0, instead.

2.4 Functions

You can declare your own functions; specifically, C++ functions, template functions, member functions, and overloaded operators will all work as you expect. Don't worry about the cost of copying arguments and returning them. References will work as expected when passing arguments, but they are not necessary.

Later, when we define shaders and functions via metaprogramming and compile them with the Sh compiler, Sh will flatten and optimize all operations. In particular, the cost of argument copying will be completely eliminated. Some cost will be incurred in immediate mode, but Sh uses a reference model for data internally. Passing a matrix type by value, for instance, does not involve copying the matrix data itself, but really only involves passing the equivalent of a pointer.

We will now introduce the use of C++ functions in Sh with some examples that will be useful later.

2.4.1 Example: Glass Support Functions

Suppose you would like to simulate the appearance of glass (or water), including reflection and refraction. You will need a function to compute a reflection vector, a refraction vector, and the Fresnel coefficient [104]. The Fresnel coefficient determines the ratio between specular reflection and refraction.

As previously discussed, reflection of a vector $\vec{v}$ can be computed as follows:

$$\vec{r} \;=\; 2(\hat{n} \cdot \vec{v})\hat{n} - \vec{v}.$$

Note that this requires $\hat{n}$ to be normalized, but $\vec{v}$ does not have to be. However, the output vector $\vec{r}$ will be normalized if the input vector $\vec{v}$ is.[1]

The refracted vector $\hat{f}$ is a little harder to compute. We use the following [134, 43]:

$$
\begin{aligned}
\cos\beta &= \hat{v} \cdot \hat{n}, \\
k &= 1 + \eta^2(\cos^2\beta - 1), \\
K &= \mathrm{pos}(\mathrm{sat}(k)), \\
\hat{f} &= \eta\hat{v} + (\eta\cos\beta + \sqrt{K})\hat{n}.
\end{aligned}
$$

The relative index of refraction is given as $\eta = n_i/n_t$, where n_i is the index of refraction of the material the ray is coming from, and n_t is the index of refraction

---

[1]The library version of this function will track these dependencies for the optimizer, but the version we present here does not.

of the material the ray is being transmitted into. Total internal reflection occurs when $k < 0$. In this case, the refracted vector should not be used. We clamp k to the $[0, 1]$ range using $pos(sat(k))$ to avoid NaN (Not-a-Number) floating-point results.

At a smooth interface between two materials, the Fresnel relationship arises due to the condition that the electric and magnetic fields must be continuous. The Fresnel coefficient indicates the portion of the light that will be reflected compared to the amount that will be transmitted. The Fresnel term tends to go to unity for glancing view angles and reaches a minimum when the surface is viewed along the normal direction. Smooth surfaces therefore tend to be more reflective near their silhouettes.

Full treatment of the Fresnel term requires a representation of the polarization of light. The Fresnel coefficient is different for different incoming polarizations, and so specular reflection tends to polarize light. This is why polarizing sunglasses are effective at selectively cutting glare. However, treatment of polarization is rarely done in graphics, even for non-real time rendering.

For unpolarized light, a good approximation has been suggested by Schlick [130, 104]:

$$\begin{aligned}
\cos\gamma &= \hat{\mathbf{h}} \cdot \hat{\mathbf{l}} \\
&= \hat{\mathbf{h}} \cdot \hat{\mathbf{v}}, \\
F(\cos\gamma) &= R_s + (1 - R_s)(1 - \cos\gamma)^5,
\end{aligned}$$

where R_s is the fraction of light reflected at normal incidence (in the direction of the normal when the light is also in the direction of the normal). This value can either be given explicitly or can be computed as a function of the relative index of refraction, η:

$$R_s = \left(\frac{\eta - 1}{\eta + 1}\right)^2.$$

Functions to compute the Fresnel term, the reflection vector, and the refraction vector are actually already in the standard library, but if you wanted to define these functions yourself, you could do it as shown in Listing 2.1. We will finish the definition of a glass shader in Chapter 4 when we discuss texture maps, since we will need to index an environment map.

These function definitions have the obvious semantics. Sh types can generally be used just like you would use any other class library for points and vectors. You can use function pointers, pass by reference to return values in arguments, overloaded operators, template functions, separate compilation, and all the usual machinery of C++.

```
ShVector3f
reflect (ShVector3f v, ShNormal3f n) {
  v = normalize(v);
  n = normalize(n);
  return ShVector3f(2.0*(n|v)*n - v);
}
ShAttrib1f
fresnel (ShVector3f v, ShNormal3f l, ShAttrib1f eta) {
  v = normalize(v);
  l = normalize(l);
  ShAttrib1f Rs = pow((eta - 1)/(eta + 1),2);
  return Rs + (1-Rs)*pow((1 - (v|l)),5);
}
ShVector3f
refract (
    ShVector3f v,
    ShNormal3f n,
    ShAttrib1f eta
) {
    v = normalize(v);
    n = normalize(n);
    ShAttrib1f c = (v|n);
    ShAttrib1f k = c*c - 1;
    k = 1 + eta*eta*k;
    k = clamp(k,0,1);
    ShAttrib1f a = eta;
    ShAttrib1f b = eta*c + sqrt(k);
    ShVector3f r = a*v + b*n;
    return r;
}
```

Listing 2.1. Glass support functions.

Sh classes are really smart pointers to data stored elsewhere. This is described in more detail in Section 14.1 on page 229. Therefore, passing Sh types by value is relatively efficient, even for matrices; operating on them is slightly slower in immediate mode than a more direct implementation, since a pointer must be dereferenced (and also because every Sh operation has to check if it *is* being used in immediate mode).

If you want to store an array of Sh types, you may want to use one of the Sh array types discussed in Chapter 4 to avoid the pointer dereferencing overhead.

However, if you *really* want to improve efficiency, you should make use of the Sh CPU metaprogramming and stream processing capabilities, which will result in much more efficient code than is possible with standard C++ class libraries. We will discuss this capability in the following chapters. When Sh's metaprogramming capability is used, Sh can apply global optimizations (such as tracking and removal of extraneous normalizations, copies, and common subexpression elimination) that are difficult or impossible to apply at C++ compile time. The same code you write in immediate mode can generally be used in metaprogrammed mode, except you should avoid data-dependent control flow decisions based on values computed by Sh expressions.

We strongly suggest that when writing Sh code that you aim for simple, readable code. Do not excessively hand optimize your code until you understand what optimizations Sh can do for you. In particular, do not worry about normalizations and common subexpressions. If a function requires a normalized vector to operate correctly, go ahead and normalize it. Don't force users of your function to do dot products for you, do them yourself, encapsulated inside the function. In fact, if you try too hard to hand optimize your code, you will make it harder to maintain *and* may make it harder for Sh to find optimizations on its own.

2.4.2   Example: Reflectance Models

We will now discuss the mathematics of a number of reflectance models that we will use for examples. After introducing them mathematically we will define Sh functions for each model, and then show how abstract classes and operator overloading can be used to encapsulate and abstract their interfaces. However, we are not defining shaders yet—we will do that in the next chapter. We will just define these lighting models in immediate mode for now, as if we were going to use them in a software renderer such as a ray tracer [134].

A lighting model in computer graphics traditionally includes several factors, including a model of attenuation from the light source. For the purposes of this chapter, we will consider reflection only: once the light has reached the surface, how do we compute the color the viewer sees?

Physically, the problem of reflectance is modelled with the bidirectional reflectance distribution function, or *BRDF*. The BRDF f of a reflection model is the differential ratio of outgoing radiance in the view direction to the incoming irradiance reaching the surface from the light source [104]. It is parameterized by the view and light vectors relative to the local surface coordinate system:

$$f(\hat{\mathbf{v}}^S, \hat{\mathbf{l}}^S) \quad = \quad \frac{dL_o(\underline{\mathbf{p}}, \hat{\mathbf{v}}^S)}{L_i(\underline{\mathbf{p}}, \hat{\mathbf{l}}^S)\, \ell_z^S \, d\omega(\hat{\mathbf{l}}^S)},$$

where L_o is the outgoing radiance, L_i is the incoming radiance, and $d\omega$ is the solid angle measure. The incoming irradiance is computed from incoming radiance L_i by multiplying by the projected area of the surface relative to the direction of the flow of light. The projected area is given by $\hat{n} \cdot \hat{l} = \ell_z$.

For *isotropic* BRDFs, that is, reflectance models that do not change if we rotate the surface around its normal, the dependency of the BRDF on the local surface frame can be reduced to a dependency on $\hat{n}$, and we can write $f(\hat{v}, \hat{l}, \hat{n})$. Of course, in general, $\hat{n}$ depends in turn on $\underline{p}$.

Anisotropic BRDFs depend on the orientation of the surface frame around the normal. Generally, we only need two of the three surface frame basis vectors. There are computational advantages to using the two tangents rather than a tangent and a normal, since tangent vectors can be transformed using the same matrix as points. We generally use $f(\hat{v}, \hat{l}, \hat{t}, \hat{s})$ for anisotropic BRDFs and generate the normal using $\hat{n} = \hat{t} \times \hat{s}$. This approach is also useful for bump mapping, in which a local surface coordinate system is also required.

If we only give $f(\hat{v}, \hat{l})$, a dependency on the local surface frame is to be understood.

Radiance L is defined as the radiative power per unit solid angle per unit projected area:

$$L(\underline{p}, \hat{v}) \quad = \quad \frac{d^2\Phi}{dA(\underline{p})_\perp \, d\omega(\hat{v})}.$$

The definition of radiance factors out both the orientation and distance to the light source, and so is constant along a ray in free space. Values in units of radiance are what we usually attach to a ray in a ray tracer, and it is what we "see" when we look at a surface.

A radiance field $L(\underline{p}, \hat{v})$ is a five-dimensional function describing the light flow everywhere in an environment. Given a BRDF f, the outgoing radiance L_o at a surface point can be computed as a linear functional of the incoming radiance:

$$L_o(\underline{p}, \hat{v}) \quad = \quad \int_\Omega f(\hat{v}, \hat{l}) \, L_i(\underline{p}, -\hat{l}) \, (\hat{n} \cdot \hat{l}) \, d\omega(\hat{l}),$$

where Ω is the hemisphere of directions above $\underline{p}$ centered about $\hat{n}$. This is called the local reflectance equation and can be interpreted as a linear functional $\mathcal{K}_f$ with kernel f acting on the incoming radiance field L_i and scattering it into an outgoing radiance field L_o:

$$L_o \quad = \quad \mathcal{K}_f L_i.$$

Physically consistent BRDFs have to satisfy a number of conditions. First, they must be positive everywhere. Second, they must be reciprocal: the linear functional $\mathcal{K}$ should be self-adjoint, so running reflectance backwards transmits the same energy as running it forward. This means, generally, that $f(\hat{\mathbf{v}}, \hat{\mathbf{l}}) = f(\hat{\mathbf{l}}, \hat{\mathbf{v}})$ for physical BRDFs; they must be symmetrical. Third, BRDFs should conserve energy (or absorb it); they cannot create it. The hemispherical reflectivity of a BRDF is defined as

$$H(\hat{\mathbf{v}}) \quad = \quad \int_\Omega (\hat{\mathbf{v}} \cdot \hat{\mathbf{n}}) \, f(\hat{\mathbf{v}}, \hat{\mathbf{l}}) \, d\omega(\hat{\mathbf{l}}).$$

In order to be energy-conserving, we must have $H(\hat{\mathbf{v}}) \leq 1$ for all $\hat{\mathbf{v}} \in \Omega$.

We can compute the lighting due to a point source by sampling the BRDF. However, several traditional reflectance models in computer graphics were not originally expressed as BRDFs and do not satisfy the above conditions of physical plausibility. Traditional lighting models, including the Blinn-Phong lighting model built into the original fixed-function pipeline of OpenGL, evaluate the complete local reflectance integral given above relative to a point source, and ignore the energy conservation and reciprocity principles. Unfortunately, physical consistency is important for global illumination.

For example, diffuse surfaces are traditionally modelled in real-time rendering with a constant reflectance equal to a value between 0 and 1. The range $[0, 1]$ was originally chosen to make it easier to predict the range of output colors and avoid having to rescale the output to fit the display range. However, to conserve energy, a constant BRDF must be at *most* $1/\pi$, which is significantly smaller than 1. The large non-physical reflectances used in traditional models can potentially cause problems with the convergence of global illumination algorithms. On the other hand, if we combine traditional and physically based reflectance models in the same rendering, we have to take the $1/\pi$ scale factors into account.

In the following, we will define a number of isotropic reflectance models using a function $\rho(\hat{\mathbf{l}}, \hat{\mathbf{v}}, \hat{\mathbf{n}})$ which will be related to the BRDF by

$$\rho(\hat{\mathbf{l}}, \hat{\mathbf{v}}, \hat{\mathbf{n}}) \quad = \quad f(\hat{\mathbf{l}}, \hat{\mathbf{v}}, \hat{\mathbf{n}}) \operatorname{pos}(\hat{\mathbf{n}} \cdot \hat{\mathbf{l}}).$$

The term $\operatorname{pos}(\hat{\mathbf{n}} \cdot \hat{\mathbf{l}})$ is factored into our definitions because, in traditional lighting models, it is omitted on specular lobes, which is wrong: it results in a non-reciprocal BRDF. On the other hand, supporting these "incorrect" lighting models is often important for backward compatibility and performance reasons.

We also use a clamped version of this dot product in our implementations. In real-time implementations, we have to avoid returning negative values for view and light vectors "below the horizon," that is, with $\hat{\mathbf{l}} \cdot \hat{\mathbf{n}} < 0$ or $\hat{\mathbf{v}} \cdot \hat{\mathbf{n}} < 0$. For real surfaces, this can never happen, and the local reflectance integral is only defined for the upper hemisphere. However, various approximations are made in real-time rendering, such as vertex normal interpolation, that can lead to under-the-horizon lighting model evaluations in practice.

The hardware might implicitly clamp to zero when you assign to a output buffer with a datatype that supports only a $[0, 1]$ range. But not clamping is a bad habit to get into, since one day you might need to render into a buffer without implicit clamping, or compose shaders in some other way with floating-point intermediate values. It's better to explicitly specify clamping and let the compiler optimize it away if possible.

With this background, we can now present a number of fundamental reflectance models: the Phong, Blinn-Phong, and Cook-Torrance models. We will also present variations of both the Phong and Blinn-Phong models that improve their physical plausibility.

Phong Reflection Model. The Phong lighting model [115] originally developed by Bui Tuong Phong is defined as follows:

$$\rho(\hat{\mathbf{l}}, \hat{\mathbf{v}}, \hat{\mathbf{n}}) \quad = \quad k_d \text{pos}(\hat{\mathbf{n}} \cdot \hat{\mathbf{l}}) + k_s \text{pos}(\hat{\mathbf{r}}(\hat{\mathbf{l}}) \cdot \hat{\mathbf{v}})^q,$$

where $\hat{\mathbf{r}}(\hat{\mathbf{l}})$ is the light vector reflected by the plane with normal $\hat{\mathbf{n}}$. The diffuse coefficient k_d is a color with components in the range $[0, 1]$ and likewise for the specular coefficient k_s. The Phong model does not generally conserve energy for coefficients given these ranges.

The Phong model also leads to a non-reciprocal BRDF because the $\text{pos}(\hat{\mathbf{n}} \cdot \hat{\mathbf{l}})$ term is included in the diffuse part of the lighting model but not the specular part. Interestingly, though, the specular lobe is itself reciprocal. This can be seen by expressing the reflectance computation using a Householder matrix R computed from $\hat{\mathbf{n}}$:

$$\begin{aligned}
\hat{\mathbf{r}}(\hat{\mathbf{a}}) &= 2\hat{\mathbf{n}}(\hat{\mathbf{n}} \cdot \hat{\mathbf{a}}) - \hat{\mathbf{a}} \\
&= (2\mathbf{n}\mathbf{n}^T - \mathbf{l})\mathbf{a} \\
&= \mathbf{R}\mathbf{a}; \\
\mathbf{R} &= 2\mathbf{n}\mathbf{n}^T - \mathbf{l} \\
&= \begin{bmatrix} 2n_x^2 - 1 & 2n_x n_y & 2n_x n_z \\ 2n_x n_y & 2n_y^2 - 1 & 2n_y n_z \\ 2n_x n_z & 2n_y n_z & 2n_z^2 - 1 \end{bmatrix}.
\end{aligned}$$

Note that $\mathbf{R} = \mathbf{R}^T$ for all $\hat{\mathbf{n}}$. The specular part of the Phong lighting model can be shown to be symmetric in $\hat{\mathbf{l}}$ and $\hat{\mathbf{v}}$ as follows:

$$\begin{aligned}
\hat{\mathbf{l}} \cdot \hat{\mathbf{r}}(\hat{\mathbf{v}}) &= \mathbf{l}^T \mathbf{r}(\mathbf{v}) \\
&= \mathbf{l}^T \mathbf{R}\mathbf{v}
\end{aligned}$$

$$\begin{aligned} &= \mathbf{l}^T \mathbf{R}^T \mathbf{v} \\ &= (\mathbf{R}\mathbf{l})^T \mathbf{v} \\ &= \mathbf{r}(\mathbf{l})^T \mathbf{v} \\ &= \hat{\mathbf{r}}(\hat{\mathbf{l}}) \cdot \hat{\mathbf{v}}. \end{aligned}$$

Therefore, we can also define the Phong lighting model as follows:

$$\rho(\hat{\mathbf{l}}, \hat{\mathbf{v}}, \hat{\mathbf{n}}) = k_d \mathrm{pos}(\hat{\mathbf{n}} \cdot \hat{\mathbf{l}}) + k_s \mathrm{pos}(\hat{\mathbf{l}} \cdot \hat{\mathbf{r}}(\hat{\mathbf{v}}))^q,$$

where $\hat{\mathbf{r}}(\hat{\mathbf{v}})$ is the reflection of the view vector $\hat{\mathbf{v}}$ (relative to $\hat{\mathbf{n}}$).

The Lafortune lobe model [75] generalizes the Phong specular lobe by using a symmetric matrix of the form $\mathbf{S}^T \mathbf{C} \mathbf{S}$ in place of $\mathbf{R}_{\hat{\mathbf{n}}}$, where $\mathbf{C}$ is diagonal and $\mathbf{S} = [\hat{\mathbf{t}}, \hat{\mathbf{s}}, \hat{\mathbf{n}}]$ is the SCS basis matrix. The Phong specular lobe is a special case of a Lafortune lobe, but Lafortune lobes can also model other effects, such as anisotropy and retroreflection. Sums of Lafortune lobes can be used to approximate other BRDFs.

An implementation of the Phong reflectance model as a C++ function using Sh code is given in Listing 2.2.

```
ShColor3f kd;   // diffuse coefficient
ShColor3f ks;   // specular coefficient
ShAttrib1f q;   // exponent

ShColor3f
phong (
  ShVector3f l,   // vector to light
  ShVector3f v,   // vector to viewer
  ShNormal3f n    // normal
) {
  l = normalize(l);
  v = normalize(v);
  n = normalize(n);
  ShAttrib1f fd = pos(l|n);
  ShVector3f r = reflect(v,n);
  ShAttrib1f fs = pow(pos(r|l),q);
  ShColor3f c = kd*fd + ks*fs;
  return c;
}
```

Listing 2.2. Phong reflectance model function.

We have defined the parameters k_d, k_s, and q as global variables. Generally, this is not a very good idea, and of course we would need different parameters for different surfaces in a scene. However, passing in these parameters as arguments would lead to a different functional interface for different reflectance models, since not all models will have the same parameters. What is needed is a way to encapsulate the parameters as well as the reflectance procedure itself. After introducing a few more reflectance models, we will introduce an object-oriented solution to this problem.

Modified Phong Reflectance Model. The Phong reflectance model has been modified to be reciprocal and energy-conserving [76]:

$$\rho(\hat{\mathbf{l}}, \hat{\mathbf{v}}, \hat{\mathbf{n}}) \;\; = \;\; \left(\frac{k_d}{\pi} + \frac{k_s(q+2)}{2\pi} \text{pos}(\hat{\mathbf{r}}(\hat{\mathbf{l}}) \cdot \hat{\mathbf{v}})^q \right) \text{pos}(\hat{\mathbf{n}} \cdot \hat{\mathbf{l}}),$$

where the diffuse and specular coefficients must now satisfy the constraint $k_d + k_s \leq 1$ in order to conserve energy. For the same values of k_d and k_s as those used in the original Phong model, this model will look roughly $1/\pi$ darker. The behavior of the specular lobe is also different as we vary q. With the original Phong model, when q is varied, the maximum value of the specular lobe remained the same, and the width of the specular lobe varied. With the modified Phong model, when q varies, the *integral* of the specular lobe remains the same. A larger q leads to a sharper and *brighter* highlight.

An Sh implementation is given in Listing 2.3. Again, note the use of global variables. Of course we would need to place these global variables in a different scope than the ones declared earlier.

```
ShColor3f kd;    // diffuse coefficient
ShColor3f ks;    // specular coefficient
ShAttrib1f q;    // exponent

ShColor3f
modphong (
   ShVector3f l,    // vector to light
   ShVector3f v,    // vector to viewer
   ShNormal3f n     // normal
) {
   l = normalize(l);    // normalize light vector
   v = normalize(v);    // normalize view vector
   n = normalize(n);    // normalize normal
   ShAttrib1f fd = pos(l|n);    // diffuse lobe
   ShVector3f r = reflect(v,n);    // reflect view vector
   ShAttrib1f fs = pow(pos(r|l),q);    // specular lobe
   ShColor3f c = (kd + 0.5*ks*(q+2)*fs)*fd/M_PI;    // combine
   return c;
}
```

Listing 2.3. Modified Phong reflectance model function.

Blinn-Phong Reflectance Model. The Blinn-Phong lighting model [14] is the standard "Phong" lighting model used in the OpenGL fixed-function pipeline. We can define the corresponding reflectance model as follows:

$$\rho(\hat{\mathbf{l}}, \hat{\mathbf{v}}, \hat{\mathbf{n}}) = k_d \mathrm{pos}(\hat{\mathbf{n}} \cdot \hat{\mathbf{l}}) + k_s \mathrm{pos}(\hat{\mathbf{n}} \cdot \hat{\mathbf{h}})^q.$$

The definition of the specular lobe in the Blinn-Phong model is somewhat different than that in the Phong model: the Blinn-Phong model uses $(\hat{\mathbf{n}} \cdot \hat{\mathbf{h}})$ rather than the $(\hat{\mathbf{l}} \cdot \hat{\mathbf{r}}(\hat{\mathbf{v}}))$ or $(\hat{\mathbf{r}}(\hat{\mathbf{l}}) \cdot \hat{\mathbf{v}})$ used in the original Phong model. The justification for this is that the half-vector $\hat{\mathbf{h}}$ is the orientation of the mirror surface that would reflect $\hat{\mathbf{l}}$ into $\hat{\mathbf{v}}$, and $\hat{\mathbf{h}} \cdot \hat{\mathbf{n}}$ measures the deviation of the surface being shaded from this ideal orientation. The closer $\hat{\mathbf{h}}$ is to $\hat{\mathbf{n}}$, the brighter we would expect the highlight to be, since the normals of the microfacets of a rough surface will have a distribution centered around the overall surface normal. In contrast, the Phong lobe is just sort of "made up" to have a lobe centered around the reflection vector.

The exponents of the two models can be roughly related by a scale factor, if necessary [6, 44]:

$$\begin{aligned} (\hat{\mathbf{r}}(\hat{\mathbf{l}}) \cdot \hat{\mathbf{v}})^q &= (\hat{\mathbf{l}} \cdot \hat{\mathbf{r}}(\hat{\mathbf{v}}))^q \\ &\approx (\hat{\mathbf{n}} \cdot \hat{\mathbf{h}})^{4q}. \end{aligned}$$

To make the Blinn-Phong model look roughly the same as the Phong model, we have to scale the exponent used in the Phong model by a factor of 4.

The specular lobe of the Blinn-Phong model is also symmetric in $\hat{\mathbf{l}}$ and $\hat{\mathbf{v}}$ since $\hat{\mathbf{h}}$ is a symmetric function of these vectors. However, the traditional form of the overall Blinn-Phong model is neither energy-conserving nor reciprocal. Here is an Sh implementation:

```
ShColor3f kd;      // diffuse coefficient
ShColor3f ks;      // specular coefficient
ShAttrib1f q;      // exponent

ShColor3f
blinnphong (
  ShVector3f l,    // vector to light
  ShVector3f v,    // vector to viewer
  ShNormal3f n     // normal
) {
  l = normalize(l);      // normalize light vector
  v = normalize(v);      // normalize view vector
  h = normalize(l+v);    // compute and normalize half vector
  n = normalize(n);      // normalize normal
  ShAttrib1f fd = pos(n|l);   // diffuse lobe
```

```
ShAttrib1f fs = pow(pos(h|n),q); // specular lobe
ShColor3f c = kd*fd + ks*fs; // combine lobes
return c;
}
```

Listing 2.4. Blinn-Phong reflectance model function.

Modified Blinn-Phong Reflectance Model. We can modify the Blinn-Phong reflectance model to be reciprocal as well, and apply similar exponent scaling to make it consistent with the modified Phong model:

$$\rho(\hat{\mathbf{l}}, \hat{\mathbf{v}}, \hat{\mathbf{n}}) \;\; = \;\; \left(\frac{k_d}{\pi} + \frac{k_s(q/4+2)}{2\pi} \text{pos}(\hat{\mathbf{n}} \cdot \hat{\mathbf{h}})^q \right) \text{pos}(\hat{\mathbf{n}} \cdot \hat{\mathbf{l}}).$$

For consistency with the modified Phong reflectance model, we should also have $k_d + k_s \leq 1$ (although we make no guarantees that this conserves energy, since the specular scaling uses only an approximate relationship between the Phong and Blinn-Phong models). Here is an Sh implementation:

```
ShColor3f kd;      // diffuse coefficient
ShColor3f ks;      // specular coefficient
ShAttrib1f q;      // exponent

ShColor3f
modblinnphong (
  ShVector3f l,    // vector to light
  ShVector3f v,    // vector to viewer
  ShNormal3f n     // normal
) {
  l = normalize(l);      // normalize light vector
  v = normalize(v);      // normalize view vector
  h = normalize(l+v);   // compute and normalize half vector
  n = normalize(n);      // normalize normal
  ShAttrib1f fd = pos(n|l);    // diffuse lobe
  ShAttrib1f fs = pow(pos(h|n),q); // specular lobe
  ShColor3f c = (kd + 0.5*(q/4+2)*ks*fs)*fd/M_PI;  // combine lobes
  return c;
}
```

Listing 2.5. Modified Blinn-Phong reflectance model function.

Cook-Torrance Reflectance Model. The Phong and Blinn-Phong reflectance models are phenomenological. While the modified forms are closer to physical reality, and the Blinn-Phong model is slightly more justified physically than the original Phong model, neither model is strongly based on any physical theory.

The Cook-Torrance model [25, 26, 104] is physically based. It is derived from a model of the probabilistic distribution of normal orientation on a rough surface, combined with the Fresnel effect and a shadowing/masking term. The overall model is defined as a combination of a diffuse part and a specular part as follows:

$$f(\hat{\mathbf{l}}, \hat{\mathbf{v}}, \hat{\mathbf{n}}) \;=\; \frac{k_d}{\pi} + \frac{k_s}{\pi}\, \frac{F(\cos\gamma)\, D(\cos\delta)\, G(\cos\alpha, \cos\beta, \cos\delta, \cos\gamma)}{\cos\alpha\,\cos\beta},$$

$$\rho(\hat{\mathbf{l}}, \hat{\mathbf{v}}, \hat{\mathbf{n}}) \;=\; f(\hat{\mathbf{l}}, \hat{\mathbf{v}}, \hat{\mathbf{n}})\, \mathrm{pos}(\hat{\mathbf{n}} \cdot \hat{\mathbf{l}}),$$

where we have defined as usual

$$\cos\alpha \;=\; \hat{\mathbf{l}} \cdot \hat{\mathbf{n}},$$
$$\cos\beta \;=\; \hat{\mathbf{v}} \cdot \hat{\mathbf{n}},$$
$$\cos\delta \;=\; \hat{\mathbf{h}} \cdot \hat{\mathbf{n}},$$
$$\cos\gamma \;=\; \hat{\mathbf{h}} \cdot \hat{\mathbf{v}}$$
$$\;=\; \hat{\mathbf{h}} \cdot \hat{\mathbf{l}}.$$

The distribution term D accounts for the variations in surface normal due to roughness. It can be modeled with the Beckmann distribution, which we give here in terms of the dot product $\cos\delta = \hat{\mathbf{h}} \cdot \hat{\mathbf{n}}$:

$$D(\cos\delta) \;=\; \frac{1}{m^2 \cos^4\delta}\, \exp\left(\frac{1 - \cos^4\delta}{m^2 \cos^2\delta}\right).$$

The roughness factor m is the mean square tangent of the slope angles; larger values give rougher surfaces. The shadowing and masking term G accounts for the occlusion of some microscopic surface features by others. The term given by Cook and Torrance is based on the assumption of V-shaped microfacets:

$$G(\cos\alpha, \cos\beta, \cos\delta, \cos\gamma) \;=\; \min\left(1, \frac{2\cos\gamma\cos\alpha}{\cos\gamma}, \frac{2\cos\gamma\cos\beta}{\cos\gamma}\right).$$

Here is a relatively straightforward implementation in Sh:

```
ShColor3f kd;      // diffuse coefficient
ShColor3f ks;      // specular coefficient
ShAttrib1f m;      // roughness
ShAttrib1f eta;    // relative index of refraction

ShColor3f
cooktorrance (
  ShVector3f l,    // vector to light
```

```
  ShVector3f v,    // vector to viewer
  ShNormal3f n     // normal
) {
  l = normalize(l);     // normalize light vector
  v = normalize(v);     // normalize view vector
  h = normalize(l+v);   // compute and normalize half vector
  n = normalize(n);     // normalize normal
  ShAttrib1f nl = pos(n|l);   // diffuse
  ShAttrib1f nh = (h|n);
  ShAttrib1f nh2 = nh*nh;
  ShAttrib1f nh4 = nh2*nh2;
  ShAttrib1f m2 = m*m;
  ShAttrib1f D = exp((1.0-nh2)/(nh2*m2))/(m2*nh4);
  ShAttrib1f vh = (v|h);
  ShAttrib1f G = min(1.0, (2*nh/vh)*nv, (2*nh/vh)*nl);
  ShAttrib1f F = fresnel(v,l,eta);
  ShColor3f c = (kd*nl + ks*F*D*G/nv)/M_PI;  // combine lobes
  return c;
}
```

Listing 2.6. Cook-Torrance reflectance model function.

Common Reflectance Model Interface. We have given a number of examples of reflectance models and their implementations in Sh. Suppose we want to use these in a renderer, but want to define a scene where each object might use any one of these models. All the reflectance model functions defined so far have a common interface for evaluation. Therefore, we could use a function pointer with a common prototype to refer to each of them, and we could give them a common interface this way. However, each reflectance model has a number of parameters that also need to be set, and these parameters are potentially different for each model. In order to carry around these parameters as well as an associated evaluation function, an object-oriented model of abstraction is appropriate.

In Listing 2.7, we define a common base class for reflectance models. This abstract base class defines a pure virtual member function `eval` which can be accessed via a pointer or reference to an instance of a class subclassed from this class. We also define the `()` operator on the base class to provide a simpler interface to the `eval` member function. This abstract class provides a common interface to all isotropic reflectance models.

```
// abstract base class of evaluable reflectance models
class Reflectance {
  public:
    virtual ShColor3f
```

```
eval (
  ShVector3f l,    // vector to light
  ShVector3f v,    // vector to viewer
  ShNormal3f n     // normal
) const = 0;   // pure virtual

ShColor3f
operator() (
  ShVector3f l,    // vector to light
  ShVector3f v,    // vector to viewer
  ShNormal3f n     // normal
) const {
  return eval(l,v,n);
}
};
```

Listing 2.7. Abstract reflectance model base class.

Now we can subclass the base class and encapsulate the parameters inside each subclass. Here is an example for PhongReflectance. We could define ModifiedPhongReflectance, BlinnPhongReflectance, Modified BlinnPhongReflectance, and CookTorranceReflectance similarly.

```
class PhongReflectance: public Reflectance {
  public:
    ShColor3f kd;    // diffuse coefficient
    ShColor3f ks;    // specular coefficient
    ShAttrib1f q;    // exponent

    PhongReflectance (
      ShColor3f kdi,
      ShColor3f ksi,
      ShAttrib1f qi
    ) : kd(kdi), ks(ksi), q(qi) {}

    virtual ShColor3f
    eval (
      ShVector3f l,    // vector to light
      ShVector3f v,    // vector to viewer
      ShNormal3f n     // normal
    ) const {
      l = normalize(l);
      v = normalize(v);
      n = normalize(n);
      ShAttrib1f fd = pos(l|n);
      ShVector3f r = reflect(v,n);
      ShAttrib1f fs = pow(pos(r|l),q);
```

```
    ShColor3f c = kd*fd + ks*fs;
    return c;
  }
};
```

Listing 2.8. Encapsulated Phong reflectance model.

Of course, we could add much more structure to this, for instance, by adding accessor methods to more strongly encapsulate the parameters. We could also define light classes and then techniques for combining light sources and reflectances. However, remember that right now, these are functions that execute in immediate mode on the host. They are not (yet) shaders. In the next chapter, we will describe how to turn functions like these into shaders and will also show how similar object-oriented data encapsulation techniques can be extended to shaders.

Chapter 3

Programs, Parameters, and Attributes

This chapter introduces the construction of Sh program objects, and in particular the implementation of GPU shaders. Sh programs are defined by putting Sh into a mode that observes and records sequences of operations on Sh types, rather than executing those operations immediately. These stored operation sequences can then be compiled for a target specified separately from the program. Sh also supports operators that act on program objects. Programs can be composed, concatenated, and specialized using these operators. Program objects in Sh are essentially treated like "first class objects" in a functional language, a theme that we will expand upon in Chapter 5.

3.1 Programs

In Chapter 2 we introduced the Sh tuple and matrix types and showed how C++ could be used to encapsulate definitions of lighting models on these types. In the "immediate mode" used in that chapter, Sh acts as if it were a simple geometry and matrix/vector utility library. If that was all Sh could do, it would not be that interesting. However, Sh can also be placed in a "retained mode" in which sequences of operations on the types it defines are stored instead of executed. We can then take these stored sequences of operations and dynamically cross compile them to another target. To capture sequences of Sh operations, we wrap the desired operations in a pair of **SH_BEGIN_PROGRAM** and **SH_END** keywords. We also annotate certain variable declarations to specify the inputs and outputs of the resulting *program object*.

The **SH_BEGIN_PROGRAM** keyword takes a string parameter that specifies the compilation target. A value of `"gpu:vertex"` indicates compilation for the vertex shading unit of the currently installed GPU, while `"gpu:fragment"` indicates compilation for the fragment shading unit. The **SH_BEGIN_PROGRAM** keyword returns an object of type **ShProgram** which represents the compiled program. Once compiled, a program object can be loaded into the shader unit it was compiled for using the `shBind` system management function.

We use the name "program" rather than "shader," because if control constructs or stream processing compilation targets are used, an **ShProgram** can, in fact, compile to a multipass implementation in order to support virtualization. Stream programs (discussed in Chapter 5) are also not limited to computing surface shading, but are instead intended for general-purpose computation. In this chapter, we will focus on the use of Sh programs for implementing single-pass GPU shaders in particular; we will assume that a shader compilation target is used. Discussion of texture mapping will also be deferred to Chapter 4; here, we will focus on the procedural aspects of shaders.

3.2   Example: Blinn-Phong Point-Source Lighting

Consider again the Blinn-Phong reflectance model discussed in Chapter 2:

$$\rho(\hat{\mathbf{v}}, \hat{\mathbf{l}}, \hat{\mathbf{n}}) \;\; = \;\; k_d \mathrm{pos}(\hat{\mathbf{n}} \cdot \hat{\mathbf{l}}) + k_s \mathrm{pos}(\hat{\mathbf{n}} \cdot \hat{\mathbf{h}})^q.$$

We will implement this model using per-pixel computation of the specular lobe and per-vertex computation of the diffuse lobe. We will do this first in a straightforward manner, by expressing the above computation directly; then we will show how the object-oriented encapsulation methods presented in Chapter 2 can be extended to shaders. For a shader, we actually need to implement a complete lighting model, not just a reflectance function. For simplicity, in our examples we will use a simple point source lighting model (without attenuation). At first, we will just support one source; then, we will use C++ metaprogramming to unroll a loop over multiple light sources and will build a version of the shader supporting variable numbers of point sources. A typical rendering (with one source) is shown in Figure 3.1.

3.2.1   Vertex Shader

The vertex shader given in Listing 3.1 computes the model-view transformation of the position, the normal, the projective transformation of the view-space position into device space, the halfvector, and the irradiance term $\mathrm{pos}(\hat{\mathbf{n}} \cdot \hat{\mathbf{l}})$. These

Figure 3.1. Example of the Blinn-Phong lighting model. See Plate 2 on page 111.

values will be interpolated by the rasterizer and the interpolated values will be
assigned to the fragments it generates.

```
ShProgram vsh = SH_BEGIN_PROGRAM("gpu:vertex") {
    // Declare input vertex attributes
    ShInputNormal3f nm;         // normal vector (MCS)
    ShInputPosition3f pm;       // position (MCS)

    // Declare output vertex attributes
    ShOutputVector3f hv;        // half-vector (VCS)
    ShOutputNormal3f nv;        // normal (VCS)
    ShOutputColor3f ec;         // irradiance
    ShOutputPosition4f pd;      // position (DCS)

    // Specify computations
    ShPoint3f pv = (MV|pm)(0,1,2);       // VCS position
    pd = VD|pv;                          // DCS position
    nv = normalize((nm|VM)(0,1,2));      // VCS normal
    ShVector3f lv = normalize(light.pv - pv);  // VCS light vector
    ec = light.c * pos(nv|lv);           // irradiance
    ShVector3f vv = normalize(-pv);      // VCS view vector
    hv = normalize(lv + vv);             // VCS half vector
} SH_END;
```

Listing 3.1. Vertex shader for Blinn-Phong point-source lighting model.

Attributes. The *Input* and *Output* binding type modifiers modify the declaration of certain variables inside each shader. The constructors of types annotated this way allocate input/output channels in the Sh compiler. The order in which these constructors are called, as well as their type, provides the necessary information for Sh to bind inputs and outputs to vertex attributes. In Sh, inputs and outputs of shaders will be called *attributes*, because they are values attached to vertices (or fragments). Attributes roughly correspond to the *varying* variables in RenderMan, because they can be different for each invocation of the shader.

Conceptually, *ShProgram* objects represent functions that are applied in parallel to streams of records, each record containing k objects of various types, and produce another stream of records, with each output record containing m objects of various types.

A vertex shader takes the vertex attributes bound to each input vertex by the user and produces another set of attributes that will be interpolated by the rasterizer, and this computation is repeated for each vertex. Likewise, a fragment shader takes as input interpolated values bound to fragments and computes output values. (In this case, only one color tuple is output per fragment, but multiple output values are possible in Sh, even if the hardware does not support them directly.)

Position Semantic Type. A special semantic type, *ShPosition*, is used to identify the output of the vertex shader to be considered the vertex position by the rasterizer. This semantic type otherwise acts like a point. The *ShPosition* type is only used for the inputs and outputs of shader programs and has a special meaning in this context. The output types from the vertex shader should match in size and type with the inputs of the fragment shader, although the *ShPosition* input is optional and can appear anywhere in the input or output declaration sequence. If no position input is given, it is assumed to have been absorbed by the rasterizer. The position output from the vertex shader should have the type *ShPosition4f* and be in homogeneous coordinates.

Temporaries. Tuples and matrices declared without qualifiers inside a shader definition are temporaries local to the shader. The same constructors are used to declare global parameters as those used to declare temporaries; the fact temporary constructors are called inside a shader distinguishes them. Temporaries are initialized to zero at the start of every invocation of a shader, which often simplifies the accumulation of contributions from multiple light sources. Of course, the compiler will declare more temporary registers internally in order to implement expression evaluation and will optimize register allocation as well. You should *not* go to great pains to "pack" temporary values together into 4-tuples, as this will only serve to confuse the optimizer.

Sh also permits reading from output attributes and writing to input attributes. The latter does not change the real input data; program objects are strictly pass by value. If the target platform does not support this directly, then Sh automatically introduces an appropriate temporary.

Parameters. Shader programs may read from instances of Sh variables created in immediate mode, but may not write to them. Such external references are called the *parameters* of the shader. Parameters roughly correspond to the *uniform* variables in RenderMan, because they must be the same for every invocation of the shader in a given pass. Outside of a shader invocation, you can modify parameters in immediate mode, and the system will automatically make the updated values available for the next invocation of the shader.

The parameters of the modified Blinn-Phong lighting model are given in Listing 3.2. Parameters are highlighted in the listings: *MV*, `light.pv`, *kd*, and so forth. In this shader, transformation matrices, the light position, and the light color are externally declared parameters in addition to the shader-specific parameters *kd*, *ks*, and *q*. Somewhere outside the shader definition, but still in scope, we need the following set of declarations. (Some of these parameters will only be used in the fragment shader.)

```
// Transformation parameters
ShMatrix4x4f MV;       // MCS to VCS
ShMatrix4x4f VD;       // VCS to DCS
ShMatrix4x4f VM;       // VCS to MCS (inverse of MV)

// Light source parameters
Light lights[NLIGHTS];
Light& light = lights[0];     // position and color of light source

// Parameters specific to the Blinn-Phong lighting model
ShColor3f ks;          // specular lobe coefficient
ShColor3f kd;          // diffuse lobe coefficient
ShAttrib1f q;          // specular lobe exponent
```

Listing 3.2. Parameters of the Blinn-Phong lighting model.

3.2.2 Fragment Shader

The fragment shader given in Listing 3.3 completes the Blinn-Phong lighting example by computing the specular lobe and adding it to the diffuse lobe. Both reflection modes are modulated by specular and diffuse colors that come from the externally declared parameters, *kd* and *ks*.

The position input to the fragment shader must have the type **ShPosition3f** and will have been projectively normalized; it represents the

(x, y, z) position of the fragment being shaded by the fragment shader. An output position can also be set in the fragment shader, but currently, replacement of the x and y values will be ignored. Replacing the z value is possible and will modify the depth of the fragment.

The exponent q specified here is another externally defined parameter. Ideally, we would antialias this lighting model by clamping the exponent as a function of distance and curvature [8], but we have not implemented this functionality in this shader.

```
ShProgram fsh = SH_BEGIN_PROGRAM("gpu:fragment") {
  // declare input fragment attributes
  ShInputVector3f hv;        // half-vector (VCS)
  ShInputNormal3f nv;        // normal (VCS)
  ShInputColor3f ec;         // irradiance
  ShInputPosition3f pd;      // fragment position (DCS) [not used]

  // declare output fragment attributes
  ShOutputColor3f c;         // fragment color

  // normalize interpolated unit vectors
  hv = normalize(hv);
  nv = normalize(nv);

  // compute Blinn-Phong lighting model
  c = kd*ec + ks*pow(pos(hv|nv),q);
} SH_END;
```

Listing 3.3. Fragment shader for Blinn-Phong lighting model.

3.2.3 Modularity

The Blinn-Phong lighting model is an example of a shader which would be a useful subprogram in other places. We would expect that many shaders in practice will be a combination of several standard parts. We could define functions as in Chapter 2 to encapsulate the desired computations, but there is still the problem that shaders also need to carry around settings of their parameters, and many parameters are shared between shaders. In other words, an object-oriented solution is probably more appropriate for modularizing shaders than simple functions.

We can better package the above Blinn-Phong shader as shown in Listings 3.4 and 3.5. Listing 3.4 defines a class to encapsulate the parameters of the model. We use a template just to make allocation of the light parameter array simpler (and to show that templated code is also possible), but you could also use a dynamically sized array or `std::vector`.

```
template <int NLIGHTS>
class BlinnPhongShader1 {
  protected:
    // Program objects
    ShProgram vsh, fsh;

  public:
    // Transformation parameters
    ShMatrix4x4f MV;        // MCS to VCS
    ShMatrix4x4f VD;        // VCS to DCS
    ShMatrix4x4f VM;        // VCS to MCS (inverse of MV)

    // Light source parameters
    Light lights[NLIGHTS];

    // Parameters specific to the Blinn-Phong lighting model
    ShColor3f ks;           // specular lobe coefficient
    ShColor3f kd;           // diffuse lobe coefficient

    BlinnPhongShader1 (float q);

    void bind () {
      shBind(vsh);
      shBind(fsh);
    }
};
```

Listing 3.4. Encapsulated shader for the Blinn-Phong lighting model

Listing 3.5 defines a constructor to build an instance of the BlinnPhong Shader1 class and defines appropriate program objects while doing so. This class manages the definition and binding of a complete multistage shader. Construction of an instance of this class defines the shaders; destruction deallocates them. We don't need explicit deallocation of each component shader, since deallocation of the corresponding *ShProgram* objects, which is performed when the whole class is destroyed, performs that task. We have also defined a single member function, bind, to load the shader into all shader units, and we have also used the class to organize all the parameters for this shader.

We have also modified the shader somewhat, using a definition-time constant for q. The use of q is worth noting: basically, each instance of the Blinn-PhongShader1 class builds a specialized shader, with a different exponent compiled in for each instance. We could just as easily have defined q as a parameter without changing the definition of the program objects (which we could, in turn, have embedded in functions if we wanted).

```
template <int NLIGHTS>
BlinnPhongShader1::BlinnPhongShader1 (float q) {
  // define vertex shader
  vsh = SH_BEGIN_PROGRAM("gpu:vertex") {
    // specify inputs
    ShInputNormal3f nm;                // MCS normal
    ShInputPosition3f pm;              // MCS position
    // specify outputs
    ShOutputVector3f hv[NLIGHTS];      // VCS half-vectors (per light)
    ShOutputNormal3f nv;               // VCS normal
    ShOutputColor3f ec;                // total irradiance
    ShOutputPosition4f pd;             // DCS position
    // specify computations
    ShPoint3f pv = (MV|pm)(0,1,2);     // VCS position
    pd = VD|pv;                        // DCS position
    nv = normalize((nm|VM)(0,1,2));    // VCS normal
    ShVector3f vv = normalize(-pv);    // VCS view vector
    // for all light sources, sum irradiance, compute half vector
    for (i=0; i<NLIGHTS; i++) {
      // first compute normalized light vector
      ShVector3f lv = normalize(lights[i].pv - pv);
      ec += lights[i].c * pos(nv|lv);  // add up irradiance
      hv[i] = normalize(lv + vv);      // VCS half-vector
    }
  } SH_END;

  // define fragment shader
  fsh = SH_BEGIN_PROGRAM("gpu:fragment") {
    // specify inputs
    ShInputVector3f hv[NLIGHTS];       // VCS half-vector
    ShInputNormal3f nv;                // VCS normal
    ShInputColor3f ec;                 // total irradiance
    ShInputPosition3f pd;              // DCS position
    // specify outputs
    ShOutputColor3f c;                 // final color
    // specify computations
    nv = normalize(nv);      // renormalize
    c = kd*ec;               // diffuse lobe
    // for each light source, add specular lobe
    for (int i=0; i<NLIGHTS; i++) {
      hv[i] = normalize(hv[i]);
      c += ks * pow(pos(nv|hv[i]),q) * lights[i].c;
    }
  } SH_END;
}
```

Listing 3.5. Constructor for the modified Blinn-Phong lighting model.

3.2.4 Shader Framework

The scope rules and modularity constructs of C++ can be used to control which parameters get bound to which shaders. Normally, we would define shaders inside a framework that encapsulates parameters and program objects. We can use the subclass capabilities of C++ to create a hierarchy of shaders and parameters.

A simple example is given in Listing 3.6. Here, we declare transformation parameters in the BaseShader abstract class, point light parameters for NLIGHT light sources in the PointLightShader templated subclass, and finally the Blinn-Phong specific parameters in the BlinnPhongShader2 subclass. The constructor for BaseShader calls an initialization method, eventually defined in the BlinnPhongShader2 concrete class, which constructs the *ShProgram* objects vsh and fsh. The bind member function loads these shaders onto the GPU when called.

Such encapsulation is not mandatory. On the other hand, more sophisticated frameworks are certainly possible, such as a framework that provides a separation between surface, light, and postprocessing shaders. The Sh library includes some optional frameworks that can provide various shader management facilities. Many other programming and encapsulation techniques are enabled by the close binding between C++ and Sh and the semantic similarity of *ShProgram* definitions to dynamic function definitions with static binding to parameters.

```
class BaseShader {
  protected:
    ShProgram vsh;
    ShProgram fsh;
  public:
    static ShMatrix4x4f VD;          // VCS to DCS
    static ShMatrix4x4f MV;          // MCS to VCS
    static ShMatrix4x4f MD;          // MCS to DCS
    static ShMatrix4x4f VM;          // MCS from VCS
    void bind();
    virtual void init() = 0;
    BaseShader() {
      init();
    }
};
template <int NLIGHTS>
class PointLightShader: public BaseShader {
  public:
    static Light lights[NLIGHTS];
    static Light& light;
```

```
    PointLightShader() {
      light = lights[0];
    }
};
template <int NLIGHTS>
class BlinnPhongShader2: public PointLightShader<NLIGHTS> {
  public:
    ShColor3f ks;       // specular color
    ShColor3f kd;       // diffuse color
    ShAttrib1f q;      // exponent
    BlinnPhongShader2();
    virtual void init();
};
```

Listing 3.6. Framework classes for managing parameters.

3.3   Shader Algebra

We have shown that we can use the modularity constructs of C++ to organize shader code. However, since Sh represents program objects internally as data, it can provide additional mechanisms for modularity by manipulating those representations explicitly.

Sh provides three additional operators that act on program objects and can be used to manage the interaction of programs and other data types in Sh. These operators are "<<," "&," and ">>," and together with program objects, they form what we call a *shader algebra*. Shader algebra operations can be used to combine existing program objects to create new program objects.

We call "<<" the *connect* operator. It implements functional composition. Given two program objects p and q, the expression "p << q" feeds the output attributes of q into the input attributes of p. These attributes must match in number and type, but type checking is done dynamically by Sh itself, not by C++. This operator is surprisingly powerful when you realize that the resulting program is run through the Sh optimizer. For instance, suppose you want to specialize a shader. You have been given a shader with two outputs and you only want to keep one of them [52]. Just define a "glue" shader that reads the input you want and copies it to its output, but ignores the other input. Connect it to the output of the shader you want to specialize. The dead code eliminator in the Sh optimizer will tear out any unnecessary code in the original shader and will leave only the operations needed to compute the output you want. Similar glue programs can be used to reorganize inputs, do type conversion, normalize things that need normalizing, perturb attributes, perform changes of coordinate systems, etc.

Certain kinds of glue programs are very common, for instance, programs that just selectively copy outputs to support specialization. Sh includes a library of *nibbles*, which are functions to generate specific kinds of glue shaders. Many of these are template functions so they can generate program objects with the correct interface types. Several nibbles support simple operations like taking the maximum of two inputs. In fact, the nibbles in conjunction with the connect operator implements a functional shader language that can itself be used to build up full shaders. There are also special classes called *manipulators* that act like programs in expressions but can infer type information. For instance, if we are discarding an output, we don't really care what its type is. Manipulators can figure out the types in the interfaces of the program objects to which they are connected and can modify the program objects they generate as appropriate.

The second operator, "&," is the *combine* operator. It simply concatenates two shaders, just as if we had concatenated the source code (with some braces around each body to avoid name collisions). Because of the way Sh is defined, this means that the input attribute declarations are concatenated, the output attribute declarations are concatenated, and all computations in both program objects are performed. The result is a program that does everything the original two shaders did and has the same total number of inputs and the same total number of outputs.

If the two source shaders involved in a combine operation have redundant computations, there is only so much the optimizer can do to simplify them. For instance, the two computations may be done just differently enough that we can't use common subexpressions to get rid of them, or they may be tied to different inputs and outputs. Fortunately glue shaders and specialization can be used to discard outputs we don't need, simplifying the results of combined shaders.

The "<<" operator can also be used to apply program objects to tuple values. If t is a tuple and p is a program, then

---

```
ShProgram q = p << t;
```

---

binds the tuple t to the first input attribute of p and creates a new program object q with one less input. This is interpreted as *partial evaluation*, but with a deferred read of the value of the tuple t. Whenever the program given by p << t runs, it will read the value of t in effect *at the time of execution*. In other words, the expression p << t converts an input "varying" *attribute* to a "uniform" *parameter* t. This is useful, but we also want to be able to go in the other

direction, so the ">>" operator, called *extract*, *removes* the dependence of a program object on a parameter and creates a new attribute. We can get back to a
program object p2 functionally equivalent to the original p as follows:

```
ShProgram p2 = q >> t;
```

However, the new program object p2 has the new attribute placed at the end
of its inputs, and so may not have the same order of inputs as the original
program p.

Tuples can also be combined into *stream records* using the " & " operator. These
records can be used to provide several inputs at once to a program. Once all the
inputs of a program are bound, it can be evaluated like a subroutine and the
result assigned to some Sh tuples. Let a, b, c, and x, y be tuples, and let p be
a program with 2 inputs and 3 outputs. The following are equivalent and both
invoke p as a subroutine (even if it was compiled for the GPU):

```
(a & b & c) = p << (x & y);
(a & b & c) = p << x << y;
```

Program object p acts like a curried function, since each application of the "<<"
operator returns a function that takes one less input. Using GPU program objects this way is not very efficient. The real power of this approach will come
in Chapter 5, when we define streams and can replace the tuples above with
large collections of data that we can operate on in parallel. However, binding
programs to parameters, extracting parameters, and connecting and combining
programs to one another provide some additional forms of modularity useful
for constructing shaders.

3.4   Example: Surfaces, Lights, and Postprocessing

The RenderMan shading language supports a division between surface, light,
and imaging (postprocessing) shaders. A similar division can be supported in
Sh by defining shader program objects with certain interfaces, and then combining them either during definition, or using shader algebra operations. This can
be supported with a suitable class framework or set of program object interface
conventions.

Figures 3.2 and 3.3 give examples. These images were generated using a
relatively small number of surface, light, and postprocessing program objects
that were combined under application control using shader algebra operations.

Figure 3.2. Surface and light shaders can be combined with shader algebra operators, and any attribute or parameter can be replaced with a texture map (or procedure). See Plate 3 on page 112.

Shader algebra operations can also be used to manipulate and modulate the attributes of shaders in general ways. For instance, to implement bump mapping, we have to perturb the normal. This can be done by modifying the vertex shader to output SCS coordinates, providing a tangent frame on input, and then modifying the normal used in the fragment shader. These operations can also be supported on relatively arbitrary fragment shaders; see Figure 3.4.

Figure 3.3. Halftoning postprocess applied with shader algebra. See Plate 4 on page 113.

Figure 3.4. The normals (and/or tangents) used for any lighting model can be perturbed to implement bump mapping. See Plate 5 on page 113.

Code for these specific examples can be downloaded from the Sh website. Download the shrike package and take a look at the Algebra shader.

Shader kernel generators that build parameterized program objects for bump mapping, postprocessing, and other transformations are provided as part of the

Sh standard library; see Section 10.7. In addition, many vertex shaders are very similar, but certain conventions have to be followed to make these fragment shader kernels work. For instance, if you want to implement bump mapping, then you need to provide a tangent frame. The Sh standard library therefore also includes a "universal" vertex shader generator that can generate generic vertex shaders suitable for these tasks.

3.5 Example: Metaprogrammed CSG Text

The shader algebra operators can be used to build up complex shaders from simple ones and provide a convenient mechanism for certain kinds of metaprogramming. We will now present a function that, given a string at runtime, can dynamically create a shader that renders glyphs representing that string as a black and white resolution-independent image. See Figure 3.5. This example scans the string and generates a tree of Boolean union, intersection, and difference operators that combine three basic shapes: rectangles, circles, and skewed rectangles.

Figure 3.5. Text implemented by a metaprogrammed shader.

First, we will define a global parameter that gives the two-dimensional texture coordinate. This is just going to be a placeholder so we can avoid routing this input to each shader in expressions. We are going to turn it into an input attribute at the end by using the ">>" operator. (This is a useful general trick.)

// Letter position. This parameter is a placeholder and will be
// converted into an input attribute before the final shader is returned.
static *ShTexCoord2f* posn;

Listing 3.7. Input parameter for metaprogrammed text example.

Next, we will define some helper functions that implement CSG operations. We use the nibbles shMin and shMax to implement the Boolean AND and OR operations, respectively. Each CSG operator takes two program objects returning Boolean values and combines them into a new one using some nibbles and shader algebra operators.

// CSG Union. We use a nibble to take the maximum of two
// Boolean functions in order to compute the CSG union.
ShProgram u (**const** *ShProgram*& a, **const** *ShProgram*& b)
{
    return shMax<*ShAttrib1f*>() << (a & b);
}

// CSG Intersection. We use a nibble to take the minimum of
// two Boolean functions in order to compute the CSG union.
ShProgram i (**const** *ShProgram*& a, **const** *ShProgram*& b)
{
    return shMin<*ShAttrib1f*>() << (a & b);
}
// CSG Difference. Take the 1's complement of the second
// argument (to compute the CSG complement) and intersect it
// with the first argument.
ShProgram s (**const** *ShProgram*& a, **const** *ShProgram*& b)
{
    return i(a, shSub<*ShAttrib1f*>() << *ShAttrib1f*(1.0) << b);
}

Listing 3.8. Two-dimensional CSG operators for metaprogrammed text.

Now we define Boolean functions for each of our basic primitives: circles, rectangles, and skewed rectangles. Each of these functions depends implicitly on the *posn* global parameter, but takes two arguments x and y giving the offset of the origin of each shape (as well as some other parameters unique to each shape):

// Boolean function for a rectangle with lower-left corner at
// (x,y) of width w and height h (program takes no inputs, depends
// only on parameter posn)
ShProgram r (**float** x, **float** y, **float** w, **float** h)

```
{
  ShProgram rect = SH_BEGIN_PROGRAM() {
    ShVector2f o = posn - ShAttrib2f(x,y);
    ShOutputAttrib1f f = min((o[0] > 0.0)*(o[1] > 0.0),
                             (o[0] < w)*(o[1] < h));
  } SH_END;
  return rect;
}

// Boolean function for a skewed rectangle.
ShProgram sr (float x, float y, float w, float h, float skew)
{
  ShProgram srect = SH_BEGIN_PROGRAM() {
    ShVector2f o = posn - ShAttrib2f(x, y);
    o[0] -= o[1] * (skew/h);
    ShOutputAttrib1f f = min((o[0] > 0.0)*(o[1] > 0.0),
                             (o[0] < w)*(o[1] < h));
  } SH_END;
  return srect;
}

// Boolean function for a circle with center at (x,y) of radius r
ShProgram c (float x, float y, float r)
{
  ShProgram circ = SH_BEGIN_PROGRAM() {
    ShVector2f o = posn - ShAttrib2f(x, y);
    ShOutputAttrib1f f = ((o|o) < ShAttrib1f(r*r));
  } SH_END;
  return circ;
}
```

Listing 3.9. Basic two-dimensional shapes for metaprogrammed text.

Finally, we define a function that will scan the input string, character by character. For each character, we build an expression of CSG operators and primitives to represent a glyph for that character. This function is only an example, and so does not build glyphs for all letters, just enough to render interesting strings like "Sh" and "Hello World." Then, we take the union of the CSG operator trees for each letter to build up a CSG expression for the entire phrase. The generators for each letter also update the origin so the letters are spaced correctly. Finally, when we are all done, we extract and discard the dependency on the *posn* parameter, resulting in a program object with a single two-dimensional texture coordinate input.

Is this an efficient way to render text? No, not really. As the string becomes longer, the tree gets larger and larger, and we exhaustively evaluate it for every texel. To build a good text renderer, we would want to implement a more sophisticated representation of regions bounded by line segments and curves, probably using information compiled and stored in texture maps. We would also want a representation that supports antialiasing (this one could be extended to do so by using signed distance functions). However, this example is interesting because it demonstrates that non-trivial shaders can be built automatically, dynamically, and reasonably conveniently at runtime. We have also implemented an algorithm to render arbitrary polygons by converting them to CSG trees [35].

```
// Create a program that evaluates the glyphs for a given string
ShProgram text (const std::string & text)
{
  // initialize cursor position and character separation
  float px = 0.0; float py = 0.0;
  float sep = 7.0; float lineheight = 60.0;
  float linesep = 20.0;

  // start with an empty shader for the phrase
  ShProgram phrase = SH_BEGIN_PROGRAM() {
    ShOutputAttrib1f f = 0.0;
  } SH_END;

  // for each character in the input string...
  std::string::const_iterator ch;
  for (ch = text.begin(); ch != text.end(); ch++) {
    // build a shader expression for each letter
    ShProgram letter;
    switch (*ch) {
      case 'H': {
        float vw = 13.0; float vh = 60.0;
        float hw = 27.0; float hy = 24.0; float hh = 11.0;
        letter = u(u(r(px,py,vw,vh),
                     r(px+vw,py+hy,hw,hh)),
                     r(px+vw+hw,py,vw,vh));
        px += vw+hw+vw;
      } break;
      case 'S': {
        float ro = 18.0; float w = 12.0;
        float ri = ro-w;
        letter = u(s(s(c(px+ro,py+ro,ro),
                       c(px+ro,py+ro,ri)),
                     r(px,py+ro,ro,ro)),
                   s(s(c(px+ro,py+ro+ro+ri,ro),
                       c(px+ro,py+ro+ro+ri,ri)),
                     r(px+ro,py+ro+ri,ro,ro)));
        px += ro+ro;
```

```
    } break;
    case 'W': {
      float vw = 13.0; float vh = 60.0; float wl = 17.0;
      letter = sr(px+wl,py,vw,vh,-wl);
      letter = u(letter,sr(px+wl,py,vw,vh,wl));
      letter = u(letter,sr(px+wl+wl+wl,py,vw,vh,-wl));
      letter = u(letter,sr(px+wl+wl+wl,py,vw,vh,wl));
      px += vw+wl*4.0;
    } break;
    case 'a': {
      float ro = 22.5;
      float ri = ro-12.0;
      letter = u(s(c(px+ro,py+ro,ro),
                  c(px+ro,py+ro,ri)),
                r(px+ro+ri,py,ro-ri,ro+ro));
      px += ro+ro;
    } break;
    case 'b': {
      float vh = 60.0; float ro = 22.5;
      float ri = ro-12.0;
      letter = u(s(c(px+ro,py+ro,ro),
                  c(px+ro,py+ro,ri)),
                r(px,py,ro-ri,vh));
      px += ro+ro;
    } break;
    case 'd': {
      float vh = 60.0; float ro = 22.5;
      float ri = ro-12.0;
      letter = u(s(c(px+ro,py+ro,ro),
                  c(px+ro,py+ro,ri)),
                r(px+ro+ri,py,ro-ri,vh));
      px += ro+ro;
    } break;
    case 'e': {
      float eh = 8.0; float ro = 22.5;
      float ri = ro-12.0;
      letter = u(s(s(c(px+ro,py+ro,ro),
                    c(px+ro,py+ro,ri)),
                  r(px+ro,py+ro-ri+ri/2.0,
                    ro,ri/2.0-eh/2.0)),
                r(px+(ro-ri),py+ro-eh/2.0,ri*2.0,eh));
      px += ro+ro;
    } break;
    case 'i': {
      float ro = 22.5; float vw = 13.0;
      float w = vw/2.0;
      letter = u(r(px,py,vw,ro+ro),
```

```
                         c(px+w,py+ro+ro+w+w,w));
      px += vw;
    } break;
    case 'h': {
      float vh = 60.0; float hs = 10.0;
      float ro = 22.5; float w = 12.0;
      float ri = ro-w;
      letter = u(u(s(s(c(px+ro,py+ro-hs,ro),
                         c(px+ro,py+ro-hs,ri)),
                       r(px,py-hs,ro+ro,ro)),
                     r(px+ro+ri,py,w,ro-hs)),
                   r(px,py,w,vh));
      px += ro+ro;
    } break;
    case 'n': {
      float ro = 22.5; float w = 12.0;
      float ri = ro-w;
      letter = u(u(s(s(c(px+ro,py+ro,ro),
                         c(px+ro,py+ro,ri)),
                       r(px,py,ro+ro,ro)),
                     r(px+ro+ri,py,w,ro)),
                   r(px,py,w,ro+ro));
      px += ro+ro;
    } break;
    case 'l': {
      float vw = 13.0; float vh = 60.0;
      letter = r(px,py,vw,vh);
      px += vw;
    } break;
    case 'o': {
      float ro = 22.5;
      float ri = ro-12.0;
      letter = s(c(px+ro,py+ro,ro),c(px+ro,py+ro,ri));
      px += ro+ro;
    } break;
    case 'r': {
      float ro = 22.5;
      float ri = ro-12.0;
      letter = u(s(s(c(px+ro,py+ro,ro),c(px+ro,py+ro,ri)),
                     r(px,py,ro+ro,ro)),
                   r(px,py,ro-ri,ro+ro));
      px += ro+ro;
    } break;
    case 'v': {
      float vw = 6.5; float vh = 45.0;
      float w1 = vw;
      letter = sr(px+w1,py,vw,vh,-w1);
```

```
          letter = u(letter,sr(px+w1,py,vw,vh,w1));
          px += vw + w1 + w1;
        } break;
      case '␣': {
          px += 21.0;
        } break;
      case '\n': {
          px = -sep;
          py -= lineheight + linesep;
        } break;
      default:
          // empty shader for unsupported letters
          letter = SH_BEGIN_PROGRAM() {
            ShOutputAttrib1f f = 0.0;
          } SH_END;
        break;
      }
      // add each new letter to the phrase and move over by the letter width
      phrase = u(phrase,letter);
      px += sep;
    }
    // extract the position parameter and make it an input attribute
    return phrase >> posn;
}
```

Listing 3.10. CSG metaprogrammed text program generator.

3.6 Control Constructs

It is an error to attempt to convert a value stored in an Sh variable into a non-Sh C++ value inside a program object definition. Therefore, you cannot use C++ control flow constructs to define data-dependent looping or conditionals in shaders. In fact, the Sh compiler never sees C++ control constructs directly; it just sees the sequences of operations they generate.

However, Sh provides a mechanism to define data-dependent imperative control constructs inside shaders. Sh defines its own keywords that are really macros. They call functions to let Sh know that a particular control construct is requested. Control constructs include the following:

```
SH_IF(cond1) {
    // do stuff if cond1 is true
} SH_ELSEIF(cond2) {
    // do stuff if cond1 is false but cond2 is true
} SH_ELSE {
```

```
    // do stuff if both are false
} SH_ENDIF;
SH_WHILE(cond) {
    // repeat stuff here as long as cond is true
} SH_ENDWHILE;
SH_FOR(init,cond,update) {
    // repeat stuff here as long as cond is true
} SH_ENDFOR;
SH_DO {
    // repeat stuff here until cond is true
} SH_UNTIL(cond);
```

3.7   Example: Julia Set

This example demonstrates the use of a conditional data-dependent loop inside a shader. It was actually implemented on a CPU simulator because at the time of writing, no available GPUs actually supported conditional iteration inside a fragment shader. However, this feature is expected in the next generation of GPUs and our compiler has been tested with the Sm simulator, which supports a similar instruction set to real GPUs. Sh also currently supports conditional control flow whenever it compiles to a CPU target.

The Julia set shader searches for points in the Julia set, which consists of the locus of points on the complex plane for which the iteration

$$ u_{i+1} \quad \leftarrow \quad u_i^2 + c $$

does *not* diverge, as a function of the initial complex number u_0. Different values of c give different Julia sets.

In fact, we will visualize the number of iterations i it takes for $|u_i|^2 > 2$ for different initial values u_0. Once the squared magnitude of u_i reaches this value, further iterations are guaranteed to diverge, but the closer we get to the true Julia set points, the more iterations it will take before this condition is met.

Figure 3.6 shows the result of applying this shader to two different objects, a sphere and a plane.

The Julia set shader will generally produce a fairly noisy picture, since it is hard to antialias a fractal function. Supersampling must be used to generate a picture of reasonable quality. We did this here by generating a high resolution image and then downsampling, but in theory it could be done in the fragment shader by evaluating the Julia set at several offset points and then averaging them.

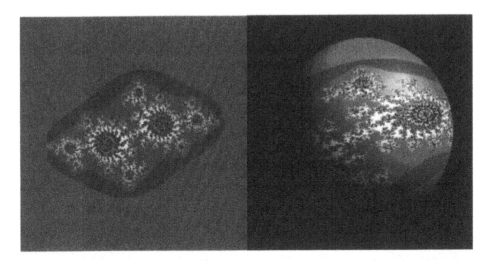

Figure 3.6. Examples of the Julia set shader, which uses a data-dependent loop in its implementation. See Plate 6 on page 114.

Our shader actually uses a texture map as a lookup table to map the iteration count to a color. We will discuss textures in more detail in Chapter 4. For now, just consider the texture object to be a (tabulated) function that maps a texture coordinate to a color.

The parameters of the Julia set shader are given in Listing 3.11. A one-dimensional texture map, $julia\_map$, and a scale factor parameter, $julia\_scale$, have been defined to map from the iteration count to the color of the final output. A parameter, $julia\_max\_iter$, has also been defined to specify the maximum number of iterations permitted. The two-dimesional parameter $julia\_c$ can be manipulated to give different Julia sets.

```
ShTexture1D<ShColor3f> julia_map(256);
ShAttrib1f julia_scale;
ShAttrib2f julia_c;
ShAttrib1f julia_max_iter;
```

Listing 3.11. Parameters of the Julia set shader.

The vertex shader in the next example, given in Listing 3.12, performs the usual transformations and also computes a diffuse lighting model. It also passes along a texture coordinate.

```
vertex_shader = SH_BEGIN_PROGRAM("gpu:vertex") {
    // declare input vertex attributes (unpacked in order given)
    ShInputTexCoord2f ui;        // texture coords
    ShInputNormal3f nm;          // MCS normal
    ShInputPosition3f pm;        // MCS position

    // declare outputs vertex parameters (packed in order given)
    ShOutputTexCoord2f uo;       // texture coords
    ShOutputColor3f ec;          // irradiance
    ShOutputHPosition4f pd;      // position (HDCS)

    // specify computations
    uo = ui;                                // copy texture coords
    ShPoint3f pv = (MV|pm)(0,1,2);          // VCS position
    ShPoint3f lv = normalize(light.pv - pv);        // VCS light vector
    ShNormal3f nv = normalize((nv|VM)(0,1,2));      // VCS normal
    ec = light.c * pos(nv|lv);              // Lambert's law
    pd = MD|pm;                             // DCS position
} SH_END;
```

Listing 3.12. Vertex shader for computing the Julia set.

```
ShProgram julia_fragment = SH_BEGIN_PROGRAM("gpu:fragment") {
    // declare input fragment attributes (unpacked in order given)
    ShInputTexCoord2f u;        // texture coordinates
    ShInputColor3f ec;          // irradiance
    ShInputPosition3f pd;       // fragment position (DCS)

    // declare output fragment parameters (packed in order given)
    ShOutputColor3f c;              // final color

    // specify computations
    ShAttrib1f i = 0.0; // iteration counter
    ShAttrib2f v;           // temporary
    SH_WHILE((u|u) < 2.0 && i < julia_max_iter) {
        v(0) = u(0)*u(0) - u(1)*u(1);
        v(1) = 2*u(0)*u(1);
        u = v + julia_c;
        i++;
    } SH_ENDWHILE;
    c = ec*julia_map(julia_scale*i); // send increment through lookup
} SH_END;
```

Listing 3.13. Fragment shader for computing the Julia set.

The fragment shader applies only the interpolated diffuse component for shading, multiplied by the color generated by the procedural Julia set texture. Of course, a more sophisticated lighting model could be used, but that's not the point of this example.

Here, we have written out the Julia set iteration explicitly and use two-vectors to store complex numbers. The shape of the Julia set can be manipulated by changing the *julia_c* parameter, and the resolution can be increased by increasing *julia_max_iter*, although at the cost of increased computation. Eventually we also run out of precision, so, if anything, this shader would be a good visual indicator of the precision available in a fragment shader implementation.

The texture map, *julia_map*, and the parameter, *julia_scale*, can be used to color the result in various interesting ways. In theory, we could also use an integer for the iteration counter i, but we assume, at present, that integer support would involve some extra clamping operations which really are not critical here.

Chapter 4

Arrays and Textures

In the original fixed-function graphics accelerator pipeline, textures were intended to hold images that would then be used to replace or modulate the diffuse component of the Blinn-Phong lighting model. In today's GPUs, texture maps are still used for this, but also can be used by any shader which needs to read from tabulated data for any purpose. Textures can be used to hold representations of reflectance models, displacement maps, light fields, volume data, and tabulated functions. Data structures have been invented that can use textures for holding sparse data, photon maps, and accelerator structures for ray tracers.

The texture support in Sh is designed to enable strong data abstraction so that these kinds of advanced applications can be better supported and combined with one another. Textures in Sh are treated semantically like arrays of parameters, and can be accessed like arrays both by the host application and by shader programs running on the GPU.

4.1 Texture Types

Texture maps in Sh are supported as template classes which take the type of the elements they store as a template argument. For instance, if we want to create a texture that stores 3-channel unsigned byte color data in a three-dimensional grid, we would declare an **ShTexture3D**<**ShColor3ub**>. If we wanted a cube map of floating-point vectors, we would declare an **ShTextureCube** <**ShVector3f**>.

Lookups on textures are supported with both the "()" and "[]" operators. These are slightly different. The "()" operator treats the lookup as if the texture is a tabulated function and the function is resolution independent. This is the traditional view of a texture lookup. The operator uses a normalized texture coordinate range of $[0, 1] \times [0, 1]$. In contrast, if "[ ]" is used, Sh places texture samples at the integers, although interpolation is still performed on the texture types that support it.

A texture type declaration consists of an *access type* chosen from **Array**, **Table**, and **Texture** and a *format type*. Several texture data format types are supported: **1D** for one-dimensional power-of-two textures, **2D** for square power-of-two two-dimensional textures, **Rect** for general rectangular two-dimensional textures, **3D** for three-dimensional volume textures, and **Cube** for cube environment-map textures indexed by a direction vector. The access types specify generally what interpolation and filtering modes are used, although trait modifiers can be used to refine these modes. The **Array** access type specifies nearest-neighbor lookup, **Table** specifies bilinear interpolation but not filtering, and **Texture** specifies both filtering and interpolation.

If support is missing for some access or format type on some platform, Sh will attempt to emulate it with shader code. For instance, on the GeForceFX 5000 series, floating point textures are not bilinearly interpolated in hardware. In Sh, *all* **ShTable** and **ShTexture** types support bilinear interpolation. Sh will insert code into the implementation of the "( )" and "[ ]" lookup operators to implement interpolation in software, if necessary.

Inserting code to support non-native access modes poses a problem, however. For instance, what if you want to change the interpolation mode of a texture after it has been used in a shader, and possibly loaded into the GPU? We *don't* want to trigger implicit recompilation and possible reloading of shaders upon such changes. Since shader compilation and loading are relatively heavyweight operations, they should not be invoked unexpectedly. On the other hand, if we allowed some dynamic mode changes and not others, we would be exposing platform dependencies. Our solution is to disallow *all* dynamic changes to access modes. Instead, all access modes are made a part of the type of a texture, and can, therefore, only be specified when the texture is created. If you want to use the same shader with different textures using two different access modes, you can always redefine and recompile the shader, using a template type or a common base type for the texture in question. If you want to share data between two textures with different access modes, for instance using nearest-neighbor interpolation in one place and bilinear interpolation in another, an explicit data-sharing facility is available to share data between two compatible texture types.

As previously mentioned, three major classes of access types are currently supported. The **ShArray** types (**ShArray1D**, **ShArray2D**, **ShArrayRect**, etc.) only support nearest-neighbor lookup and no filtering. These types are useful for the storage of data structures or for array processing. The **ShTable** types support bilinear interpolation, but not filtering. They are useful for the representation of tabulated functions. Finally, **ShTexture** types support MIP-map filtering with trilinear interpolation and are intended for the traditional uses of texture maps: pasting images on surfaces. Other minor modes or variations on these modes are supported with template trait modifiers. Suppose you want a MIP-filtered **ShArray2D**, but without interpolation. Then you could use the type **ShMIPFilter<ShArray2D<T> >**. Other trait modifiers can be used to set wrap-and-edge clamping modes and detailed interpolation modes. Trait modifiers are smart enough to avoid adding extra code if they are invoked more than once on a given type and will enable hardware features to support their semantics, if possible.

4.2   Example: Texture Mapped Blinn-Phong

An example using texture lookups is given in Listing 4.1; this is a modification of the shaders given in Listings 3.1 and 3.3. We made a few other changes, such as moving computations down to the fragment shader to avoid an excessive number of interpolants. However, the main change important here is that we have passed through texture coordinates in the vertex shader (demonstrating the *InOut* binding type, which declares *both* an input and an output) and converted ks and kd to textures. An example rendering is given in Figure 4.1.

Figure 4.1. Textured Blinn-Phong lighting model. See Plate 2 on page 111.

```
template <int NLIGHTS>
class TexturedBlinnPhongShader
  : public PointLightShader<NLIGHTS> {
public:
  ShTexture2D<ShColor3f> ks;      // specular texture
  ShTexture2D<ShColor3f> kd;      // diffuse texture
  ShAttrib1f q;                   // exponent
  TexturedBlinnPhongShader();
  void init() {
   vsh = SH_BEGIN_PROGRAM("gpu:vertex") {
    // declare input vertex attributes
    ShInOutTexCoord2f u;          // texture coordinate
    ShInputNormal3f nm;           // normal vector (MCS)
    ShInputPosition3f pm;         // position (MCS)
    // declare output vertex attributes
    ShOutputNormal3f nv;          // normal (VCS)
    ShOutputPoint3f pv;           // position (VCS)
    ShOutputPosition4f pd;        // position (DCS)
    // specify computations
    pv = (MV|pm)(0,1,2);          // VCS position
    pd = VD|pv;                   // DCS position
    nv = normalize((nm|VM)(0,1,2));   // VCS normal
   } SH_END;
   fsh = SH_BEGIN_PROGRAM("gpu:fragment") {
    // declare input fragment attributes
    ShInputTexCoord2f u;       // texture coordinate
    ShInputNormal3f nv;        // normal (VCS)
    ShInputPoint3f pv;         // position (VCS)
    ShInputPosition3f pd;      // fragment position (DCS)
    // declare output fragment attributes
    ShOutputColor3f c;         // fragment color
    // compute unit normal and view vector
    nv = normalize(nv);
    vv = normalize(-pv);
    // process each light source
    for (int i=0; i<NLIGHTS; i++) {
     // compute per-light normalized vectors
     ShVector3f lv = normalize(lights[i].pv - pv);
     ShVector3f hv = normalize(lv + vv);
     ShColor3f ec = lights[i].c * pos(nv|lv);
     // sum up contribution of light source
     c += ec*kd(u) + ks(u)*pow(pos(hv|nv),q);
    }
   } SH_END;
  }
};
```

Listing 4.1. Textured Blinn-Phong shader.

If you look carefully at this example, you will see that we seem to be doing more work than necessary. For instance, we include texture lookups ks(u) and kd(u) inside a loop, which means we do lookups at the same place in these texture maps more than once. You might be tempted to hoist those lookups out of the loop to avoid repeated texture evaluations. In the short term, this may improve performance. In the long term, the compiler will notice those repeated lookups too and can make that optimization for you, so you may not want to mangle your code.

One advantage that Sh has over a more general compiler is that we can make stronger assumptions about what will and won't change. Here although we are reading from the ks and kd "arrays," we know that the contents of this array *cannot change* during the invocation of the shader, and so we will always read the same value for the same index. This assumption could not be made in a general C program which has the ability to write to any memory location at any time (perhaps hidden inside some function). Sh program objects can *only* modify the outside world through a well-defined interface, and we don't have to worry about things like pointer aliasing; thus, much more aggressive optimization can be performed.

4.3   Example: Encapsulated BRDF Representation

Previously we demonstrated that you can use C++ constructs to perform data abstraction by encapsulating the parameters to shaders inside objects. Since textures are treated essentially like array-valued parameters by Sh, you can also form data abstractions using textures.

For instance, consider Listing 4.2, which implements homomorphically factorized reflectance models [88]. We use a parabolically tabulated representation of the hemispherically parameterized functions involved. Figure 4.2 shows some images rendered using homomorphically factorized materials.

```
class HfShader: public PointLightShader<1> {
public:
 ShTexture2D<ShColor3f> p;
 ShTexture2D<ShColor3f> q;
 ShColor3f a;
 HfShader ();
 void init() {
  vsh = SH_BEGIN_PROGRAM("gpu:vertex") {
   // declare input vertex attributes (unpacked in order given)
   ShInputVector3f tm;          // primary tangent (MCS)
   ShInputVector3f sm;          // secondary tangent (MCS)
```

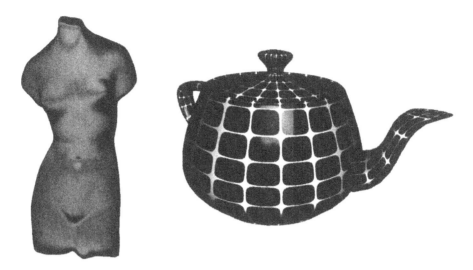

Figure 4.2. Homomorphically factorized materials. On the left, anisotropic satin; on the right, a combination of three materials (garnet red, satin, and mystique). See Plate 8 on page 115.

```
ShInputPosition3f pm;          // position (MCS)
// declare output vertex attributes (packed in order given)
ShOutputVector3f vs;           // view vector (SCS)
ShOutputVector3f ls;           // light vector (SCS)
ShOutputColor3f ec;            // irradiance
ShOutputPosition4f pd;         // position (HDCS)
// compute transformations
ShPoint3f pv = (MV|pm)(0,1,2);    // VCS position
pd = MD|pv;                        // DCS position
// find surface frame
ShVector3f tv = normalize((MV|tm)(0,1,2));  // transform tangents
ShVector3f sv = normalize((MV|sm)(0,1,2));
ShNormal3f nv = normalize(tv^sv);           // compute normal
// compute irradiance
ShVector3f lv = normalize(light.pv - pv);
ec = light.c * pos(nv|lv);
// compute SCS view and light vectors
ShVector3f vv = normalize(-pv);
ls = ShVector3f(tv|lv,sv|lv,nv|lv);
vs = ShVector3f(tv|vv,sv|vv,nv|vv);
} SH_END;
fsh = SH_BEGIN_PROGRAM("gpu:fragment") {
  // declare input fragment attributes (unpacked in order given)
```

```
ShInputVector3f vs;      // view vector (SCS)
ShInputVector3f ls;      // light vector (SCS)
ShInputColor3f ec;       // irradiance
ShInputPosition3f pd;    // fragment position (DCS)
// declare output fragment attributes (packed in order given)
ShOutputColor3f c;       // final color
// compute normalized vectors
ls = normalize(ls);
vs = normalize(vs);
ShVector3f hs = normalize(ls + vs);
c = a * ec * p(parabolic(vs))
            * q(parabolic(hs))
            * p(parabolic(ls));
} SH_END;
}
};
```

Listing 4.2. Vertex and fragment shaders for homomorphic factorization.

With only slightly more effort, we can encapsulate the representation of the BRDF in a class, as shown in Listing 4.3.

```
// Texture abstraction: radially symmetric 2D texture
template <typename ELEM>
class RadialTexture2D {
 ShTexture1D<ELEM> tex;
 ELEM operator() (ShTexCoord2f u) const {
    ShTexCoord1f r = 2.0*length(u-ShTexCoord2f(0.5,0.5));
    return tex(r);
 }
};
// BRDF abstraction: HF representation
template <typename TEXTURE>
class HfBRDF: public BRDF {
public:
 TEXTURE p, q;
 ShColor3f a;
 HfBRDF();
 ShColor3f operator() (ShVector3f vs, ShVector3f ls) const {
  ls = normalize(ls);
  vs = normalize(vs);
  ShVector3f hs = normalize(ls + vs);
  ShColor3f c = p(parabolic(vs))
              * q(parabolic(hs))
              * p(parabolic(ls));
  return c * a;
 }
};
```

```
template <typename F>
class BRDFShader: public PointLightShader<1> {
public:
 BRDFShader();
 void init() {
  vsh = SH_BEGIN_PROGRAM("gpu:vertex") {
   ...   // as before
  } SH_END;
  fsh = SH_BEGIN_PROGRAM("gpu:fragment") {
   // declare input fragment attributes (unpacked in order given)
   ShInputVector3f vs;       // view vector (SCS)
   ShInputVector3f ls;       // light vector (SCS)
   ShInputColor3f ec;        // irradiance
   ShInputPosition3f pd;     // fragment position (DCS)
   // declare output fragment attributes (packed in order given)
   ShOutputColor3f fc;       // fragment color
   // multiply BRDF by irradiance
   fc = ec * F(vs,ls);
  } SH_END;
 }
};
```

Listing 4.3. Data abstraction for factorized BRDF.

The fact that this reflectance model is implemented using a texture map is completely hidden. In fact, we could use another representation of a BRDF in place of the homomorphically factorized BRDF. Also, we have created a new type for radially symmetric two-dimensional textures. This is suitable for isotropic BRDFs under homomorphic factorization, and a considerable optimization, but cannot be used for anisotropic BRDFs. For isotropic BRDFs we would therefore use

```
BRDFShader< HfBRDF< RadialTexture2D<ShColor3f> > >
```

while for anisotropic BRDFs we would use

```
BRDFShader< HfBRDF< ShTexture2D<ShColor3f> > >
```

If we wanted, we could also include the call to the `parabolic` function as part of our texture abstraction.

4.4   Example: Shiny Bump Map

A bump map reflecting an environment map is a common example, so we will give our version here. In the following, we assume *normal_map* is a texture

map of normals represented with respect to the surface coordinate system, and
env_map is an environment map represented as a cube map. We also assume
that we wish to transform the surface for rendering in the usual way by a *MV*
affine transformation and a projective *MD* transformation. However, the environment map is represented relative to the world space, and so we also need
to use a model to world transformation *MW* and a view to world transformation
VW. We will only give a shader for a purely reflective surface here.

4.4.1 Vertex Shader

The vertex shader for the shiny bump mapped surface is given in Listing 4.4.
To define the local surface frame, we have chosen to only pass in two tangents,
rather than a normal. This makes transformation easier, as we will only need
the forward transformation matrices. On the other hand, we have to use two
more matrices to go from model to world coordinates, and from view to world
coordinates.

```
vsh = SH_BEGIN_PROGRAM("gpu:vertex") {
  // declare input vertex attributes (unpacked in order given)
  ShInputVector3f tm;          // primary tangent (MCS)
  ShInputVector3f sm;          // secondary tangent (MCS)
  ShInputTexCoord2f ui;        // texture coords
  ShInputPosition3f pm;        // position (MCS)

  // declare output vertex attributes (packed in order given)
  ShOutputVector3f vw;         // view vector (WCS)
  ShOutputVector3f tw;         // primary tangent (WCS)
  ShOutputVector3f sw;         // secondary tangent (WCS)
  ShOutputTexCoord2f uo(ui);   // texture coordinates
  ShOutputPosition4f pd;       // position (HDCS)

  // specify computations
  tw = (MW|tm)(0,1,2);                    // transform tangents
  sw = (MW|sm)(0,1,2);
  ShPoint3f pv = (MV|pm)(0,1,2);     // compute VCS position
  vv = -ShVector3f(pv);             // unnormalized view vector
  vw = (VW|vv)(0,1,2);              // WCS unnormalized view vector
  pd = VD|pv;                       // compute DCS position
} SH_END;
```

Listing 4.4. Vertex shader for shiny bump-mapped surface.

4.4.2 Fragment Shader

The fragment shader, given in Listing 4.5, looks up the surface normal in a texture map, but this normal is expressed relative to the surface frame. Using the WCS tangents interpolated from the vertices, we can construct a version of the normal in world coordinates (WCS). Using this normal, we can reflect the WCS view vector for indexing into the cube map. The `reflect` function defined in the standard library will be used to compute the reflection vector. If we use cube maps, we do not need to normalize the view vector, and the `reflect` function will still work correctly with an unnormalized incident vector. In Figure 4.3, we show the shiny bump-mapped surface next to a mirrored surface without bumps.

```
fsh = SH_BEGIN_PROGRAM("gpu:fragment") {
    // declare input fragment parameters (unpacked in order given)
    ShInputVector3f vw;         // view vector (WCS)
    ShInputVector3f tw;         // primary tangent (WCS)
    ShInputVector3f sw;         // secondary tangent (WCS)
    ShInputTexCoord2f u;        // texture coordinates
    ShInputPosition3f pd;       // fragment position (DCS)

    // declare output fragment parameters (packed in order given)
    ShOutputColor3f c;          // final color

    // specify computations
    ShNormal3f ns = normal_map(u);    // look up SCS normal
    ShNormal3f nw = ns(0) * tw        // transform from SCS to WCS
                  + ns(1) * sw
                  + ns(2) * (tw^sw);
    nw = normalize(nw);
    c = env_map(reflect(vw,nw));      // look up reflection in cube map
} SH_END;
```

Listing 4.5. Fragment shader for shiny bump-mapped surface.

4.5 Example: Glass

In Chapter 2, we defined the functions `reflect`, `refract`, and `fresnel`. All three of these functions are actually in the standard library. We have already used the `reflect` function to implement the shiny bump-map shader. Now we will implement a glass shader and a lucite shader, both of which will use first-surface refraction. In first surface refraction, we refract the view vector only at the first surface encountered, and then just index into the environment map, ig-

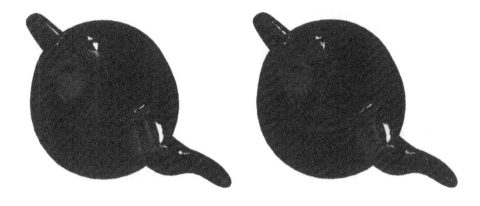

Figure 4.3. Shiny bump-mapped shader. See Plate 9 on page 115.

noring refraction upon leaving the object and possible internal reflections. Even though this is a terrible hack, the results look pretty good; see Figure 4.4. For glass, we assume one relative index of refraction for all wavelenths of light. For lucite, we want some color fringing due to dispersion, so we use slightly different refractive indices for each of R, G, and B, compute three separate refraction vectors, and make three separate lookups for each color channel.

Here are the shader parameters specific to glass. Only one index of refraction is needed if we assume non-dispersive glass.

```
ShTextureCube<ShColor3f> env_map;
ShAttrib1f eta = ShAttrib1f(1.3f);
```

Listing 4.6. Glass parameters.

Now we define the vertex shader. The reflection and refraction vectors and the Fresnel term all vary relatively gradually, so we will compute them in the vertex shader and interpolate them. As with the shiny bump-map shader, we need transformation to world space and need to represent the refraction and reflection vectors in the WCS, since that is the space in which the environment map is defined.

```
vsh = SH_BEGIN_PROGRAM("gpu:vertex") {
  ShInputPosition4f pm;      // MCS position
  ShInputNormal3f nm;        // MCS normal
```

```
ShOutputPosition4f pd;        // DCS position
ShOutputVector3f rw;          // WCS reflection vector
ShOutputVector3f fw;          // WCS refraction vector
ShOutputAttrib1f F;           // Fresnel term

pd = MD|pm;                              // DCS position
ShPoint3f pv = (MV|pm)(0,1,2);           // VCS position
ShPoint3f vv = normalize(-pv);           // VCS view vector
ShVector3f vw = normalize((VW|vv)(0,1,2)); // WCS view vector
ShNormal3f nw = normalize((nm|WM)(0,1,2)); // WCS normal
rw = reflect(vw,nw);                     // WCS reflection vector
fw = refract(vw,nw,eta);                 // WCS refraction vector
F = fresnel(vw,nw,eta);                  // Fresnel term
} SH_END;
```

Listing 4.7. Glass vertex shader.

Since we have done all the hard work at the vertex level, the fragment shader is relatively simple. In fact, it boils downs to only a few instructions at the assembly level: two texture lookups and a linear interpolation!

```
fsh = SH_BEGIN_PROGRAM("gpu:fragment") {
  ShInputPosition4f pd;
  ShInputVector3f rw;          // WCS reflection vector
  ShInputVector3f fw;          // WCS refraction vector
  ShInputAttrib1f F;           // Fresnel term

  ShOutputColor3f c;

  c = lerp(F,env_map(fw),env_map(rw));
} SH_END;
```

Listing 4.8. Glass fragment shader.

4.6   Example: Lucite

Lucite is similar to glass, except now in our parameters we need three separate indices of refraction:

```
ShTextureCube<ShColor3f> env_map;
ShAttrib3f eta = ShAttrib3f(1.32f,1.3f,1.28f);
```

Listing 4.9. Lucite parameters.

The vertex shader is similar to that for glass, except we compute three refraction vectors. We pack the three different Fresnel factors together into one

3-tuple to save on interpolants and because, later, we want to use component-wise multiplication with the reflected color.

```
vsh = SH_BEGIN_PROGRAM("gpu:vertex") {
  ShInputPosition4f pm;       // MCS position
  ShInputNormal3f nm;          // MCS normal

  ShOutputPosition4f pd;       // DCS position
  ShOutputVector3f rw;          // WCS reflection vector
  ShOutputVector3f fw[3];      // WCS refraction vectors (per RGB channel)
  ShOutputAttrib3f F;           // fresnel terms (per RGB channel)

  pd = MD|pm;                            // DCS position
  ShPoint3f pv = (MV|pm)(0,1,2);        // VCS position
  ShPoint3f vv = -normalize(pv);        // VCS view vector
  ShVector3f vw = normalize((VW|vv)(0,1,2));  // WCS view vector
  ShNormal3f nw = normalize((nm|WM)(0,1,2));  // WCS normal
  rw = reflect(vw,nw);                  // WCS reflection vector
  for (int i=0; i<3; i++) {
    fw[i] = refract(vw,nw,eta[i]);      // WCS refraction vectors
    F[i] = fresnel(vw,nw,eta[i]);       // Fresnel terms
  }
} SH_END;
```

Listing 4.10. Lucite vertex shader

Again, the fragment shader is relatively simple. We make a total of four texture lookups. We can weight the reflection with a componentwise multiplication with the Fresnel term. The results of the wavelength-dependent refractions have to be weighted by the complement of the Fresnel term component-by-component.

```
fsh = SH_BEGIN_PROGRAM("gpu:fragment") {
  ShInputPosition4f pd;
  ShInputVector3f rw;          // WCS reflection vector
  ShInputVector3f fw[3];      // WCS refraction vectors (per RGB channel)
  ShInputAttrib3f F;           // Fresnel terms (per RGB channel)

  ShOutputColor3f c;

  c = F * env_map(rw);
  for (int i=0; i<3; i++) {
    c[i] += (1-F[i]) * env_map(fw[i])(i);
  }
} SH_END;
```

Listing 4.11. Lucite fragment shader.

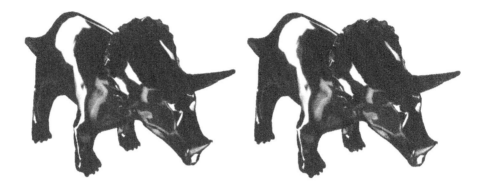

Figure 4.4. Glass and lucite shaders. See Plate 11 on page 116.

4.7   Example: Wood and Marble

To implement marble, wood, and similar materials, we can use the simple parameterized model for such materials proposed by John C. Hart et al. [56]. This model is given by

$$t(\mathbf{x}) = \sum_{i=0}^{N-1} \alpha_i |n(2^i \mathbf{x})|,$$

$$\mathbf{u} = \mathbf{x}^T \mathbf{A}\mathbf{x} + t(\mathbf{x}),$$

$$k_d(\mathbf{x}) = c_d(\mathbf{u}),$$

$$k_s(\mathbf{x}) = c_s(\mathbf{u}),$$

where n is a bandlimited signed noise function such as Perlin noise [113], t is the "turbulence" noise function synthesized from it, A is a 4×4 symmetric matrix giving the coefficients of the quadric function $\mathbf{x}^T \mathbf{A}\mathbf{x}$ (Note, that this matrix can include transformation of the model space position.), c_d and c_s are one-dimensional MIP-mapped texture maps functioning as filtered color lookup tables, and x represents the model-space (normalized homogeneous) position of a surface point. The outputs need to be combined with a lighting model, so we will combine them with the Blinn-Phong lighting model. We build this model into the shader; really, we should support an abstract BRDF interface such as that defined earlier in this chapter.

Figure 4.5. Wood and marble shaders. See Plate 12 on page 117.

Generally speaking, we would use fractal turbulence and would have $\alpha_i = s2^{-i}$ for some scale factor s. For the purposes of this example, we will permit the α_i values to vary arbitrarily to permit further per-material noise shaping and will bind them to named parameters. Likewise, various simplifications would be possible if we fixed A (marble requires only a linear term, wood only a cylinder) but we have chosen to give an implementation of the more general model and will bind A to a named parameter. One nice thing about this approach is that you can leave a single shader bound and render a lot of different materials in your environment just by changing a few parameters.

4.7.1 Parameters

The framework for the parameterized noise shaders is given in Listing 4.12.

```
template <int NLIGHTS>
class ParameterizedNoiseShader
  : public PointLightShader<NLIGHTS> {
public:
  ShTexture1D<ShColor3f> cd;       // diffuse color lookup table
  ShTexture1D<ShColor3f> cs;       // specular color lookup table
  ShMatrix4x4f A;                  // quadric coefficient matrix
  ShAttrib4f alpha;                // turbulence frequencies
  ShAttrib1f q;                    // blinn-phong exponent

  ParameterizedNoiseShader ();
};
```

Listing 4.12. Parameters of the parameterized noise model.

4.7.2   Vertex Shader

The vertex shader given in Listing 4.13 sets up the Phong lighting model.

```
vsh = SH_BEGIN_PROGRAM("gpu:vertex") {
  // declare input vertex attributes (unpacked in order given)
  ShInputNormal3f nm;          // normal vector (MCS)
  ShInputPosition3f pm;        // position (MCS)

  // declare output vertex attributes (packed in order given)
  ShOutputPoint3f x(pm);              // position (MCS)
  ShOutputVector3f hv[NLIGHTS];       // half-vector, per light (VCS)
  ShOutputNormal3f nv;                // normal (VCS)
  ShOutputColor3f ec;                 // irradiance
  ShOutputPosition4f pd;              // position (HDCS)

  // specify computations
  ShPoint3f pv = (MV|pm)(0,1,2);   // VCS position
  pd = VD|pv;                      // DCS position
  nv = normalize((nm|VM)(0,1,2)); // VCS normal
  vv = normalize(-pv);            // VCS view vector
  for (int i=0; i<NLIGHTS; i++) {
    // Compute VCS light vector
    ShVector3f lv = normalize(lights[i].pv - pv);
    ec += lights[i].c * pos(nv|lv); // accumulate irradiance
    hv[i] = normalize(lv + vv);
  }
} SH_END;
```

Listing 4.13. Vertex shader for parameterized noise model.

4.7.3   Fragment Shader

The fragment shader given in Listing 4.14 performs the computation of the quadric and the turbulence function and passes their sum through the color lookup table. Two different lookup tables are used to modulate the specular and diffuse parts of the lighting model, which will permit, for example, dense dark wood to be shinier than light wood (with the appropriate entries in the lookup tables).

We use a noise function here, specifically, sturbulence. This function is part of the standard library. On hardware accelerators without built in noise functions, noise can be stored in textures. All that is really needed is the ability to hash a point in space to a determinisitic, but random-seeming, value. This

```
fsh = SH_BEGIN_PROGRAM("gpu:fragment") {
  // declare input fragment attributes
  ShInputPoint3f pm;                    // position (MCS)
  ShInputVector3f hv[NLIGHTS];          // half vector, per light (VCS)
  ShInputNormal3f nv;                   // normal (VCS)
  ShInputColor3f ec;                    // irradiance
  ShInputPosition3f pd;                 // fragment position (DCS)

  // declare output fragment attributes
  ShOutputColor3f c;                    // final color

  // specify computations
  ShTexCoord1f u = (pm|A|pm)            // perturb texture coordinates
                 + sturbulence<1>(pm,alpha);
  nv = normalize(nv);
  c = cd(u)*ec;
  ShColor3f ks = cs(u);
  for (int i=0; i<NLIGHTS; i++) {
    c += ks*pow(hv[i]|nv,q);  // Blinn-phong specular lobes
  }
} SH_END;
```

Listing 4.14. Fragment shader for parameterized noise model.

can be supported using a one-dimensional nearest-neighbor texture lookup (Perlin's original implementation of his noise function, in fact, uses such an approach for implementing a hash function [38, 113]) or a "hash" procedure or instruction. In the noise functions for Sh, we have implemented procedures to compute a hash function completely procedurally, so noise can even be used on existing vertex units without texture mapping. With the hash values in hand, the rest of the computation to support noise functions can be performed using arithmetic operations already supported by the shading unit.

4.8   Example: Worley Noise Shaders

While we are on the subject of noise functions, we have also implemented the Worley noise basis functions [151]. Construction of the Worley basis functions starts with a random distribution of points. The original paper used a Poisson distribution (a completely random distribution of points) but, for efficiency, we use a jittered grid. Then the kth Worley basis function is equal to the distance to the kth nearest neighbor from the evaluation location to the jittered points. We first determine what cell we are in, then compute the positions of the jittered

Figure 4.6. Worley shaders. See Plate 14 on page 118.

sample points in this cell and neighboring cells using a hash of each cell's coordinates. In two dimensions, this gives us nine sample points. We then compute the distance to each of them and sort these distances, using a tuple-sort routine also provided in the standard library. The resulting tuple gives values for all basis functions.

Various linear and non-linear combinations of these functions can be used to get different effects. It is also interesting to use different distance metrics, and map the basis functions through color lookup tables implemented with texture maps. Various obtainable effects are demonstrated in Figure 4.6.

4.9   Example: Wood from Phong

In Section 4.7, a wood/marble shader based on a quadric function perturbed by noise was developed. Now we will show how such a shader can be based on any reflectance model via use of shader algebra operators. We will start with a simple Phong lighting model, extract the kd and ks parameters, and replace them with one-dimensional texture lookups. We will then feed these texture lookups with a perturbed quadric to obtain results similar to what we had before. We show this process on Phong but with only a little more work, something similar could be done with practically any parameterized lighting model. Also, as shown previously, with small changes in the noise model and color lookup tables (stored in texture maps) a variety of effects can be obtained.

Listing 4.15 gives the function that computes wood from Phong. This listing is given relative to the Phong lighting model defined in Listing 4.16. We modify both the vertex shader and the fragment shader. The original Phong vertex shader did not pass through model space position to the fragment shader, so we first modify the vertex shader to pass through the model space position. We do this with a keep nibble (glue program object generator) and some shader algebra operations. To generate the fragment shader, we first define a shader program that generates a noise function. We then convert *phong_kd* and *phong_ks* parameters in the Phong shader to attributes and rebind them to the results of one-dimensional texture accesses. We finally duplicate the output of our noise function generator and feed it into both texture lookup inputs. A diagrammatic representation of all the operations is shown in Figure 4.7.

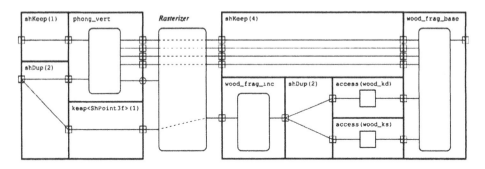

Figure 4.7. Diagram of expression to compute wood from Phong.

```
ShAttrib2f wood_freq;
ShAttrib1f wood_scale;
ShAttrib1f wood_noise_scale;
ShTexture1D<ShColor3f> wood_kd(256);
ShTexture1D<ShColor3f> wood_ks(256);
ShProgram wood_vert, wood_frag;

void wood_init() {
```

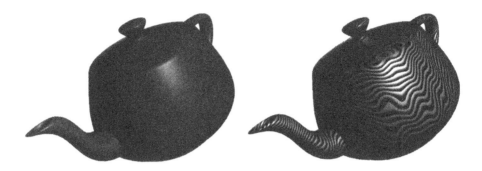

Figure 4.8. Images generated with Phong and a wood shader derived from it using shader algebra operators. See Plate 13 on page 117.

```
// modify phong_vert to pass through model space position
wood_vert = phong_vert & keep<ShPoint3f>();
wood_vert = wood_vert << (shKeep(1) & shDup(2));

// define kernel to generate texture coords from noise
ShProgram wood_frag_inc = SH_BEGIN_PROGRAM("gpu:fragment") {
  ShInputPoint3f x;          // IN(0): model space position
  ShOutputTexCoord1f u;      // OUT(1): texture coordinate
  ShPoint3f scaled_x = x*wood_scale*0.5;
  ShAttrib1f nse = sturbulence(scaled_x);
  u = frac(wood_scale*(x(1,2)|x(1,2))+wood_noise_scale*nse);
} SH_END;

// make two copies of texture coords (one for ks, one for kd)
wood_frag = shDup(2) << wood_frag_inc;
// feed texture coords into texture lookups for ks and kd
wood_frag = (shAccess(wood_kd) & shAccess(wood_ks))
            << wood_frag;
// convert ks and kd parameters to input attributes
ShProgram wood_frag_base = phong_frag
                                >> phong_kd >> phong_ks;
// replace new inputs with our noise-based texture lookups.
wood_frag = wood_frag_base << (shKeep(4) & wood_frag);
}
```

Listing 4.15. Converting a Phong shader to a wood shader.

```
ShColor3f phong_kd;         // diffuse color
ShColor3f phong_ks;         // specular color
ShAttrib1f phong_q;         // specular exponent
ShProgram phong_vert, phong_frag;

void phong_init () {
  phong_vert = SH_BEGIN_PROGRAM("gpu:vertex") {
    ShInputNormal3f nm;         // IN(0): normal vector (MCS)
    ShInputPosition3f pm;       // IN(1): position (MCS)

    ShOutputNormal3f nv;        // OUT(0): normal (VCS)
    ShOutputVector3f lv;        // OUT(1): light-vector (VCS)
    ShOutputVector3f vv;        // OUT(2): view vector (VCS)
    ShOutputColor3f ec;         // OUT(3): irradiance
    ShOutputPosition4f pd;      // OUT(4): position (HDCS)

    ShPoint3f pv = (MV|pm)(0,1,2);
    pd = VD|pv;
    vv = normalize(-pv);
    lv = normalize(light.pv - pv);
    nv = normalize((nm|VM)(0,1,2));
    ec = light.c * pos(nv|lv);
  } SH_END;
  phong_frag = SH_BEGIN_PROGRAM("gpu:fragment") {
    ShInputNormal3f nv;         // IN(0): normal (VCS)
    ShInputVector3f lv;         // IN(1): light-vector (VCS)
    ShInputVector3f vv;         // IN(2): view vector (VCS)
    ShInputColor3f ec;          // IN(3): irradiance

    ShOutputColor3f c;          // OUT(0): fragment color

    vv = normalize(vv);
    nv = normalize(nv);
    ShVector3f rv = reflect(normalize(lv),nv);
    c = phong_kd*ec + phong_ks*pow(pos(rv|vv),phong_q);
  } SH_END;
}
```

Listing 4.16. Phong shader (wood source shader).

Plate 1: Some example shaders. See Figure 1.1 on page 6.

Plate 2: Examples of the Blinn-Phong lighting model. See Figure 3.1 on page 65 and Figure 4.1 on page 91.

Plate 3: Surface and light shaders can be combined with shader algebra operators, and any attribute or parameter can be replaced with a texture map (or procedure). See Figure 3.2 on page 75.

113

Plate 4: Halftoning postprocess applied with shader algebra. See Figure 3.3 on page 76.

Plate 5: Bump mapping applied with shader algebra. See Figure 3.4 on page 76.

114

Plate 6: Examples of the Julia set shader, which uses a data-dependent loop in its implementation. See Figure 3.6 on page 85.

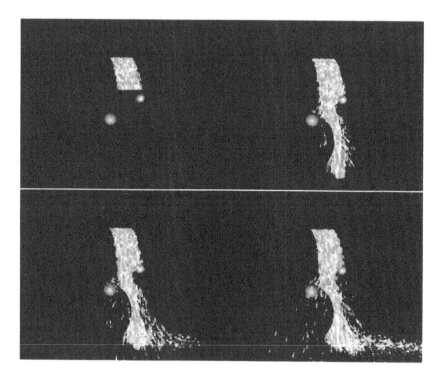

Plate 7: Frames from the particle system animation. See Figure 5.1 on page 125.

Plate 8: Homomorphically factorized materials. On the left, anisotropic satin, on the right, a combination of three materials (garnet red, satin, and mystique). See Figure 4.2 on page 94.

Plate 9: Shiny bump-mapped shader. See Figure 4.3 on page 99.

Plate 10: Cel shading and Gooch Shading

Plate 11: Glass and lucite shaders. See Figure 4.4 on page 102.

Plate 12: Wood and marble shaders. See Figure 4.5 on page 103.

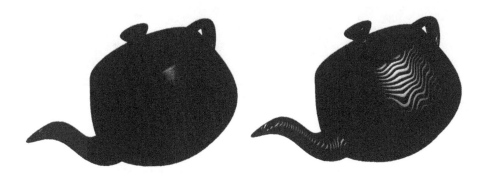

Plate 13: Images generated with Phong and a wood shader derived from it using shader algebra operators. See Figure 4.8 on page 108.

118

Plate 14: Worley shaders. See Figure 4.6 on page 106.

Chapter 5

Streams and Channels

Sh supports a stream model of computation. Program objects that are compiled with the "gpu:stream" or "cpu:stream" compilation targets can be applied to data directly without invoking a graphics API. This mode of execution of Sh program objects is intended to support general-purpose computation.

5.1 Channels

Data for the stream model of computation is stored in channels. Declarations for channels are similar to those for textures; the *ShChannel* template class takes a template argument which is the type of the element it stores, which may be any Sh tuple type:

```
ShChannel<ShPoint3f> pos;
ShChannel<ShPoint3f> pos_tail;
ShChannel<ShVector3f> vel;
```

A channel stores a sequence of data, but the actual representation is hidden. In particular, the data stored in a channel may be packed internally into a two-dimensional texture, several textures, or a vertex buffer. It may also be shadowed on both the host and the video memory.

5.2 Combining Channels into Streams

Channels store elements of a particular type and are themselves typed. Streams are containers for sequences of channels and are untyped (or rather, dynamically typed by Sh, like program objects). A stream is created by combining channels with the "&" operator. For instance:

```
ShStream state = pos & pos_tail & vel;
```

Streams can also be combined with other streams using the "&" operator, but this does not create a hierarchy; it just concatenates the channels, and each stream object refers to a flat sequence of channels. Streams only refer to channels; they do not copy them. Channels can be referenced by more than one stream at the same time and may be accessed independently of any stream by which they are referenced. For convenience, a channel object can also be referred to as if it were a single-channel stream.

All the elements at the same relative offset in the channels participating in a stream are called a *record* of that stream. Stream data can be seen either as an ordered sequence of channels or an ordered sequence of records.

5.3   Applying Programs to Streams

When a program object has been compiled with a `stream` target, it can be applied to stream data using "<<." Such an application will invoke, conceptually, the stream program on all records of the stream in parallel and generate a new stream. The output of a program can be assigned to another stream object, even an anonymous one constructed solely for the purpose of output splitting. Since a single channel can be used as a stream, the output from programs with a single output can also be assigned to a single channel.

For instance, suppose we have channels a, b, c, x, and y. We also have a stream program p with two input attributes and three output attributes. This program can be invoked as follows:

```
(a & b & c) = p << (x & y);
```

This constructs stream (x & y) and invokes program p on all elements of this stream. The three output channels are then split up and directed to a, b, and c. Stream program objects are also curried and partial evaluation is supported. The following expression is equivalent to the one we just considered:

```
(a & b & c) = p << x << y;
```

Here x is first bound to p, but the resulting program p << x requires one more input, which is obtained when y is bound. The bound program is now ready to execute, and execution is triggered when the result is assigned to another stream. Inputs bound this way are bound *by reference*. The data is not copied when it is bound, it is only referenced and read when the program executes. This is actually convenient, because the relationships between a network of stream programs can be compiled into the program objects and then executed efficiently later in the inner loop of an algorithm. Also note that the deferred read semantics is also applied to tuples when they are used in place of channels, and a program can be applied to a mixture of tuples and channels.

5.4 Example: Particle Systems

Particle systems [123, 124] are a classic and useful technique for modelling certain phenomena, including explosions and wave spray. A particle system consists of a large set of particles, each of which carries a *state*. Associated with each particle system is a state update function, a render function, a birth process, and death process. The state update function computes the new state of each particle from the current state. The render function takes the current state and computes a visible representation of the particle. The birth process initializes the state of new particles, and the death process terminates particles. If the number of particles is kept constant, then the birth and death processes can be integrated with the state update. Part of the state can be a life time, which is incremented on every state update. When the particle reaches its maximum time to live, it is reinitialized (so the old particle dies, but a new one is immediately born).

Particle systems can be classified into independent and interacting. In an independent particle system, the state of each particle evolves separately from all other particles. Particles may still interact with the environment, but not with one another. In an interacting particle system, the new state of a particle depends on the state of other particles, typically the k particles closest to it. Interacting particle systems can be used to model (viscous) fluid [141], cloth [19, 20], and herding behaviour [125], but they are more expensive to compute. One advantage of independent particle systems is that the state of all particles can be updated in parallel, without communication. Implementing interacting particles requires communication of the state between particles. The interaction pattern can be fixed (for instance, in the case of cloth), but generally, requires a solution to the k nearest-neighbor (KNN) problem. The KNN problem, however, has been solved or approximated on GPUs [121, 82].

In this example, we only demonstrate the implementation of an independent particle system, which is still suitable for rendering explosions or water spray. Our example will also be able to handle collisions with a ground plane and an arbitrary number of spheres. We use an $O(n)$ implementation, testing each particle against every sphere. A more sophisticated implementation would use an accelerator structure stored in a texture map to limit the number of spheres. For simplicity, we also do not integrate a birth and death process.

The particles will interact with a scene consisting of a collection of spheres and a ground plane. We define these parameters as follows:

```
int num_spheres;
struct Sphere {
  ShPoint3f center;
  ShAttrib1f radius;
};
Sphere spheres[num_spheres];
```

Listing 5.1. Sphere-collider parameters for particle system simulation.

Using these parameters, the code in Listing 5.2 defines a stream program to update the state of a particle system in parallel [137].

```
ShProgram particle = SH_BEGIN_PROGRAM("gpu:stream") {
  // Unbound parameters (to be curried)
  ShInputVector3f A;        // acceleration vector
  ShInputAttrib1f delta;    // timestep

  // Particle state (inputs AND outputs)
  ShInOutPoint3f Ph;    // head position
  ShInOutPoint3f Pt;    // tail position
  ShInOutVector3f V;    // velocity vector

  // Basic state update
  Pt = Ph;    // copy head position to tail (line segment rendering later)
  // clamp acceleration to zero if particles at or below ground plane
  A = cond(abs(Ph(1)) < 0.05, ShVector3f(0.,0.,0.), A);
  // integrate acceleration to get velocity
  V += A * delta;
  // clamp velocity to zero if small to force particles to settle
  V = cond((V|V) < 1.0, ShVector3f(0.0, 0.0, 0.0), V);
  // integrate velocity to update position
  Ph += (V - 0.5 * A) * delta;

  // Sphere collisions
  ShAttrib1f mu(0.1), eps(0.3);
  for (int i = 0; i < num_spheres; i++) {    // for each sphere...
    // retrieve parameters defining sphere
    ShPoint3f C = spheres[i].center;
    ShAttrib1f r = spheres[i].radius;
    // compute vector from center of sphere
```

```
ShVector3f PhC = Ph - C;
// normalize to get sphere normal
ShVector3f N = normalize(PhC);
// find position of surface point of sphere closest to particle
ShPoint3f S = C + N * r;
// determine if collision has occured
ShAttrib1f collide = ((PhC|PhC) < r * r) * ((V|N) < 0);
// update state by reflection off sphere if collision
Ph = cond(collide, Ph - 2.0 * ((Ph - S)|N) * N, Ph);
ShVector3f Vn = (V|N) * N;
ShVector3f Vt = V - Vn;
V = cond(collide, (1.0 - mu) * Vt - eps * Vn, V);
}

// Handle collision with ground
ShAttrib1f under = Ph(1) < 0.0;  // check if below ground level
// clamp to ground level if necessary
Ph = cond(under, Ph * ShAttrib3f(1.0, 0.0, 1.0), Ph);
// modify velocity in case of collision
ShVector3f Vn = V * ShAttrib3f(0.0, 1.0, 0.0);
ShVector3f Vt = V - Vn;
V = cond(under, (1.0 - mu) * Vt - eps * Vn, V);
Ph(1) = cond(min(under, (V|V) < 0.1),
             ShPoint1f(0.0f), Ph(1));
// make sure lines have a minimum length (modifies Pt)
ShVector3f dt = Pt - Ph;
Pt = cond((dt|dt) < 0.02,
          Pt + ShVector3f(0.0, 0.02, 0.0), Pt);
} SH_END;
```

Listing 5.2. Particle system simulation.

The input attributes of the `particle` stream program consist of two cate-gories. First, the attributes A (acceleration) and `delta` (time-step) are designed to be bound to parameters by currying. We will just use a constant acceleration, but in theory, we could also use a procedure to compute acceleration procedu-rally (for instance, using a wind field). The second set of input attributes is the actual state: Ph (head position), Pt (tail position), and V (velocity). Both a head and a tail position are maintained, since we plan to render our particles as line segments to avoid temporal aliasing. Note that these attributes are defined us-ing the *InOut* binding type: we map the old state to the new state, and both have the same format.

We now bind these attributes to inputs using partial evaluation. First, we bind the `particle` program to acceleration and time-step parameters to cre-ate the update function. Here we just use gravity for the acceleration. Then, for maximum efficiency in our inner loop, we bind the update function to its stream state input as well, creating update_stream. This stream function requires no more inputs to execute, but does not execute right away because we have specified no output stream.

```
// bind particle function to additional parameters
ShVector3f gravity(0.0,-9.8,0.0);
ShAttrib1f delta_t(0.001);
ShProgram update = particle << gravity << delta_t;
// define state stream by combining channels
ShStream state = (pos & pos_tail & vel);
// bind update operator to state input
ShProgram update_state = p << state;
```

Listing 5.3. Binding inputs to particle system simulation.

In the inner loop of our application, we can now efficiently update the state of our particle system by assigning the procedural stream update_state to the state stream. The input to update_state, which is also the state stream, has already been compiled in.

```
// execute state update (update state stream input )
state = update_state;
```

Listing 5.4. Inner loop of particle system simulation.

A very important feature to note in this code is that we are writing to the same stream from which we are reading. Recall that in Sh, we use parallel evaluation semantics. Conceptually, when we evaluate a stream function, we evaluate the stream kernel independently and in parallel on all records of the stream.

On the GPU, streams are stored in texture maps and buffers, and, in general, we can't read from the same buffer to which we are writing without getting undefined results due to the way the texture caches work. Even if that worked (and it would be highly platform-dependent), we need to break stream functions into multiple passes to virtualize certain resources. On the NVIDIA GeForceFX, for instance, only one output can be written per pass. The particle stream function has three outputs, so on the NVIDIA platform the Sh virtualizer will need to create three specialized functions, one for each output. When executing one of these specialized functions, we don't want to accidentally read the new state computed in a previous pass when we need the old state.

Therefore, Sh checks if a source is the same as a target, and if so, allocates temporary buffers for the destination channels. These temporary buffers are then swapped with the original input buffers once the computation is complete. In other words, Sh double-buffers as needed to get the correct semantics. It also tries to reuse such temporary buffers when necessary; it will not allocate a new buffer every time through the loop, but will use a previously allocated buffer from previous stream invocations. In particular, an allocation will only be performed the first time a certain computation is specified. Later invocations of the same computation will end up efficiently and automatically alternating between two previously allocated buffers.

The inner loop is therefore very simple and fast. All shader compilation and optimization is done during setup (with perhaps final optimization deferred until the first invocation), and all buffer allocation is done only on the first invocation of the stream operation. In general, Sh is designed to cache setup work under the assumption that similar work will be done every frame. Therefore, there may be a small amount of setup work done on the first frame (as

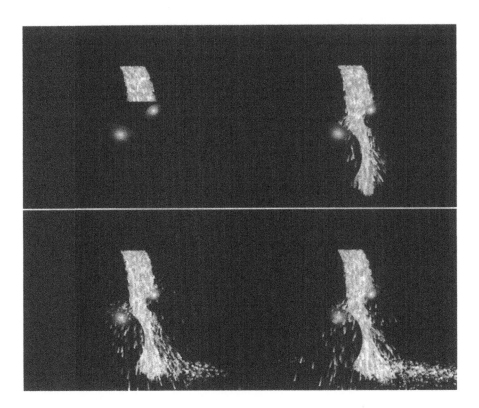

Figure 5.1. Frames from the particle system animation. See Plate 7 on page 114.

Sh "learns" the sequence of operations that will be used for a frame), but later frames will be faster if they are consistent with the first frame. If you want to force final optimization to happen earlier, however, you can use the `shCompile` function on the `update_state` function, but this is probably not necessary in most situations.

Once the state has been updated, the particles are rendered as shaded line segments by feeding the positions of the particles back through the GPU as a vertex array (code for this is not shown). Screenshots are shown in Figure 5.1.

Part II

Reference

Chapter 6

Reference Overview

The Sh reference manual provides a detailed guide to the functions, classes, and program object generators provided by Sh. In this chapter, we describe the basic steps needed to set up Sh for use as well as some basic test applications provided as part of the Sh distribution.

6.1 Setup

To use Sh, some setup is required. First, you have to include the Sh header file. Assuming you have set up your include paths correctly, this is usually done as follows:

```
#include <sh/sh.hpp>
```

All Sh functions and classes are enclosed in the `SH` namespace. Explicitly qualifying each class or function in Sh would be rather tedious, but it is useful in some circumstances. However, to make it easier to write shaders, you can isolate shader code in particular files and place the following clause in such files right after the inclusion of the header file:

```
using namespace SH;
```

Sh names are defined to avoid conflicts with other common libraries, in particular the standard libraries.

Before you can make any other Sh calls, you have to initialize the library. This is done by calling the function `shInit` before making any other Sh calls.[1]

---

[1] It would be nice to do this automatically as a side effect of the construction of a singleton class inside the library. Unfortunately, this doesn't work for some platforms in combination with dynamic libraries, so we have elected for the reliability and portability of explicit initialization.

You can now use Sh for stream computing. If you want to use it for shaders, however, you will need two other calls. First, shBind will load a program into the shading unit given in the program's definition. The shUpdate function should also be called after textures and uniform parameters have been modified but before rendering with the standard graphics API takes place. This will ensure that the Sh uniform parameters have been synchronized with the graphics API state.

Finally, you have to link your application to the libsh library, which can be used as a shared library.

6.2   Sample OpenGL GLUT Application

If you plan to use Sh with OpenGL to program shaders, you should take a look at glutex, a simple application that combines GLUT, OpenGL, and Sh. This application is available from the Sh website.   The main program of glutex is given in its entirety in Listing 6.1. Note, in particular, the use of shInit, shBind, and shUpdate. You can use this program as a starting point for developing your own applications. For development and testing of shaders, however, shrike provides much more functionality.

```
#include <sh/sh.hpp>
#include <GL/glut.h>
#include <GL/glext.h>
#include <GL/glu.h>
#include "Camera.hpp"

using namespace SH;

ShMatrix4x4f MV, MD, VM;    // transformations
ShPoint3f light_pv;         // VCS light source position

Camera camera;    // camera object (see Camera.hpp)

ShProgram vsh, fsh;  // vertex and fragment shader objects

// Glut data
int buttons[5] = {GLUT_UP, GLUT_UP, GLUT_UP, GLUT_UP, GLUT_UP};
int cur_x, cur_y;   // for trackball

// initialize program objects for shaders
void init_shaders()
{
  vsh = SH_BEGIN_PROGRAM("gpu:vertex") {
    ShInputNormal3f nm;         // MCS normal
```

```
    ShInputPoint4f pm;          // MCS position

    ShOutputNormal3f nv;        // VCS normal
    ShOutputVector3f lv;        // VCS light vector
    ShOutputPosition4f pd;      // DCS position

    ShPoint3f pv = (MV|pm)(0,1,2); // Compute viewspace position
    lv = light_pv - pv; // Compute light direction in view space
    pd = MD|pm; // Transform position to device space
    nv = normalize((nm|VM)(0,1,2)); // Transform normal to view space
  } SH_END;

  // declare and initialize diffuse color
  ShColor3f kd = ShColor3f(0.5, 0.7, 0.9);

  fsh = SH_BEGIN_PROGRAM("gpu:fragment") {
    ShInputNormal3f nv;     // VCS normal
    ShInputVector3f lv;     // VCS light vector

    ShOutputColor3f c;      // fragment color

    // normalize interpolated vectors to unit length
    nv = normalize(nv);
    lv = normalize(lv);
    // per-pixel diffuse lighting model
    c = kd * pos(nv|lv);
  } SH_END;
}


// GLUT callback
// draw using glut teapot (which has several faults, but)
void display ()
{
  // make sure Sh uniform parameters are synchronized
  shUpdate();

  // clear framebuffer
  glClear(GL_COLOR_BUFFER_BIT | GL_DEPTH_BUFFER_BIT);

  // draw teapot
  glFrontFace(GL_CW);
  glutSolidTeapot(2.5);
  glFrontFace(GL_CCW);

  // swap front and back buffers
  glutSwapBuffers();
}
```

```cpp
void setup_view ()
{
  MV = camera.shModelView();
  VM = inverse(MV);
  MD = camera.shModelViewProjection(ShMatrix4x4f());
}

// GLUT callback
// called on window resize
void reshape (int width, int height)
{
  glViewport(0, 0, width, height);
  setup_view();
}

// GLUT callback
// called on mouse movement
void motion (int x, int y)
{
  const double factor = 20.0;
  bool changed = false;

  // process UI events
  if (buttons[GLUT_LEFT_BUTTON] == GLUT_DOWN) {
    // rotate camera orientation using left mouse button
    camera.orbit(cur_x, cur_y, x, y,
                 glutGet(GLUT_WINDOW_WIDTH),
                 glutGet(GLUT_WINDOW_HEIGHT));
    changed = true;
  }
  if (buttons[GLUT_MIDDLE_BUTTON] == GLUT_DOWN) {
    // track camera forward and back using middle mouse button
    camera.move(0, 0, (y - cur_y)/factor);
    changed = true;
  }
  if (buttons[GLUT_RIGHT_BUTTON] == GLUT_DOWN) {
    // pan camera using right mouse button
    camera.move((x - cur_x)/factor, (cur_y - y)/factor, 0);
    changed = true;
  }

  // update everything
  if (changed) {
    setup_view();
    glutPostRedisplay();
  }
```

```
}

void mouse (int button, int state, int x, int y)
{
  buttons[button] = state;
  cur_x = x;
  cur_y = y;
}

int main (int argc, char** argv)
{
  // set up GLUT
  glutInit(&argc, argv);
  glutInitDisplayMode(GLUT_RGB | GLUT_DOUBLE | GLUT_DEPTH);
  glutInitWindowSize(512, 512);
  glutCreateWindow("glutex: Sh Example");

  // register callback functions
  glutDisplayFunc(display);
  glutReshapeFunc(reshape);
  glutMouseFunc(mouse);
  glutMotionFunc(motion);

  // initialize Sh
  shInit();
  // set up default GPU backend (optional)
  shSetBackend("arb");

  // initialize OpenGL state, turn on shader support
  glEnable(GL_DEPTH_TEST);
  glEnable(GL_VERTEX_PROGRAM_ARB);
  glEnable(GL_FRAGMENT_PROGRAM_ARB);
  glClearColor(0.0, 0.0, 0.0, 1.0);
  setup_view();

  // Place the camera at its initial position
  camera.move(0.0, 0.0, -15.0);

  // Set up the light position
  light_pv = ShPoint3f(5.0, 5.0, 5.0);

  // define our shader programs
  init_shaders();

  // bind shaders
  shBind(vsh);
  shBind(fsh);
```

```
// hand over event processing to GLUT
glutMainLoop();
}
```

Listing 6.1. Example Sh application using GLUT and OpenGL.

6.3   The `shrike` Testbed

The `shrike` application, available as a free download from the Sh website, is shown in Figure 6.1. The `shrike` application is a testbed environment for developing and tuning shaders.

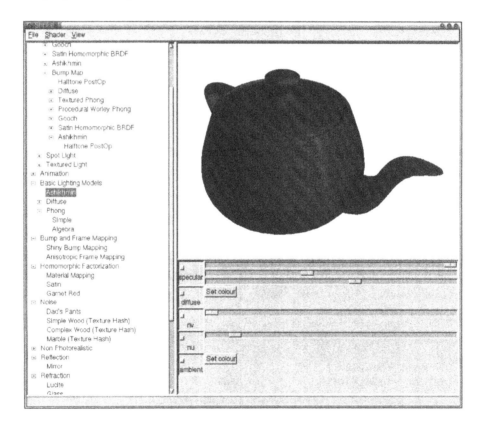

Figure 6.1. Ashikhmin shader demonstrated inside `shrike`. This application can automatically determine the parameters of a given shader and build a user interface to manipulate those parameters.

It provides a class framework for shaders, a browser interface to compare multiple shaders, and a generic interface for loading models and texture maps. A simple user interface is available for rotating models and moving them relative to light sources, storing definition-time constants, and reinitializing meta-programmed shaders as needed. It uses introspection to determine the parameters used for each shader and uses the metadata for each parameter to build a suitable user interface for those parameters. Support for visual debugging of shaders, including computation and visualization of intermediate values in shaders and a visual programming and visualization interface, are also under development and will eventually be included in the shrike application. As shrike is still under active development, please refer to the website for online documentation.

6.4   API Documentation

This reference manual does not go into great detail on the API of Sh. For example, we do not give full prototypes of all functions. This is because detailed and accurate information is available using HTML documentation generated by doxygen from structured comments in the codebase itself. Precompiled versions of this documentation are available from the Sh website, but you can also generate them yourself from the downloadable distribution.

The documentation generated by structured comments should be considered the definitive reference for all functions, classes, frameworks, and program object generators implemented by the Sh library. Since Sh is still under active development, it is also likely that new functions and classes will be added over time that are not (yet) discussed in this manual.

Chapter 7

Types

Many types are supported by the Sh library. Two general categories of types exist: classes that provide control of constructed objects such as shaders and textures, and those that represent numerical values manipulated by expressions. There is some overlap between these two. In particular, program objects can be used in expressions as subroutines, and texture objects can be used with the array-access operator to indicate texture lookups inside shaders.

7.1 Programs

Instances of the *ShProgram* type represent compiled shader programs. To create an *ShProgram*, sequences of Sh operations are wrapped in a pair of *SH_BEGIN_PROGRAM* and *SH_END* keywords. Programs are dealt with in depth in Chapter 10.

Each program has a default target, which is a string passed to *SH_BEGIN_PROGRAM*. This target specifies the backend and type of program being compiled. Example targets for GPU programs include gpu:vertex, gpu:fragment and gpu:stream. For more detail, refer to Section 10.1.

You can also generate a stream function to run on the CPU using a "cpu:stream" argument to *SH_BEGIN_PROGRAM*. This can be used to implement run-time, just-in-time code generation for the CPU. Typically this option will generate code in a high-level language such as C++, compile it, and dynamically link it back in. In the future, a more lightweight approach might be used, for instance, using libtcc [13]. However, use of external compilation means that the well-developed optimizers in existing compilers can be exploited.

By specifying a backend directly instead of a general type of backend, it is possible to cross-compile programs. For instance, you may want to cross-

137

compile for an NVIDIA GPU from a system with an ATI GPU, in which case you would need to explictly specify the "nv" backend, with possible further elaboration as to the specific video card, rather than use the default (the currently installed GPU) provided by the generic "gpu" option. Of course you cannot run such a shader immediately, but you can save it and restore it later. This might be used, for instance, to avoid start-up shader compilation costs by precompiling a number of shaders for each possible platform on which an application might run. In the future there may also be multiple ways to compile a program to the CPU with different performance characteristics (i.e., using branches vs. using multipass SIMD stream execution).

Several functions exist that act on *ShProgram* objects. The most important for GPU applications is shBind(*ShProgram* p), which loads a program p into the shader unit for which it was compiled and makes it active. This function also initializes the constant registers of the shading unit with the current values of all the parameters the shader program references; the function also binds all the textures the shader uses to the same shading unit and loads them onto the GPU's local memory if necessary. To update the textures and uniforms for an already bound shader, an update should be forced using shUpdate(). Parameters may be automatically updated as they are changed if they are used by the currently bound shader, but shUpdate() will force this to be the case. Since texture updates are expensive, they are deferred until shUpdate() is called. These calls are only needed when using Sh with a separate rendering interface (as is the case on OpenGL). When running stream computations using Sh, it is not necessary to bind a shader and buffer updates happen automatically. More details on these calls are provided in Section 10.2.

7.2 Tuples

Tuples are short arrays with elements of the same basic type. Tuples have a semantic type, a size, and a storage type. For instance, an *ShPoint3f* is a three-dimensional geometric point stored using three single-precision floating-point numbers.

7.2.1 Semantic Types

The generic semantic type is *ShAttrib*, but semantic types *ShPoint*, *ShNormal*, *ShVector*, *ShPlane*, and *ShTexCoord* are also supported. The special semantic type *ShPosition* may be used inside shaders to indicate the special input/output slots for vertex and fragment positions, but this type is otherwise equivalent to a point. See Table 7.1 for a listing of semantic types.

Semantic Types	
Name	Meaning
ShAttrib	generic tuple
ShColor	color
ShVector	direction
ShNormal	covector (tangent plane orientation)
ShPoint	non-homogeneous position
ShPlane	half-space equation
ShTexCoord	non-homogeneous texture coordinate
ShPosition	position (special point)

Table 7.1. Semantic types. A semantic type indicates what kind of geometric or numerical object a tuple represents. All semantics types are subclasses of the *ShAttrib* type.

There are actually few differences in how library functions and operators treat the different semantic types. Sh has intentionally been defined *not* to overly restrict operations on tuples based on semantic type. For instance, addition and scalar multiplication of the *ShPoint* semantic type is supported in Sh, even though it is geometrically invalid. This is because because affine combinations of points *are* valid and are built up out of these operations. Some operators do cause type conversions, for example subtracting two points gives a vector, but most do not.

Operations generally act the same on all semantic types as well, for instance the arithmetic operators "+," "−," "∗," and "/" act componentwise on all basic semantic types. However, there are a few exceptions that would otherwise be errors in which the semantic types are treated differently (for instance, inferral of homogeneous coordinates), and in some cases (e.g. matrices) the multiplication and division operators are specialized. These issues are dealt with at greater length in Chapter 8.

7.2.2   Storage Types

Storage types indicate how the numeric values stored in a tuple are represented internally. The storage type is indicated by a suffix that roughly mimics (but does not duplicate) the conventions of OpenGL. The available storage types are shown in Table 7.2. The "double-precision" storage type may actually be implemented using a single precision value on some compilation targets. GPUs currently do not support double precision, but we might want to use the same stream program and compile it to both a CPU (where double precision is no

Suffix	Name	Sign/Exponent/Significand
	Floating-Point Types			
d	double-precision float	1/8/15	to	1/11/52
f	single-precision float	1/8/15	to	1/8/23
h	half-precision float	1/5/10	to	1/8/23
	Signed Integer Types			
i	signed integer	1//15	to	1//31
s	signed short integer	1//10	to	1//15
b	signed byte	1//7		
	Unsigned Integer Types			
ui	unsigned integer	0//15	to	0//32
us	unsigned short integer	0//10	to	0//16
ub	unsigned 8-bit byte	0//8		
	Signed Fraction Types			
fi	signed fraction in $[-1, 1]$	1//15	to	1//31
fs	signed short fraction in $[-1, 1]$	1//10	to	1//15
fb	signed byte fraction in $[-1, 1]$	1//7		
	Unsigned Fraction Types			
fui	unsigned fraction in $[0, 1]$	0//15	to	0//32
fus	unsigned short fraction in $[0, 1]$	0//10	to	0//16
fub	unsigned byte fraction in $[0, 1]$	0//8		

Table 7.2. Storage types. A storage type, indicated with one of the given suffixes, gives both the size of data stored and how it is interpreted.

problem) and a GPU (where it is). Double precision in Sh therefore really means "as much precision as feasible."

A storage type may automatically be upgraded to the next available storage type if there is no cost or if a particular type is not available. For instance, if half floats are not available on a given target or would be unreasonably expensive, they will be upgraded to single-precision floats.

The integer storage formats are mostly useful for defining textures holding values of these types. Inside shaders, they will generally be represented using a combination of floats and clamping instructions, which may be more expensive than you expect and may also cause some range restrictions. This is the reason for the 10-bit precision limit on short integers and the 15-bit precision limit on integers. These limits are due to the simulation of integers on various platforms using the worst-case floating point precision. Using the 1/8/15-bit floating point in the fragment shader on ATI 9700 series GPUs, for instance, means that short, regular, and long integers alike will be simulated inside shader computations using only 15 bits of precision, since this is the maximum length of the significand supported by that target. On NVIDIA GeForceFX GPUs, simulation of long and regular integers with single-precision floats will lead to 23-bit limits, and short integers (simulated using half floats) will have a limit of 10 bits.

Under no condition should you assume anything about the wraparound behavior or sign representation of "integers." Since, on the current generation of GPUs, integers must be simulated with floating point numbers, exceeding the range restrictions means that "integers" will start to lose low-order bits, not wrap around. Also, if we must simulate integers using floating point, the sign representation will be sign-magnitude, not two's complement. Future GPUs may add better support for integer types.

The fraction types are used to reflect the usual representation of colors in texture maps. In the case of an unsigned byte fraction, we would store an 8-bit integer in the texture, but divide its value by 255 when reading it into the floating-point unit to get a number in the range of $[0, 1]$ inclusive [15]. This is called a scaled-integer representation, and is usually the most efficient texture storage format on GPUs. Other representations actually require us to insert shader code to transform the retrieved value (for instance, to scale by 255 to get integer bytes, or subtract 0.5 and multiply by 2 to get signed fractions).

The $[0, 1]$ and $[-1, 1]$ range restrictions on fractions are *not* enforced inside shaders. If you really need that behavior, use a library function to clamp the value. Sh will optimize away such functions if they are not really needed, but by default will not insert extra clamping code for fraction storage types if it is implementing them using floating-point values inside a shader.

7.2.3 Binding Types

Tuples can be used in several different situations. If they are declared outside of a shader definition, they are considered to be *parameters*. Such tuples can be acted upon using all the operators and functions defined in Sh, but the computations will take place on the host. In this way, Sh tuples (and matrices and textures) can be used as a host-based "immediate mode" library. It should be noted that shaders can actually be debugged this way using a standard IDE.

However, a more usual use of parameters is as global variables inside shader definitions. Nothing special is required to import a parameter into a shader: the shader definition just needs to use the parameter, and the Sh runtime will automatically track which parameters are used by which shaders and will allocate

Binding Types		
Name	Token	Meaning
default	**SH_TEMP**	parameter or temporary variable
Const	**SH_CONST**	definition-time constant
Input	**SH_INPUT**	input attribute
Output	**SH_OUTPUT**	output attribute
InOut	**SH_INOUT**	input and output attribute

Table 7.3. Binding types. A binding type indicates where a value is stored. The interpretaton of the local type (the default) depends on whether it is used inside or outside a program definition.

and load constant registers as needed. Parameters, however, cannot be updated inside shaders.

If a tuple is declared inside a shader, then it is considered to be a local temporary and is allocated to a temporary register.

Any tuple may also be declared with an **Input**, **Output** or **InOut** prefix, such as **ShInputColor3f**. These are used to declare the input and outputs of a shader and are called *attributes*. The binding of inputs and outputs is both by semantic type and order and depends on the backend being used. For example, under OpenGL the first **ShInputTexCoord** declared is bound to GL_TEXTURE0, the second to GL_TEXTURE1, etc., as explained in Section 12.1.

InOut tuples internally correspond to an input and an output tuple. This is useful in many situations, e.g., if one is transforming a position between two coordinate frames, or simply passing through a value without changing it, in which case one only needs to declare an appropriate **InOut** variable.

Const tuples are Sh program compile-time (i.e., backend compile time) constants. It is in fact possible to assign to these types, but unlike uniform parameters, the change will have no effect on previously defined programs. The Sh compiler can use this information as a hint to make a more efficient program, because it can assume that the value will never change.

7.2.4 Template Declaration

Normally, we only use sizes 1, 2, 3, and 4 for tuples, and we know in advance whether we want to use them for input or output. However, a template-based mechanism for declaring tuples is also supported that can be convenient in some situations. An **ShAttrib** tuple with five components, for instance, can be declared using **ShAttrib**<5>. The template declaration also has a second argument giving the binding type, which can be one of **SH_TEMP**, **SH_CONST**, **SH_INPUT**, **SH_OUTPUT**, or **SH_INOUT**. A third template argument gives the storage type. (The default is single-precision floating-point.)

```
template <ShBindingType IO>
struct BlinnPhongVertFrag {
  ShVector<3,IO> hv;        // half-vector (VCS)
  ShTexCoord<2,IO> u;       // texture coords
  ShNormal<3,IO> nv;        // normal (VCS)
  ShColor<3,IO> ec;         // irradiance
};
```

Listing 7.1. Vertex/fragment I/O template for Blinn-Phong lighting model.

These are useful in template declarations of inputs and outputs from shaders. For example, the output types of a vertex shader must match the input types of the corresponding fragment shader. Consider Listing 7.1, which uses a template type to make this explicit. The corresponding vertex and fragment shaders are given in Listing 7.2 and Listing 7.3.

```
ShProgram blinnphong_vertex = SH_BEGIN_PROGRAM("gpu:vertex") {
  // declare input vertex parameters
  ShInputTexCoord2f ui;        // texture coords
  ShInputNormal3f nm;          // normal vector (MCS)
  ShInputPosition3f pm;        // position (MCS)

  // declare outputs vertex parameters
  BlinnPhongVertFrag<SH_OUTPUT> out;
  ShOutputPosition4f pd;       // position (HDCS)

  // specify computations
  ShPoint3f pv = (MV|pm)(0,1,2);               // VCS position
  pd = VD|pv;                                  // DCS position
  out.nv = normalize((nm|VM)(0,1,2));          // VCS normal
  ShVector3f lv = normalize(light.pv - pv);    // VCS light vector
  out.ec = light.c * pos(nv|lv);
  ShVector3f vv = normalize(-pv);              // VCS view vector
  out.hv = normalize(lv + vv);                 // VCS half vector
  out.u = ui;
} SH_END;
```

Listing 7.2. Vertex shader for templated Blinn-Phong lighting model.

```
ShProgram blinnphong_fragment = SH_BEGIN_PROGRAM("gpu:fragment")
  {
    // declare input fragment parameters (unpacked in order given)
    BlinnPhongVertFrag<SH_INPUT> in;
    ShInputPosition3f pd;     // fragment position (DCS)

    // declare output fragment parameters (packed in order given)
    ShOutputColor3f c;                       // fragment color

    // compute texture-mapped Blinn-Phong model
    c = in.ec * kd[in.u]
      + ks[in.u] * pow((normalize(in.hv)|normalize(in.nv)),q);
  } SH_END;
```

Listing 7.3. Fragment shader for templated Blinn-Phong lighting model.

The default binding type is **SH_TEMP** and is used for normal parameters (when a tuple is declared outside a shader) and for local temporaries (when a tuple is declared inside a shader).

Compile time constants have binding type **SH_CONST** and, as mentioned above, act like uniforms whose values are never updated, allowing certain optimizations.

Note that tuples can be of any fixed length greater than zero. The compiler will break them into 4-tuples (or smaller values) if that is what the hardware requires, but the shader writer does not have to worry about it.

Another thing the shader writer does not have to worry about is writing to inputs or reading from outputs. Both are legal in Sh even if the hardware does not support these operations; the Sh compiler just transforms the program as necessary. Finally, inside shader programs, temporaries are always initialized to zero. This initialization is normally optimized away if it is not used (or if the hardware initializes the corresponding register to zero anyway).

7.3   Matrices

Matrices in Sh are supported for the representation of linear, affine, and projective transformations. As with tuples, sizes of 1, 2, 3, and 4 in both dimensions are the most common and are supported with explicit names, although a template mechanism is provided for matrices of larger dimensionality if necessary.

Matrices are *not* just arrays of tuples; they may include alternative internal representations of, for instance, diagonal matrices. Sh may also try to avoid computing and storing the transpose of a matrix; instead, it might swizzle the accesses to a matrix appropriately. Run-time access to elements is limited to constant indices supported using the "[ ]" and/or "( )" operators, to be described later.

Matrices are defined with declarations of the form **ShMatrix***RxCs* where *R* gives the number of rows, *C* the number of columns, and *s* the storage format. For instance **ShMatrix4x4f** is a legal (and common) matrix declaration.

General matrices can also be declared using template syntax by writing **ShMatrix**<*R, C, b, s*>, where *b* is the binding type (as in tuples) and has a default value of **SH_TEMP**. Matrices can be used and declared as parameters, input, output or input-output attributes, or local temporaries.

Special rules are applied when using matrices in expressions with tuples using the "|" matrix multiplication operator, which promotes sizes as necessary to make it possible to combine, for instance, a 3×4 affine matrix with a 4×4 projective matrix. Basically, the smaller matrix is enlarged by the number of rows (or columns) from an identity matrix necessary to make matrix multiplication possible.

Assigning a scalar to a matrix initializes that matrix with the identity matrix scaled by that value. Therefore, to initialize a matrix with the identity matrix, assign the value of 1 to it. Diagonal matrices can also be constructed using the diag constructor function, and matrices can be built from tuples interpreted as rows (using the rowmat constructor) or as columns (using the colmat constructor).

Many library functions exist to manipulate matrices, including det (to compute the determinant), trace (to compute the trace), inverse, transpose, and adjoint (to compute the transpose of the cofactor matrix, which when divided by the determinant gives the inverse, but does not itself require divisions to compute). These operations are described in detail in Section 8.8.

7.4   Arrays, Tables, and Textures

Sh has built-in support for arrays, tables and textures. These types represent some large indexed set of tuples; they are all templates taking a regular Sh tuple type as an argument. These types are indexed using the [ ] and ( ) operators. The former uses integer-based (element) indexing, whereas the latter performs $[0, 1]$-based (tabulated) lookups.

The only difference between the **ShArray**, **ShTable**, and **ShTexture** classes is their default interpolation and filtering modes. Arrays use simple nearest neighbor lookups; tables add linear interpolation, textures use both linear interpolation and MIP-mapped filtering. Arrays, tables, and textures can be wrapped in template types which modify these and other traits. For more detail on arrays, tables and textures, please refer to Chapter 9.

7.5   Contexts

An instance of the **ShContext** type encapsulates information relevant to the current execution state of Sh. This includes information about which programs are currently bound as well as some global settings, such as the current optimization level.

The current **ShContext** can be obtained by calling the static member function **ShContext**::current(). The initialization function shInit constructs the first context and activates it.

The optimization level under a particular context may be set using the optimization(**int**) member function. A value of zero is taken to mean that no optimizations at all should be performed; a larger number adds additional optimizations. The default value is two, which implies that a reasonable "safe" set of optimizations should be performed. More experimental optimizations may be enabled by setting this function to a larger number.

7.6   Exceptions and Error Handling

All Sh errors are represented by exception classes. All of these classes derive from **ShException**, which primarily just provides a single message explaining the error. This message can be obtained by calling the message() member function.

Errors are raised by calling the global shError() function. This function checks the current **ShContext**'s throw_errors() setting. If this is **true** (which is the default), it will throw an exception. Otherwise, it will merely output the message on std::cerr and continue as if no error occured.

If throw_errors() is turned off, the system may be in an inconsistent state after an error occurs. We recommend that all errors be caught as exceptions.

7.7   Metadata

Most Sh types support storing *metadata* with their instances. This is data that is not necessary for the object itself to function, but provides potentially useful information relating to the object that might be used by other parts of the system or by the user. Sh automatically generates some metadata (such as the type), but other kinds of metadata are specified by the user.

There are two major reasons to have metadata in Sh. The first is documentation. By providing information, such as a name, a title, and a description of a tuple, a user interface containing widgets to manipulate uniform parameters and attributes can be constructed automatically and can operate on arbitrary programs by querying the metadata. This sort of information can also be useful for debugging purposes.

The second major reason to have metadata is to provide information to the backends. Because the Sh frontend is designed to be as separate from its backends as possible, we do not wish to expose interfaces that rely on particular backend properties at the API level. To provide a clean separation, we allow backends to define and access arbitrary string-based metadata that can be attached to objects with special-purpose meanings. Backends can then be updated or changed without having to change the Sh API and hence without breaking backward compatibility. This comes at the cost of having to establish conventions for naming this metadata. We expect backends to document the metadata they make use of appropriately and to use common conventions whenever possible.

All types containing metadata inherit from the *ShMeta* class. This class provides the following member functions:

std::string name() const: Obtain the name of an object. This may return an internal name if the name has not been set. Normally, this should be set to the name of the object in the C++ program, but unfortunately this name cannot be obtained automatically by Sh (see below). This name should not contain spaces and should follow the C++ conventions for identifiers. Longer human readable names can be specified using title.

void name(std::string): Set the name of an object.

bool has_name() const: Returns true if and only if the object's name has been set explicitly.

bool internal() const: Determine whether an object is to be considered internal (for example, should not be exposed in a user interface).

void internal(bool): Set whether an object is considered internal.

std::string title() const: Obtain the human-readable name of an object.

void title(std::string): Set the human-readable name of an object. This name can be longer than the C++ name and can include spaces.

std::string description() const: Obtain a longer description of an object.

void description(std::string): Set a longer description of an object. This description may be roughly a paragraph in length and might be used in a tooltip, for instance.

std::string meta(std::string key) const: Obtain arbitrary metadata associated with key. Returns an empty string if no data has been assigned to that key.

void meta(std::string key, std::string value): Set the arbitrary metadata associated with key to value.

Note that for "thin wrapper" classes, such as **ShVariable** and **ShProgram**, the above member functions are defined to forward any queries to the actual reference-counted node object to which they refer. This is done by inheriting from the **ShMetaForwarder** class.

7.7.1   Object Names

Variables in C++ are usually named. It would be nice if Sh could return these variable names by default when name() is called. Unfortunately C++ has no standard way to access these names at run time.

It would be theoretically possible to open up a program's executable file at run time and search through the symbol table to find the name corresponding to a particular variable address. However, such code would be extremely unportable, and there are many cases where this would not work (e.g., if debugging information were not present in the executable and, possibly, in the case of shared libraries).

Another alternative would be to preprocess the source somehow and add in code to mark variable declarations with appropriate calls to name(). This is non-trivial though and adds another level of indirection to the compilation process. We specifically try to avoid having to add external dependencies when using Sh, as one of its prime advantages is that it is merely a C++ library that can easily be added to a project.

Therefore, for portability reasons, we currently recommend that the name() property be set explicitly. Names are used for several introspection purposes besides documentation, and these names unfortunately cannot be set automatically in a reliable fashion.[1] Sh provides several macros that make assigning names to objects more convenient. These macros are:

```
#define SH_NAME(x)          x.name( # x )
#define SH_DECL(x)          x; x.name( # x ); x
#define SH_NAMEDECL(x, n)   x; x.name(n); x
```

Each of these macros take some variable and name it using the name as it appears in the source program. **SH_NAME** is intended to be used at some point after declaring a variable. It simply sets the given variable's name to its C++ name. Writing **SH_NAME**(foo) is somewhat nicer than having to write foo.name("foo") and avoids mistakes like foo.name("bar").

The **SH_DECL** and **SH_NAMEDECL** macros allow a variable to be named at the same time as it is declared in a function (but not, unfortunately, in a class). The **SH_NAMEDECL** allows the metadata name to differ from the actual C++ variable name.

Here's an example of the different ways in which variables can be named:

```
// Example of SH_NAME
ShAttrib3f unnamed;            // Unnamed. name() returns something like u1234.
ShAttrib3f x; x.name("x");     // Call name() directly.
ShAttrib3f y; SH_NAME(y);      // A little more convenient

// Examples of SH_DECL and SH_NAMEDECL.
// Note how these still allow initializing the object with a value.
// Consider their definitions to see why this works.
ShAttrib3f SH_DECL(z) = ShAttrib3f(1.0, 0.0, 1.0);
ShAttrib3f SH_NAMEDECL(lv, "lightvec");
```

We recommend that you get into the habit of using **SH_DECL** wherever possible. This will save you from having to go back later and add the appropriate calls.

One limitation of these macros is that they cannot be used for class member declarations. You have to set the name in the constructor, since methods cannot be called at the same time as declarations in classes.

---

[1]This is a surprising and irritating gap in Sh's ability to do things automatically. It would be nice if the C++ RTTI system provided this information.

Chapter 8

Standard Operators and Functions

Operations are specified in Sh by applying operators and functions to instances of Sh types. Outside of a program definition, these operations execute immediately on values stored on the host. However, inside an **ShProgram** definition block enclosed by **SH_BEGIN_PROGRAM** and **SH_END**, the standard functions and operators instead build up a symbolic representation of the desired operations for later consideration by the compiler.

The built-in functions mirror and extend the support provided in other shading languages. Wherever possible, we have tried to be consistent with the definitions of similar function libraries in other shading languages. Hopefully, this will make it easier to port shaders back and forth to these languages.

The collection of functions described in this chapter can be referred to as the "standard library," but these functions are as much a part of the language as the operators. In fact, the operators and the standard library functions are implemented in almost exactly the same way, except operators take advantage of the operator overloading functionality provided by C++.

You can define your own functions (and operators and types) to extend the ones given here. However, whenever possible, use of the standard library functions is encouraged, since these functions have highly tuned implementations and have optimization support in the compiler.

For instance, repeated application of `normalize` is pointless, since normalization is idempotent. Therefore, if the compiler can prove that a tuple is already normalized, it can ignore any extra normalizations of that tuple. This particular optimization is very important, since normalization is expensive. You can take advantage of this optimization to improve the modularity and robustness of your code without sacrificing performance. In particular, you can always put in a normalization if you aren't sure an input will be normalized. As long as the optimization works, the compiler will only actually perform the normalization if necessary.

All the functions and operators in the standard library can be compiled on hardware without branch support, unless specified otherwise. Certain functions, however, might use branching for some compilation targets *if* it is available *and* it is the best way to implement that function.

In general, the implementation of library functions and operators may vary by compilation target. An example is noise. The noise function might use a texture-based hash function on a fragment unit, a procedural hash on a vertex unit without texture support, and maybe a built-in instruction (hopefully) on future hardware. In fact, noise is special since it may not return the same value on different targets for the same inputs! But in most cases, for deterministic computations, we try to achieve numerical equivalence when using different implementations on different targets. The general goal of the compiler is to implement the desired computation in the most efficient and numerically stable way on each supported compilation target.

The rest of this chapter provides detailed descriptions of the library of operators and functions supported by Sh. The discussion is grouped into sections using a set of categories. Each section includes a table summarizing the operators and functions in alphabetical order. In these tables, we will often give mathematical definitions of the computation performed by a function. The mathematical definitions refer to values labelled r, a, b, and c. The value r is the return value of the function being defined, while a, b, and c refer to its arguments. In this chapter we give mathematical definitions, not implementations. The actual form of an implementation may differ significantly from its clearest mathematical definition to improve efficiency or numerical stability.

For each table entry, the tuple size that may be used is indicated. Generally, each function returns the same type as was given to it. For example, adding two vectors results in another vector. Also, when a scalar (1-tuple) is used in an input that can also be used for an n-tuple, the scalar is usually promoted to a tuple by replication. For example, in $s*a$, with s a scalar and a an n-tuple, the value of s is replicated to form an n-tuple and then componentwise multiplication is performed, giving the expected meaning of scalar-vector multiplication. Scalar promotion is common but not universal: it depends on the particular operator or function involved. The tables indicate where scalar arguments are permitted.

Most functions work on all semantic types as noted, but some functions only work on particular semantic types. These execeptions are indicated in the respective sections.

Operators are also provided that act on **ShProgram** objects. These operators are used to manipulate **ShProgram** objects in various useful ways and to apply programs to streams and tuples. These operators also permit the use of **ShProgram** objects as subroutines inside other **ShProgram** objects. However, since the implementation and use of these operators is substantially different from those of the basic operators on tuples and matrices, we defer their discussion to Chapter 10. Likewise, the access operators for textures will only be discussed in Chapter 9.

Since the parser for expressions in Sh is built upon C++ operator overloading, of course the available operators, their precedence, and their associativity is exactly the same as in C++. We do not describe these details here, only the new semantics of these operators that are in effect when at least one argument is a subclass of an Sh class type. However, for convenience, we summarize the precedence and associativity of the operators used in Sh in Table 8.1.

8.1   Swizzling and Write Masking

Swizzling refers to the extraction, rearrangement, and possible duplication of elements of tuple types. On many GPUs, swizzling is free or at least cheap, and smart use of swizzling can make your code more efficient. However, inappropriate use of swizzling can also make your code incredibly hard to read and may make it hard for the compiler to optimize it.

Swizzling is expressed in Sh using the function call operator " () " with a sequence of integer arguments. For example, suppose a is an instance of an RGB color **ShColor3f**. Then the expression a(2,1,0) represents the corresponding color with components in BGR order.

> GPUs only directly support 4-tuples, while Sh supports n-tuples. Swizzles of tuples of length greater than the hardware-supported tuple length will be decomposed into a number of swizzled and write-masked move operations.

Components are numbered starting at 0, and the components of the output tuple are listed in the order specified in the swizzle. Components can be ignored or duplicated, and swizzling can also change the tuple size. For instance, suppose an LA (luminance-alpha) color b is represented using **ShColor2f**. A corresponding 4-channel RGBA color could be represented using the expression b(0,0,0,1), or a grayscale RGB color could be expressed using b(0,0,0).

Operators				
Symbol	Associativity	Arity	Meaning	Reference
( )	postfix	1	swizzle/access/apply	8.1–153, 9–177, 10–183
[ ]	postfix	1	access	8.1–153, 9–177
++	prefix/postfix	1	increment	8.2–156
--	prefix/postfix	1	decrement	8.2–156
~	prefix	1	complement	8.2–156
!	prefix	1	clamped complement	8.2–156
*	LR	2	multiplication	8.2–156
/	LR	2	division	8.2–156
%	LR	2	modulus	8.2–156
+	LR	2	addition	8.2–156
−	LR	2	subtraction	8.2–156
−	prefix	1	negation	8.2–156
<<	LR	2	connect/apply	10–183
>>	LR	2	extract	10–183
<	LR	2	less than	8.9–171
<=	LR	2	less than or equal	8.9–171
>	LR	2	greater than	8.9–171
>=	LR	2	greater than or equal	8.9–171
==	LR	2	equals	8.9–171
!=	LR	2	not equals	8.9–171
&	LR	2	combine	10–183
|	LR	2	dot/matrix product	8.7–166, 8.8–167
^	LR	2	cross product	8.7–166
&&	LR	2	and/min	8.9–171
||	LR	2	or/max	8.9–171

Table 8.1. Operator index. This table is arranged in order from highest to lowest precedence.

Repeated swizzling is permitted. For instance, a(2,1,0)(2,1,0) on a 3-tuple just returns the original component order, since it reverses the components twice. Swizzles are applied left to right. In general these kinds of expressions should be avoided, since they look like matrix swizzles (discussed below). However repeated swizzles are occasionally useful if you need to compute a complex permutation and it is easier to express it as a sequence of simpler permutations. The compiler will, of course, collapse such decomposed swizzles into a single operation.

The () notation only expresses swizzling when used on the right side of an assignment or in an expression used as an argument to a control construct. However, the same notation may also be used on the left side of an assignment statement, where it expresses something different: write masking, or selective component update.

For write masking, the numbers indicate which components should be written. The number of components mentioned in a write mask expression on the left of an assignment should have the same number of components as the result of the expression on the right. It does not make sense to duplicate a value in a write mask (this would imply writing twice to the same location), so assignments such as t(1,1) = x(0,1) are illegal and will cause a program definition time exception.

Reordering components in a write mask performs a permutation of the elements written. The way to think of this is that the write mask computes a sequence of references to elements in the order requested. Swizzles can be applied to computed values as well as to individual tuples. Thus, a(0,1) = (b + c)(1,0) is perfectly reasonable: it adds tuples b and c, extracts and swaps their first two components, and writes the result to the first two components of tuple a. Given the interpretation of permuted write masks, this could also be written as a(1,0) = b + c, assuming b and c are both two-tuples.

The "[]" operator may be used for swizzling one element. This is equivalent to treating the tuple as an array of scalars. On the right-hand side, it reads from a particular component of a tuple, and on the left-hand side, it writes to a component element. Like the "()" swizzle, this operator can be applied to computed values as well as variables, so a[0] = (b + c)[1] computes the sum of tuples b and c, extracts component 1 from the intermediate result, and writes it to component 0 of a.

> Currently swizzle and write mask arguments must be program definition-time constants. They can be generated by C++ code but not by Sh expressions. In the future, we might permit shader-computed swizzles, but such swizzles would be relatively expensive on current hardware.

Matrices may also be swizzled, but they require two swizzle operations in sequence. The first (leftmost) swizzle is a swizzle on rows, the second (rightmost) swizzle is a swizzle on columns. This notation permits permutation of rows and columns as well as the extraction of submatrices.

On matrices, the "[]" and "()" operators have slightly different interpretations. Applying the "[]" operator to a matrix extracts a row of the matrix and makes it accessible as an **ShAttrib**. Applying an additional "[]" operator to this tuple extracts an element of this tuple, and thus an element of the matrix, as expected. For instance, M[1][2] extracts the scalar at row 1, column 2.

You could also extract row 1 of the matrix using just M[1], or column 1 using transpose(M)[1]. Both rows and columns are numbered starting at 0.

On matrices, the "()" operators must always be applied in pairs, since the first swizzle operator applied results in a special type whose only legal operation is a column swizzle. To make matrix expressions simpler, a swizzle with no arguments is interpreted as doing nothing (the identity swizzle). For instance, the expression M(3,2,1,0)(3,2,1,0) computes the transpose of a 4 × 4 matrix by reversing both rows and columns (although a transpose function is provided). The expression M(3,2,1,0)() reverses only the rows and leaves the columns alone, while M()(3,2,1,0) reverses the columns and leaves the rows alone.

When used on the left-hand side of an expression, the "[]" operator can be used to select an element (or row) to write to and the "()" notation can be used to specify a submatrix to assign new values to. The same restrictions apply as mentioned for tuple swizzles. In particular, in a matrix write mask as in a tuple write mask, repeating a component index is an error.

Our swizzling and write masking syntax differs from the syntax used in most other real-time shading languages, which use expressions like a.rgba. This alphabetic syntax is *not* supported in Sh, for several reasons:

1. It would be quite painful to define in C++. We *could* predefine a (large) number of member variables pointing back at each object instance, each representing a different swizzle, but the cost would be horrific.

2. The alphabetic swizzle names depend on the type and number of arguments. How would you swizzle a 9-tuple?

3. The alphabetic syntax interferes with the syntax for member access. To be fair, our syntax interferes with the syntax for constructors, but it's unambiguous in practice.

4. Using numerical arguments means that we can use computed values as swizzle arguments.

The [] and () operators are also used on texture objects for lookup and on program objects for function application. See Chapters 9 and 10, respectively.

8.2   Arithmetic

The standard arithmetic operators "+," "−," "*," and "/" are overloaded to support the natural arithmetic operations on each supported Sh type. For most types, these operators work componentwise and support scalar promotion by replication on both arguments. However, for quaternions, matrices, and complex numbers, the multiplication and division operators are more specialized, and these types also have special scalar promotion rules.

The modulo operator "%" is also supported with a generalized meaning suitable for floating-point numbers:

$$a \% b \;=\; a/b - \lfloor a/b \rfloor.$$

Basically, the modulo operation computes a floating-point remainder. This operation is not defined on quaternions, complex numbers, or matrices. It always operates component wise. Scalar promotion via replication is supported on both arguments. The modulo operation is useful in several contexts in shaders, for instance, to compute sawtooth stripe functions or to wrap coordinates.

Any numerical type in Sh may be prefixed with a "-," indicating a negation. At this point, all types in Sh compute negation the same way: componentwise. It should be noted that componentwise negation is free or very inexpensive on common GPUs.

Modifying forms of the "+," "−," "*," "/," and "%" operators are also defined. For example, the expression x *= 5.0 multiplies all components of x by five, storing the result in x. This example also uses scalar promotion, which is supported on the right for modifying operators. For non-commutative operations, such as matrix multiplication, the modifying forms use right multiplication, so a *= b is equivalent to a = a * b.

Matrices use different definitions of multiplication and division. As described in Section 8.8, the "*" operator on matrices is overloaded to mean matrix multiplication, *not* componentwise multiplication.

All arithmetic operations return the same type as their arguments, if the arguments are the same type, with the exceptions that subtracting two **ShPoint**s yields an **ShVector**, and similarily adding an **ShVector** to an **ShPoint** returns an **ShPoint**. An **ShAttrib** can be combined with any other type while retaining that type, so for instance an **ShAttrib** can be added to an **ShPoint** and the result will be a point.

In general, Sh is permissive and its type propagation rules are designed to be easy to remember and trace, rather than always being geometrically meaningful. For instance, addition of **ShPoint** objects is permitted, although unless the addition is part of an affine blend (with weights that are a partition of unity) addition of points is geometrically meaningless. However, attempting to disallow these kinds of geometrically invalid operations would burden the programmer, make certain common operations (such as affine combination) hard to express, and complicate the language. Hence, we have chosen not to enforce these rules strictly.

Operation	$r \leftarrow a, b, c, \ldots$	Description
+	$N \leftarrow N, N$	addition
+	$N \leftarrow 1, N$	addition to replicated scalar
+	$N \leftarrow N, 1$	addition of replicated scalar
−	$N \leftarrow N, N$	subtraction
−	$N \leftarrow 1, N$	subtraction from replicated scalar
−	$N \leftarrow N, 1$	subtraction of replicated scalar
−	$N \leftarrow N$	negation
$\star$	$N \leftarrow N, N$	multiplication
$\star$	$N \leftarrow 1, N$	scalar multiplication
$\star$	$N \leftarrow N, 1$	scalar multiplication
/	$N \leftarrow N, N$	division
/	$N \leftarrow N, 1$	division by a scalar
/	$N \leftarrow 1, N$	scaled reciprocal
%	$N \leftarrow N, N$	modulo $$r_i \leftarrow a_i/b_i - \lfloor a_i/b_i \rfloor$$
%	$N \leftarrow N, 1$	modulo a replicated scalar $$r_i \leftarrow a_i/b - \lfloor a_i/b \rfloor$$
%	$N \leftarrow 1, N$	replicated scalar modulo $$r_i \leftarrow a/b_i - \lfloor a/b_i \rfloor$$

Table 8.2. Arithmetic operators.

Operation	$r \leftarrow a, b, c, \ldots$	Description
++	$N \leftarrow (N)$	increment
--	$N \leftarrow (N)$	decrement
+=	$N \leftarrow (N), N$	modifying addition
+=	$N \leftarrow (N), 1$	modifying addition of scalar
−=	$N \leftarrow (N), N$	modifying subtraction
−=	$N \leftarrow (N), 1$	modifying subtraction of scalar
$\star$=	$N \leftarrow (N), N$	modifying multiplication
$\star$=	$N \leftarrow (N), 1$	modifying multiplication by scalar
/=	$N \leftarrow (N), N$	modifying division
/=	$N \leftarrow (N), 1$	modifying division by scalar
%=	$N \leftarrow (N), N$	modifying modulo
%=	$N \leftarrow (N), 1$	modifying modulo by scalar

Table 8.3. Modifying arithmetic operators.

> Even though we don't strictly enforce geometric rules at the level of C++ types, we are considering adding a capability to Sh that will analyze the internal representation of a program and provide warnings about geometrically improper operations.

If we do not enforce geometric consistency, you may wonder why we bother defining all these semantic types. One major reason is attribute binding. When shaders are written, input and output attributes need to be assigned to concrete backend attribute slots somehow. By providing types such as **ShNormal**, we can allow the backend to match Sh attributes to backend slots semantically.

Secondly, the semantic types also provide implicit documentation. They make the code easier to read than shader code written in languages without semantic types, as the intent of a variable can be inferred from its type. Furthermore, having multiple semantic types permits programs performing introspection (for example, the shrike shader browser program provided with Sh, or a debugger) to present the user with a better user interface. For example, shrike provides the user with a color widget to change uniform color parameters, while the user interface for more general attributes is a slider or input box.

Sh allows scalars to be promoted to tuples in the basic arithmetic operations. Generally, this is done by replication of the scalar value, although the rules are more specialized for matrices. Tables 8.2, 8.3, and 8.4 indicate when scalar operands are permitted by giving forms of the operators or functions where one of the inputs has one element only. Automatic promotion of tuples of other sizes is not supported; a cast must be used (see Section 8.11).

In addition to the operators, Sh provides several library functions for performing generic arithmetic. The sum function adds all the elements of a tuple, the prod function multiplies them. The mad function performs a multiply-accumulate operation. The reciprocal rcp function computes $1/x$, the reciprocal square root funcion rsqrt function computes $1/\sqrt{x}$, the square root sqrt function computes $\sqrt{x}$, and the cube root function cbrt function computes $\sqrt[3]{x}$. Note that mad, rcp, rsqrt, sqrt and cbrt all operate componentwise (unlike their GPU assembly counterparts).

All arithmetic operators available in Sh are listed in Tables 8.2 and 8.3. Functions for general-purpose arithmetic are summarized in Table 8.4.

8.3 Derivatives

The ability to take derivatives of functions relative to screen-space position is important for shader antialiasing. Sh offers functions to compute derivatives of

Operation	$r \leftarrow a, b, c, \ldots$	Description
sum	$1 \leftarrow N$	sum of components $$r \leftarrow \sum_i a_i$$
prod	$1 \leftarrow N$	product of components $$r \leftarrow \prod_i a_i$$
mad	$N \leftarrow N, N, N$	multiply and add $$r_i \leftarrow a_i b_i + c_i$$
mad	$N \leftarrow 1, N, N$	multiply and add $$r_i \leftarrow a b_i + c_i$$
mad	$N \leftarrow N, 1, N$	multiply and add $$r_i \leftarrow a_i b + c_i$$
rcp	$N \leftarrow N$	reciprocal $$r_i \leftarrow 1/a_i$$
rsqrt	$N \leftarrow N$	reciprocal square root $$r_i \leftarrow 1/\sqrt{a_i}$$
sqrt	$N \leftarrow N$	square root $$r_i \leftarrow \sqrt{a_i}$$
cbrt	$N \leftarrow N$	cube root $$r_i \leftarrow \sqrt[3]{a_i}$$

Table 8.4. Arithmetic functions.

any value with respect to screen-space derivatives, but these can *only* be used inside a fragment shader. Also, derivatives may be approximated with differences on some platforms (or, unfortunately, may be unavailable). A summary of the derivative functions is provided in Table 8.5.

The dx and dy functions compute the derivative of their argument with respect to screen-space position x and y, respectively. If an n-tuple is given as an argument, an n-tuple is returned, with each component being the derivative of the corresponding component in the input. The jacobian function computes a matrix. The first row is basically the result of applying dx to the input, the second row the result of dy applied to the input. The fwidth function computes

Operation	$r \leftarrow a, b, c, \ldots$	Description
dx	$N \leftarrow N$	derivative with respect to screen-space x coordinate
dy	$N \leftarrow N$	derivative with respect to screen-space y coordinate
fwidth	$N \leftarrow N$	maximum absolute value of derivatives: $$r_i \leftarrow \max\left(\left\|\frac{da_i}{dx}\right\|, \left\|\frac{da_i}{dy}\right\|\right).$$
gradient	$2 \leftarrow 1$	compute pair of screen-space derivatives for a scalar
jacobian	$2 \times N \leftarrow N$	compute the Jacobian matrix with respect to screen-space x and y

Table 8.5. Derivative functions: only defined inside fragment shaders.

the componentwise maximum of the absolute values of dx and dy. This is the usual rule used to select a MIP-map level in a texture. Finally, the gradient function only takes a scalar as an argument and returns a 2-tuple which is the result of taking the derivative of the provided quantity in the x and y directions.

8.4 Noise

The available noise functions are given in Tables 8.6, 8.7, and 8.8. Noise functions are useful in many situations, for instance, to give a surface an organic appearance. Each of these functions can compute N channels of noise on an M-dimensional input space.

The hash function procedurally computes a floating-point number which is a deterministic function of its input. Inputs with different integer parts will result in outputs that appear to be unrelated to one another. The texhash function is similar, but uses a lookup table stored in a texture. It may be faster to use texhash on some targets, although this limits the resolution of the hash function. Neither function is guaranteed (at present) to be the same on all platforms. Both hash functions depend only on the integer part of their inputs.

The cellnoise function is an interface to either hash or texhash, depending on compilation target and a global option. For instance, on GPU vertex shader targets that don't support texture maps, cellnoise *must* use the procedural function hash. The rest of the noise functions are built on top of cellnoise.

Operation	$r \leftarrow a, b, c, \ldots$	Description
cellnoise<N>	$N \leftarrow M$	generic hash based on only the integer part of a; may be implemented using either hash or texhash, depending on a program definition-time constant or the target
scellnoise<N>	$N \leftarrow M$	signed version of cellnoise
hash<N>	$N \leftarrow M$	procedural hash function
texhash<N>	$N \leftarrow M$	texture-based hash function

Table 8.6. Hash functions.

Operation	$r \leftarrow a, b, c, \ldots$	Description
linnoise<N>	$N \leftarrow M, [K]$	compute b-weighted sum of K octaves of bi-linearly interpolated cellnoise
noise<N>	$N \leftarrow M, [K]$	compute b-weighted sum of K octaves of Perlin's original noise function, implemented using cubic interpolation
perlin<N>	$N \leftarrow M, [K]$	compute b-weighted sum of K octaves of Perlin's improved noise function, implemented using a fifth-degree polynomial
turbulence<N>	$N \leftarrow M, [K]$	compute b-weighted sum of K octaves of the absolute value of snoise
worley<K>	$K \leftarrow M, f$	Worley noise function; Compute distances to the K nearest centers (points on a jittered grid) to a, using distance function f (default is distance).

Table 8.7. Noise functions.

Operation	$r \leftarrow a, b, c, \ldots$	Description
slinnoise<N>	$N \leftarrow M, [K]$	signed version of linnoise
snoise<N>	$N \leftarrow M, [K]$	signed version of noise
sperlin<N>	$N \leftarrow M, [K]$	signed version of perlin
sturbulence<N>	$N \leftarrow M, [K]$	signed version of turbulence

Table 8.8. Signed noise functions.

The noise function implements the original Perlin noise function [113], and the perlin function implements the "new and improved" (but more expensive) Perlin noise function [114]. A cheaper noise function that can replace Perlin noise in some circumstances is provided by linnoise, which just linearly interpolates cellnoise.

These noise functions can compute and sum several octaves of noise, with a different weight for each octave. For instance, if `noise(a)` is the basic Perlin noise, we support a generalization as follows:

$$\texttt{noise}(\mathbf{a}, \mathbf{b}) \;=\; \sum_{i=0}^{K-1} b_i \texttt{noise}(2^i \mathbf{a}).$$

The basic noise functions return values in the range $[0, 1]$. The versions prefixed with "s" return values in the range $[-1, 1]$.

The `turbulence` function computes a weighted sum of octaves of absolute values of `snoise`:

$$\texttt{turbulence}(\mathbf{a}, \mathbf{b}) \;=\; \sum_{i=0}^{K-1} b_i \left| \texttt{snoise}(2^i \mathbf{a}) \right|.$$

The weight vectors are optional and if not given, a weight of 1 is assumed and one octave is computed.

The `worley` function approximates the Worley basis functions [151], which are based on the Kth distance to randomly placed points (centers). Our implementation currently uses a jittered grid of centers rather than a true random distribution. The `worley` function returns a tuple of K distances and takes an optional distance function as a second argument. The maximum size of K is 3^M.

Some of these noise functions may be quite expensive, especially at higher input dimensionalities. The `worley` and `perlin` functions, as well as related functions such as `turbulence`, may compile to a large number of instructions on backends which do not have a hash function or noise built in (which is all of them at the time this was written). In fact, the implementation of `worley` will grow exponentially with dimension.

8.5   Trigonometric and Exponential Functions

Sh provides a variety of useful transcendental math functions. The names of these functions follow those in the C standard math library. However, generally they have been extended to operate componentwise, as with arithmetic instructions.

Supported trigonometric functions are listed in Table 8.9. These functions operate componentwise on tuples. This means that if you take the sine of an n-tuple, you will compute n sines in parallel. A special case is `sincos`, which computes sine and cosine in one function. It returns a tuple twice as long as

Operation	$r \leftarrow a, b, c, \ldots$	Description
acos	$N \leftarrow N$	arccosine
acosh	$N \leftarrow N$	hyperbolic arccosine
asin	$N \leftarrow N$	arcsine
asinh	$N \leftarrow N$	hyperbolic arcsine
atan	$N \leftarrow N$	arctangent
atan2	$N \leftarrow N, N$	arctangent of b/a
atanh	$N \leftarrow N$	hyperbolic arctangent
cos	$N \leftarrow N$	cosine
cosh	$N \leftarrow N$	hyperbolic cosine
sin	$N \leftarrow N$	sine
sinh	$N \leftarrow N$	hyperbolic sine
tan	$N \leftarrow N$	tangent
tanh	$N \leftarrow N$	hyperbolic tangent

Table 8.9. Trigonometric functions. Some of these functions may be replaced with approximations if the compilation target does not support them directly.

Operation	$r \leftarrow a, b, c, \ldots$	Description
exp	$N \leftarrow N$	natural (base-e) exponential
expm1	$N \leftarrow N$	natural (base-e) exponential of $a - 1$
exp2	$N \leftarrow N$	base-2 exponential
exp10	$N \leftarrow N$	base-10 exponential
log	$N \leftarrow N$	natural (base-e) logarithm
logp1	$N \leftarrow N$	natural (base-e) logarithm of $a + 1$
log2	$N \leftarrow N$	base-2 logarithm
log10	$N \leftarrow N$	base-10 logarithm
pow	$N \leftarrow N, N$	power $r_i \leftarrow (a_i)^{b_i}$
pow	$N \leftarrow 1, N$	power $r_i \leftarrow (a)^{b_i}$
pow	$N \leftarrow N, 1$	power $r_i \leftarrow (a_i)^{b}$

Table 8.10. Exponential and logarithmic functions. Some of these functions may be replaced with approximations if the compilation target does not support them.

the input tuple. Normally you would just apply it to a 1-tuple, but if a larger tuple is given to it, multiple invocation will be made and packed together into the output tuple. All trigonometric functions take radians as their arguments. The helper function `radians` converts from degrees to radians and `degrees` converts from radians to degrees.

Functions for exponentiation and logarithms to the bases of e, 2, and 10 are listed in Table 8.10. The exponential functions also work on complex numbers and return a complex number.

Operation	$r \leftarrow a, b, c, \ldots$	Description
`bernstein<N>`	$N \leftarrow 1$	evaluation of the Bernstein (Bézier) basis functions of order N at parameter a: $$r_i \quad \leftarrow \quad B_i^N(a)$$ $$= \quad \binom{N-1}{i}(1-a)^{N-1-i}a^i$$
`bezier`	$N \leftarrow 1, N, N, \ldots$	Bézier spline of degree M evaluated at parameter a using control points $p_0 = b$, $p_1 = c$, $\ldots p_M$: $$r \quad \leftarrow \quad \sum_{j=0}^{M} B_i^{M+1}(a)p_j$$
`hermite`	$N \leftarrow 1, N, N, N, N$	cubic Hermite spline evaluated at parameter a interpolating b at 0 with tangent c and d at 1 with tangent e
`lerp`	$N \leftarrow N, N, N$	linear interpolation: $$r_i \quad \leftarrow \quad a_i b_i + (1-a_i)c_i$$
`lerp`	$N \leftarrow 1, N, N$	linear interpolation with scalar promotion: $$r_i \leftarrow ab_i + (1-a)c_i$$
`poly`	$N \leftarrow N, M$	evaluation of polynomial of order M at a using coefficients in b: $$r_i \leftarrow \sum_{j=0}^{M-1} a_i^j b_j$$

Table 8.11. Spline and polynomial functions.

Not all functions are supported natively on all compilation targets, but in this case Sh will implement the function using other existing capabilities. For example, trigonometric functions like `sin` are not available in the OpenGL ARB vertex program assembly language. Sh will evaluate a polynomial or rational approximation for these functions.

8.6   Interpolation and Approximation

Spline functions are useful for interpolating and approximating data or functions. Sh provides implementations of several basic spline types as well as evaluation of polynomials; see Table 8.11. Linear interpolation is the most basic interpolation method supported, but Sh also supports Bézier and Hermite splines. Bézier splines can be evaluated either by first evaluating the Bernstein basis functions and then forming an affine combination of control points, or by calling one of the overloaded direct evaluation functions for each supported order. The cubic Hermite spline permits the interpolation of a pair of data points with specified tangents.

Evaluation of polynomials relative to the power basis is also supported, given a tuple of coefficients.

8.7   Geometry

Sh provides several functions to make geometric operations convenient. Some of these are supported directly and very efficiently by GPU hardware, dot products being the most commonly used operation in this class. Use of these functions is encouraged, since this enables the compiler to perform domain-specific optimizations. Tables 8.12, 8.13 and 8.14 list these functions.

For **ShVector**s and **ShNormal**s, a short-hand notation for dot products is (v1|v2), which takes the dot product of v1 and v2. The cross product of two three-dimensional vectors may be computed as (v1^v2). If both arguments

Operation	$r \leftarrow a, b, c, \ldots$	Description
^	$3 \leftarrow 3, 3$	cross product of $\vec{a}$ and $\vec{b}$: $$\vec{r} \quad \leftarrow \quad \begin{bmatrix} a_1 b_2 - a_2 b_1 \\ a_2 b_0 - a_0 b_2 \\ a_0 b_1 - a_1 b_0 \end{bmatrix}.$$
|	$1 \leftarrow N, N$	dot product: $$r \leftarrow (\vec{a} \cdot \vec{b}) = \sum_{i=0}^{N-1} a_i b_i$$
cross	$3 \leftarrow 3, 3$	cross-product of a and b (equivalent to "^" operator)
dot	$1 \leftarrow N, N$	Dot product of a and b (equivalent to "|" operator)

Table 8.12. Cross and dot products.   See also the matrix functions described in Section 8.8.

Operation	$r \leftarrow a, b, c, \ldots$	Description
`distance`	$1 \leftarrow N, N$	Euclidean (L_2) distance between $\underline{a}$ and $\underline{b}$: $$\vec{v} = \underline{a} - \underline{b},$$ $$r \leftarrow |\vec{v}|_2 = \sqrt{\vec{v} \cdot \vec{v}}$$
`distance_1`	$1 \leftarrow N, N$	Manhattan (L_1) distance between $\underline{a}$ and $\underline{b}$: $$\vec{v} = \underline{a} - \underline{b},$$ $$r \leftarrow |\vec{v}|_1 = \sum_{i=0}^{N-1} |v_i|$$
`distance_inf`	$1 \leftarrow N, N$	Inf (L_∞) distance between $\underline{a}$ and $\underline{b}$: $$\vec{v} = \underline{a} - \underline{b},$$ $$r \leftarrow |\vec{v}|_\infty = \max_{i=0}^{N-1} |v_i|$$
`length`	$1 \leftarrow N$	Euclidean (L_2) length of $\vec{a}$: $$r \leftarrow |\vec{a}|_2 = \sqrt{\vec{a} \cdot \vec{a}}$$
`length_1`	$1 \leftarrow N$	Manhattan (L_1) length of $\vec{a}$: $$r \leftarrow |\vec{a}|_2 = \sum_{i=0}^{N-1} |a_i|$$
`length_inf`	$1 \leftarrow N$	Inf (L_∞) length of $\vec{a}$: $$r \leftarrow |\vec{a}|_2 = \max_{i=0}^{N-1} |a_i|$$

Table 8.13. Length and distance functions. See also the matrix functions described in Section 8.8.

are **ShVectors**, the cross product returns an **ShNormal**. If one of the components is an **ShNormal**, it returns an **ShVector**.

8.8 Linear Algebra

Matrices use both the "*" and "|" operator for matrix-matrix multiplication, matrix-vector products, and vector-matrix products. Matrix-vector and vector-

Operation	$r \leftarrow a, b, c, \ldots$	Description
`faceforward`	$N \leftarrow N, N$	make vector $\vec{b}$ face in same direction as $\vec{a}$: $$\vec{r} \leftarrow \begin{cases} \vec{a} & \text{if } (\vec{a} \cdot \vec{b}) > 0, \\ -\vec{a} & \text{otherwise} \end{cases}$$
`lit`	$4 \leftarrow 1, 1, 1$	compute lighting coefficients: $$\begin{aligned} r_0 &\leftarrow 1 \\ r_1 &\leftarrow \max(a, 0) \\ r_2 &\leftarrow \begin{cases} b^c & \text{if } a > 0 \text{ and } b < 0, \\ 0 & \text{otherwise} \end{cases} \\ r_3 &\leftarrow 1 \end{aligned}$$
`normalize`	$N \leftarrow N$	normalize vector to unit Euclidean length: $$\hat{r} \leftarrow \text{norm}(\vec{a}) = \vec{a}/|\vec{a}|_2.$$
`reflect`	$N \leftarrow N, N$	reflection of $\vec{a}$ on surface with (possibly un-normalized) normal $\vec{b}$. The vector $\vec{r}$ is only normalized if $\vec{a}$ is: $$\begin{aligned} \hat{b} &\leftarrow \text{norm}\left(\vec{b}\right), \\ \vec{r} &\leftarrow 2(\vec{a} \cdot \hat{b})\hat{b} - \vec{a} \end{aligned}$$
`refract`	$N \leftarrow N, N, 1$	refraction vector for incoming vector $\vec{a}$ on surface with normal $\vec{b}$ and relative index of refraction $\eta = c$

Table 8.14. Lighting functions. See also the matrix functions described in Section 8.8.

matrix products actually apply to all matrix-tuple and tuple-matrix products, but special rules are used for **ShTexCoord, ShVector, ShNormal, ShPlane,** and **ShPoint** types to infer missing homogeneous coordinates and the use of matrices to represent affine and projective transformations. In matrix-vector and vector-matrix products, the output tuple type is the same as the input type.

On matrix-tuple products with the tuple on the right, the tuple (i.e. any subclass of **ShAttrib**) is treated as a column vector and the usual rules of matrix-vector multiplication are applied. The dimensions of the matrix and tuple must match; in particular, for this situation, the number of columns in the matrix must match the number of elements in the tuple, and the matrix-tuple product describes a linear combination of the columns of the matrix. The result is

Operation	$r \leftarrow a, b, c, \ldots$	Description
+	$N \times M \leftarrow$ $N \times M, N \times M$	componentwise addition
−	$N \times M \leftarrow$ $N \times M, N \times M$	componentwise subtraction
−	$N \times M \leftarrow N \times M$	componentwise unary negation
*	$N \times P \leftarrow$ $N \times M, M \times P$	matrix product
|	$N \times P \leftarrow$ $N \times M, M \times P$	matrix product
inverse	$N \times N \leftarrow N \times N$	inverse of a square matrix
transpose	$N \times M \leftarrow M \times N$	transpose of a matrix
adjoint	$N \times N \leftarrow N \times N$	adjoint of a square matrix (the transpose of the cofactor matrix)
det	$1 \leftarrow N \times N$	determinant of a square matrix
trace	$1 \leftarrow N \times N$	trace of a square matrix

Table 8.15. Matrix functions. Compute various quantities for matrices or operate on matrices.

Operation	$r \leftarrow a, b, c, \ldots$	Description
*	$N \times M \leftarrow 1, N \times M$	scalar-matrix product
*	$N \times M \leftarrow N \times M, 1$	matrix-scalar product
*	$N \leftarrow N \times M, M$	matrix-column vector product
*	$M \leftarrow N, N \times M$	row vector-matrix product
|	$N \leftarrow N \times M, M$	matrix-column vector product
|	$M \leftarrow N, N \times M$	row vector-matrix product

Table 8.16. Matrix-vector functions. Various functions related to combining matrices and vectors together.

Operation	$r \leftarrow a, b, c, \ldots$	Description
rowmat	$M \times N \leftarrow N_1, \ldots, N_M$	build a matrix, using the given tuples as rows
colmat	$N \times M \leftarrow N_1, \ldots, N_M$	build a matrix, using the given tuples as columns
diag	$N \times N \leftarrow N$	build a matrix, using the given tuple as diagonal

Table 8.17. Matrix constructors. Functions to construct matrices from tuples.

Operation	$r \leftarrow a, b, c, \ldots$	Description
rotate	$4 \times 4 \leftarrow 3, 1$	build a 4×4 affine transformation matrix representing a 3D rotation, given an axis vector in a (which does not need to be normalized) and an angle (in radians) about that axis in b; the generated matrix will rotate column vectors by the given angle about the given axis, using the right-hand rule
rotate	$3 \times 3 \leftarrow 1$	build a 3×3 affine transformation matrix representing a 2D rotation, given an angle (in radians); the generated matrix will rotate column vectors counter-clockwise by the given angle
translate	$4 \times 4 \leftarrow 3$	build a 4×4 affine transformation matrix representing a 3D translation, given a 3D translation vector in a
translate	$3 \times 3 \leftarrow 2$	build a 3×3 affine transformation matrix representing a 2D translation, given a 2D translation vector in a
scale	$4 \times 4 \leftarrow 3$	build a 4×4 affine transformation matrix representing a 3D non-uniform scale, given a three-tuple of scale factors in a
scale	$3 \times 3 \leftarrow 2$	build a 3×3 affine transformation matrix representing a 2D non-uniform scale, given a two-tuple of scale factors in a
scale<N>	$N \times N \leftarrow 1$	build a $N \times N$ affine transformation matrix representing a $(N-1)$D uniform scale, given a single scale factor in a

Table 8.18. Matrix transformations. Functions to construct primitive transformation matrices.

a tuple of the same type as the rightmost argument that is a result of a linear combination of the columns of the matrix.

Exceptions to the size-matching rule are made for the *ShTexCoord*, *ShVector*, *ShNormal*, *ShPlane*, and *ShPoint* types to account for missing homogeneous coordinates. If an *ShVector* or *ShNormal* is the argument on the right and the matrix has one more column than the number of elements in the vector, the weight on the last column of the matrix is assumed to be zero, i.e. the *ShVector* or *ShNormal* is automatically promoted by one dimension and the extra homogeneous element given the value of zero. For an *ShTexCoord*, *ShPoint*, or *ShPlane*, something similar happens, but the inferred homogeneous element is given a value of one.

When tuples are given on the left side and matrices on the right, similar rules apply, but the tuple is interpreted as a *row* vector and the result is a linear combination of the *rows* of the matrix.

The "|" operator can also be used for matrix multiplication.

In order to support the convenient composition of affine and projective transformation matrices, if rows are missing on the bottom of a matrix or columns on the left they are automatically drawn from an identity matrix of the correct size. This is also true for matrix functions such as "inverse", shown in Table 8.15. Matrix-vector functions and operators are listed in Table 8.16. Matrix constructors are listed in Table 8.17, and matrix transformations are given in Table 8.18.

Normally we would multiply vectors and points on the right of matrices and normals and planes on the left. However, we permit the placement of these types on the "wrong" side of expressions to avoid the use of explicit transposes in expressions like x * Q * x, which computes the quadratic form $x^T Q x$ if x is a point and Q is a coefficient matrix. This works correctly even if x is a **ShPoint3f** and Q is a **ShMatrix4x4f** due to the homogeneous promotion rules outlined above, which work on both the right and the left.

8.9   Logical and Comparison Functions

It is often useful to compare values. Sh implements all the usual comparison and logical operations, but these are generalized to act over tuples. In addition, we implement some useful functions to deal with tuples of Booleans. The comparison operators are presented in Table 8.19, while logical operations are presented in Table 8.20.

Many GPUs do not have real support for Booleans or condition registers, and for this reason we use an interpretation of true and false that is appropriate for floating point types. Values greater than zero are interpreted to be "true," whereas values less than or equal to zero are taken to mean "false." The comparison operators all return 1.0 if the comparison succeeds, and 0.0 if it does not.

Sh does not at present distinguish between Boolean types and other kinds of data. We are, however, considering adding **ShBool** as a new semantic type — similar to **ShVector** and **ShTexCoord** — to represent a Boolean value. This would allow us to take advantage more easily of conditional registers available on certain GPUs.

Operation	$r \leftarrow a, b, c, \ldots$	Description
<	$N \leftarrow N, N$	$r_i \leftarrow a_i < b_i$
<	$N \leftarrow 1, N$	$r_i \leftarrow a < b_i$
<	$N \leftarrow N, 1$	$r_i \leftarrow a_i < b$
<=	$N \leftarrow N, N$	$r_i \leftarrow a_i \leq b_i$
<=	$N \leftarrow 1, N$	$r_i \leftarrow a \leq b_i$
<=	$N \leftarrow N, 1$	$r_i \leftarrow a_i \leq b$
==	$N \leftarrow N, N$	$r_i \leftarrow a_i = b_i$
==	$N \leftarrow 1, N$	$r_i \leftarrow a = b_i$
==	$N \leftarrow N, 1$	$r_i \leftarrow a_i = b$
!=	$N \leftarrow N, N$	$r_i \leftarrow a_i \neq b_i$
!=	$N \leftarrow 1, N$	$r_i \leftarrow a \neq b_i$
!=	$N \leftarrow N, 1$	$r_i \leftarrow a_i \neq b$
>=	$N \leftarrow N, N$	$r_i \leftarrow a_i \geq b_i$
>=	$N \leftarrow 1, N$	$r_i \leftarrow a \geq b_i$
>=	$N \leftarrow N, 1$	$r_i \leftarrow a_i \geq b$
>	$N \leftarrow N, N$	$r_i \leftarrow a_i > b_i$
>	$N \leftarrow 1, N$	$r_i \leftarrow a > b_i$
>	$N \leftarrow N, 1$	$r_i \leftarrow a_i > b$

Table 8.19. Comparison functions. Each component of the output vector is set to 0 or 1 to represent the result of the comparison on each component.

Operation	$r \leftarrow a, b, c, \ldots$	Description
!	$N \leftarrow N$	$r_i \leftarrow 1 - (a_i > 0)$
&&	$N \leftarrow N, N$	$r_i = \min(a_i, b_i)$
||	$N \leftarrow N, N$	$r_i = \max(a_i, b_i)$
all	$1 \leftarrow N$	$r = \min(a_0, a_1, \ldots, a_{N-1})$
any	$1 \leftarrow N$	$r = \max(a_0, a_1, \ldots, a_{N-1})$
cond	$N \leftarrow N, N, N$	componentwise conditional: $$r_i \leftarrow \begin{cases} b_i & \text{if } a_i > 0 \\ c_i & \text{otherwise} \end{cases}$$
cond	$N \leftarrow 1, N, N$	tuple conditional: $$r \leftarrow \begin{cases} \mathbf{b} & \text{if } a > 0 \\ \mathbf{c} & \text{otherwise} \end{cases}$$

Table 8.20. Logical functions. Values greater than zero mean "true" and all others mean "false."

This leads to a natural definition of "and" and "or." The operator "and" is defined as the minimum of its arguments, whereas "or" is defined as the maximum. The operators && and || are defined correspondingly in Sh. Furthermore, Boolean negation of a value x is defined as its one's complement: $1 - (x > 0)$.

The all and any functions collapse a Boolean tuple to a single Boolean. They are especially useful in the arguments of control constructs and to control conditional assignment functions. The function all returns true only if all components of its argument are true; this is implemented by taking the minimum of these values. The function any returns true if any of the components of its argument are true; this is implemented by taking the maximum of these components.

The cond function provides a useful operation that allows for the componentwise selection of one of two computations depending on a Boolean value. It corresponds very closely to C++'s ternary ?: operator, which, unfortunately, can not be overloaded. Note that cond only *discards* one of the two values it might return; it still calculates both (although the optimizer might turn it into a real branch on some compilation targets).

8.10 Discontinuities

There are several functions which "clamp" their inputs in various ways, i.e., potentially lose some information in their inputs and introduce discontinuities. These are documented in Tables 8.21, 8.22, and 8.23. The first two sets of functions are sharp discontinuities, the last set supports smoothed discontinuities, as required in shaders for antialiasing. The smoothed version of a function typically has smooth in front of the name and an extra parameter for setting the width of the transition region.

8.11 Miscellaneous Functions

Finally we come to the functions that don't exactly fit anywhere else. These are shown in Table 8.24.

The functions cast<M> and fillcast<M> are both useful in situations where one needs to turn an N-tuple into an M-tuple. The former pads remaining values with zero, the latter replicates the last element. So, to get a 9-vector filled with ones, one might write fillcast<9>(**ShVector1f**(1.0)).

The discard function only makes sense in fragment or stream programs. It conditionally discards the current fragment or stream element, not writing any

Operation	$r \leftarrow a, b, c, \ldots$	Description
abs	$N \leftarrow N$	componentwise absolute value: $r_i \leftarrow \lvert a_i \rvert$
ceil	$N \leftarrow N$	componentwise ceiling: $r_i \leftarrow \lceil a_i \rceil$
clamp	$N \leftarrow N, N, N$	componentwise clamping of a_i between b_i and c_i
clamp	$N \leftarrow N, 1, 1$	componentwise clamping of a_i between b_i and c_i
floor	$N \leftarrow N$	componentwise floor: $r_i \leftarrow \lfloor a_i \rfloor$
frac	$N \leftarrow N$	componentwise fractional part: $r_i \leftarrow a_i - \lfloor \lvert a_i \rvert \rfloor$
mod	$N \leftarrow N, N$	componentwise floating-point modulus: $r_i \leftarrow a_i / b_i - \lfloor a_i / b_i \rfloor$
round	$N \leftarrow N$	componentwise nearest integer: $r_i \leftarrow \lfloor a_i + 1/2 \rfloor$
sign	$N \leftarrow N$	componentwise sign: $r_i \leftarrow a_i / \lvert a_i \rvert$

Table 8.21. Clamping functions. These operations all potentially lose information and introduce discontinuities.

Operation	$r \leftarrow a, b, c, \ldots$	Description
max	$N \leftarrow N, N$	componentwise maximum: $r_i \leftarrow \max(a_i, b_i)$
max	$1 \leftarrow N$	tuple maximum: $r \leftarrow \max(a_0, a_1, \ldots, a_{N-1})$
min	$N \leftarrow N, N$	componentwise minimum: $r_i \leftarrow \min(a_i, b_i)$
min	$1 \leftarrow N$	tuple minimum: $r \leftarrow \min(a_0, a_1, \ldots, a_{N-1})$
pos	$N \leftarrow N$	componentwise maximum with 0
sat	$N \leftarrow N$	componentwise minimum with 1

Table 8.22. Minimum and maximum functions.

Operation	$r \leftarrow a, b, c, \ldots$	Description
smoothstep	$N \leftarrow N, N, N$	linear smooth step of a_i centered around b_i with width c_i
smoothpulse	$N \leftarrow N, N, N, N$	linear smooth pulse of a_i between b_i and c_i with width d_i

Table 8.23. Smooth clamping functions.

Operation	$r \leftarrow a, b, c, \ldots$	Description
cast<M>	$M \leftarrow N$	tuple resize: for $M > N$, pads extra components with 0; for $M < N$, discards extra components
fillcast<M>	$M \leftarrow N$	right-filled tuple resize: for $M > N$, pads extra components with a_N; for $M < N$, discards extra components
groupsort<S>	$\leftarrow N[S]$	sorts S tuples' components based on the components of $a[0]$
join	$M + N \leftarrow M, N$	forms tuple filled with a's, then b's, components
discard	$\leftarrow N$	discards fragment if *any* $a_i > 0$
sort	$N \leftarrow N$	sort components of a into r

Table 8.24. Miscellaneous functions.

output. On fully SIMD processors (which most GPUs are) this will generally not save any processing time, as all instructions will still be evaluated, but it can be useful to generate certain effects or, for instance, to ignore edge cases in stream computations. Note that discard takes an N-tuple. It will discard the current fragment or element if *any* of the tuple's components are true (i.e., greater than zero).

Chapter 9

Arrays, Tables, and Textures

Textures are encapsulated in opaque objects allocated by the system rather than by number or texture unit number. This permits the specification of textures separately from the allocation of texture units. The run-time system will bind textures on demand to the appropriate texture units when needed by a particular shader.

Textures are supported in Sh through the use of **ShArray**, **ShTable**, and **ShTexture** objects. Use of these objects permits the use of the "[]" and "()" operators to perform lookups in shader programs and provides a unified interface to textures (so the same interface works for all target platforms).

The **ShArray** types support nearest-neighbor lookup, the **ShTable** types support linear interpolation but without filtering, and the basic **ShTexture** types support both linear interpolation and filtering.

The "[]" lookup operator places texels at integer coordinates, but still performs interpolation between them (on the **ShTable** and **ShTexture** types only). The "()" operator scales the lookup so the lower-left texel is at $(0, 0)$ and the upper-right texel is at $(1, 1)$, as is usual in OpenGL. The "[]" operator can also be used on the left-hand side of an expression (outside a shader definition) to update a particular texel of a shader. The update is actually done to a copy of the texture stored in the host's memory; updates to the version of the texture stored on the video card are deferred until necessary.

The basic texture object type is the **ShArray** type, with different interpolation and filtering modes supported with template-based type modifiers.

If **template typedef**s were allowed in C++, we might define the **ShTexture2D** type, which supports both bilinear interpolation and MIP-mapped filtering, as follows:

```
template <typename T>
typedef ShMIPFilter< ShInterp<1, ShArray2D<T> > > ShTexture2D<T>;
```

Type modifiers are smart enough to check if the underlying hardware texture can support interpolation or filtering with a simple mode change. If so, that mode is simply enabled when the texture is used. Otherwise, shader code is generated. These modifiers also avoid repeatedly generating code (applying **ShMIPFilter** twice is no different than applying it once) by seeing if a given mode is already turned on when it is applied.

Modes are indicated with type modifiers like this rather than publicly accessible run-time switches to avoid having to recompile shaders implicitly. Unfortunately, certain filtering and interpolation modes might require the insertion of shader code as well as particular settings in the underlying system texture object, and shaders might also depend on the particular interpolation modes implemented by a texture. For instance, suppose we wanted to support cubic interpolation. We might want to build upon linear interpolation supported by the hardware texture. Another example of this is simple linear interpolation, which on the GeForceFX, for instance, is supported for byte textures but not floating point textures. Sh is designed to hide these dependencies from the user by inserting shader code as needed. Because Sh inserts this code only upon compilation to a particular target, preserving the original code, the user can recompile an existing program for different targets (e.g., for cross-compilation or to switch between a GPU and CPU implementation at run time) without having to redefine the program.

9.1   Texture Formats

There are several different subtypes of textures, differing by the element type stored, the dimensionality of the texture, and the format of the data. In the following descriptions, T can be any tuple type and indicates the type stored in a texel and returned upon lookup.

In the future, we hope to support more general element types, such as composite C++ types containing a number of Sh tuple types. For now, however, textures can only store a single tuple channel, although you can always define your own classes to simplify the interface to multi-channel "textures."

To specify a texture using byte-oriented types, for instance, you must use tuple types with that storage class: **ShAttrib3ub**, in the case of unsigned byte textures. In addition to taking less space, such textures may also require fewer shader resources to support interpolation and filtering. If a floating-point storage type is used, then a floating-point texture will be allocated, but this is often overkill.

In discussing the various data formats below, we will use the *ShTexture* name, although this really relates specifically to linearly interpolated and filtered textures. The same data formats are also available for *ShArray*s and *ShTable*s.

ShTexture1D<*T*>(int r): A one-dimensional texture holding type T. The parameter r gives the size in texels. Hardware textures usually must have sizes that are an integral power of two in order to support MIP-mapping.

ShTexture2D<*T*>(int rs, int rt): A two-dimensional texture holding type T. The construction parameters rs and rt give the size in texels of the s and t dimensions, respectively. In hardware, two-dimensional textures usually are a power of two in size.

ShTextureRect<*T*>(int rs, int rt): A two-dimensional texture holding type T. Semantically, this texture type is the same as *Texture2D*. It uses a rectangular texture type internally, which allows non-square sizes that are not a power of two. However, such texture types usually do not support filtering natively, so shader code may need to be generated to support this functionality. The overhead to support filtering can be high, so use of a *TableRect* or *ArrayRect* is recommended whenever possible.

ShTexture3D<*T*>(int rx, int ry, int rz): As with two-dimensional textures, these three-dimensional volumetric textures must have resolutions that are a power of two in size. Different platforms may or may not support trilinear interpolation completely in hardware, but the Sh version does (even if it requires additional shader code). Normally, hardware supports three-dimensional textures only with rx, ry and rz being powers of two.

ShTextureCube<*T*>(int rs, int rt): Cube maps support six faces which are specified by setting six memories. All of these textures should be the same size and powers of two.

Cube maps are indexed by a three-dimensional vector whose length is ignored. Instead, the ray from the origin of the cube in the direction of the given vector is intersected with a cube and one of the six faces is referenced.

Cube maps are useful for environment maps and other functions defined over a sphere. The Sh cube-mapped texture class automatically sets up the correct border conditions and MIP-map levels for cube maps (whenever possible).

> Note that on most hardware, rectangular textures are internally indexed by $[0, w] \times [0, h]$ coordinates, whereas other textures are indexed using $[0, 1]^n$ coordinates. If you use the "[]" operator on non-rectangular textures, or the "()" operator on rectangular textures, be aware that Sh may have to insert additional scaling code, making the shader slightly slower. Whenever possible, to maximize performance you should use the native access mode for texture lookups.

9.2   Trait Modifiers

As mentioned earlier, there are several traits that can be modified for textures. In their descriptions, T refers to some other texture type that is to be amended by the modifier.

ShBorderClamp<T>: Clamp texture lookups with extreme texture coordinates to a border value.

ShEdgeClamp<T>: Clamp texture lookups with extreme texture coordinates to the edge of the texture (*default*).

ShWrapRepeat<T>: Repeat the texture for texture lookups outside its range.

ShInterp<N, T>: Set the degree of interpolation to N. Useful values for N are 0 for nearest-neighbor lookups, 1 for linear interpolation, and 3 for cubic (Catmull-Rom) interpolation. A value of 2 will be upgraded to 3, anything higher than 3 will be reduced to 3.

ShMIPFilter<T>: Use MIP-mapped filtering (turn it on if it is off).

ShNoMIPFilter<T>: Do not use MIP-mapped filtering (turn it off if it is on).

9.3   Texture Memory and Storage

All textures must be stored somewhere, and several copies may be stored in several places (e.g., the host memory or memory on board the graphics card). Sh abstracts this by providing an **ShMemory** class. Such a class only *represents* memory; it is connected to other objects (**ShStorage**s) that take care of where the memory is stored. The system automatically keeps track of how up-to-date each storage is and only transfers memory from one storage to another if necessary. Setting up a texture that shares memory with another texture is as simple as writing `texture2.memory(texture1.memory())`. Sh also provides an

ShImage class that can be used to load PNG image files and then attach the image's memory to a texture. For example:

```
ShImage image;                          // Declare an image
image.load_PNG("monalisa.png");         // Load a PNG and set up a new memory
// Now, declare a texture
ShTexture2D<ShColor3f> texture(image.width(), image.height());
texture.memory(image.memory());  // And share memory
```

Like most objects in Sh, memory is reference counted. It will stay around as long as the texture is used in an existing shader, even if the instance of the **ShImage** class used to load the image goes away.

9.4   Texture and Array Access

Texture accesses use both the "[]" and "()" operators. In both cases, this operator has one argument which is used as the lookup index. The argument to this operator may be a shader run-time variable.

For textures, this argument need not be a **ShTexCoord** (although that would be common) but should either be the same dimension as the declared texture coordinate dimension or one larger. If it is one larger, the last coordinate is assumed to be a homogeneous component and is divided out for lookup. This factor is simply ignored for cube-map lookups. For the **ShArray** types, only the integer part of the parameter is considered.

The "()" and "[]" operators differ in that "()" scales the texture coordinate range to the declared size of the texture while "[]" uses integer coordinates. The scale on "()" is defined so that (0,0) picks up the texel in the lower left and (1,1) picks up the texel in the upper right. This makes these lookups independent of the resolution of the texture. The "[]" operator accesses texels centered at each integer. This access operator is most useful with the **ShArray** type when it is used to implement data structures.

Chapter 10

Programs and Streams

Program objects in Sh contain records of sequences of operations on Sh types and a representation of Sh control constructs. They can be compiled to multiple compilation targets, combined with other program objects to create new program objects, applied to stream data, and loaded into GPU shader units. A number of built-in program object generators, called kernels and nibbles, are built into the Sh library. These can be combined with other kernels, nibbles, or user-defined programs to generate new programs.

10.1 Defining Programs

Program definitions are enclosed by a pair of *SH_BEGIN_PROGRAM* and *SH_END* keyword macros. The *SH_BEGIN_PROGRAM* keyword returns an *ShProgram* object.

The *SH_BEGIN_PROGRAM* keyword macro takes an argument specifying the compilation target for the program. This target is used to match the program to a backend and, in some cases, specify the kind of program being compiled. Valid choices include "gpu:vertex" and "gpu:fragment" for vertex and fragment programs to be run on a (generic) GPU. These particular modes are also supported by macros:

```
#define SH_BEGIN_VERTEX_PROGRAM\
     SH_BEGIN_PROGRAM("gpu:vertex")
#define SH_BEGIN_FRAGMENT_PROGRAM\
     SH_BEGIN_PROGRAM("gpu:fragment")
```

Using an empty string as a target indicates that the program does not (yet) have a specific target. This is useful in conjunction with the shader algebra operators (see Section 10.4).

The target identifier is split into two parts by a colon. The first part, before the colon, gives the backend name or type. Backends register themselves with a particular name and a set of more generic backend types for which they are instances. For example, all backends which involve running code on the GPU are also instances of the gpu backend type. Those running code on the CPU (e.g., with dynamic compilation or interpretation) will be instances of the cpu type.

The second part of the target specifies the kind of program being defined. Valid choices currently include "vertex", "fragment", and "stream". In the future there may be more possibilities, such as "shader", to support a unified vertex and fragment program automatically virtualized across both shader units. However, this is currently not supported.

If no colon is present in the target, the string given is assumed to be the kind of program to compile; any available backend is matched to the program, starting with GPU backends (if available) and then CPU backends.

Once *SH_BEGIN_PROGRAM* has been called, Sh changes from immediate mode to retained mode. In retained mode, any Sh expression, such as an arithmetic operation, a library function call, or a texture access, is not evaluated but *collected*. A list of computations is built and attached to the program currently being constructed. Chapter 14 provides more details on how this is done. Once *SH_END* is called, control constructs in the program are parsed, optimized, and possibly compiled if a matching backend has been specified.

10.1.1 Compiling Programs

If a program has been defined, and it has been given a target which can be directly compiled on the current backend, it will be *compiled* right away as soon as *SH_END* is called. In our terminology, we call the initial step of parsing and optimization *definition* and the act of translating the Sh intermediate representation to real GPU or CPU assembly, or another high-level language, *compilation*.

It is possible to force compilation of a program by invoking the shCompile function, which take an *ShProgram* as an argument. This compiles the given program object under the backend selected by its definition target, forcing recompilation of the program, even if it has been previously compiled.

By passing an optional second string argument to the shCompile function, a program can be recompiled for a particular target different from its original definition target. The internal representation of the program is designed to be platform independent to support this. Users should avoid using metaprogramming to put in hooks to particular platforms, unless they are willing to redefine shaders from scratch every time. To support platform-dependent features, it is better to extend the intermediate representation instead. Metaprogramming can be used to adapt programs to target platforms, but it is recommended that this only be used to adapt to performance, not features.

By calling the `is_compiled` member function with a string argument on a program object, it is possible to tell whether or not that program object has been successfully compiled to a particular target. Although Sh makes every effort to compile program objects to all platforms, compilation currently can fail if certain features are used that cannot yet be supported on all platforms, for instance, unbounded data-dependent iteration.

10.2   Binding Programs and Data

Eventually, Sh will have a rendering interface to specify geometry and initiate rendering passes without the user having to make low-level graphics API calls. However, this is not yet the case, and even if Sh had its own rendering API, we would still want to be able to use it with existing graphics APIs, such as OpenGL or DirectX.

In order to use Sh programs with existing graphics APIs, we provide some interfaces to *bind* programs to the GPU so that they will be run when actual geometry is sent to the graphics card externally to Sh.

None of these functions are necessary for stream programs, as the interface to stream execution is always managed through Sh regardless of compilation target.

10.2.1   Binding Programs

A GPU program is bound by calling `shBind` on a previously defined **ShProgram** object. This will bind the program object to its target using its currently selected backend. If necessary, this completes the optimization of the program (if it was deferred for more efficient execution of program manipulation operators) and uploads it to the appropriate shader unit of the GPU. Subsequent calls to draw geometry using the standard API of the current backend will then use this program as a shader.

It is possible to bind a program to a different target than it was compiled for by using a second (string) argument to `shBind()`. This may be useful to select a more specific backend than the one declared at program definition time, or to pass in some extra target compilation targets. Program targets are explained in more detail in Section 10.1.

10.2.2   Binding and Updating Data

As soon as a program is bound, all of the textures and uniform parameters it accesses will be downloaded to the GPU (if necessary). One might, however, want to change some uniform values or textures without rebinding the entire shader. Sh tries to avoid uploading new values for every little change to a parameter; instead, it defers them until it is sure that the user is done. This optimization is particularly important for textures. For this reason, the shUpdate() function is provided. It basically warns Sh that the user is about to start rendering with the standard API and that Sh should resolve any outstanding deferred updates.

Called without arguments, shUpdate will upload any textures and uniform parameters which are out-of-date but required on all compilation targets that currently have any programs bound. Depending on whether textures have been changed, this may be a fairly expensive operation or may have almost no cost at all. Sh may in fact upload uniforms earlier (for instance, as they are modified), but shUpdate() should always be called before rendering to ensure that all uniforms and textures are completely up-to-date. In particular, once we implement uniform lifting, even uniform update may be deferred to avoid redundant computation on the host.

As with shBind, the shUpdate function can take an optional string argument specifying a compilation target. If this is given, only uniforms and textures used by programs bound to the specified target will be updated. As stated earlier, if no argument is given, *all* targets in use will be updated.

10.2.3   Unbinding

The shUnbind function takes a string argument specifying a target. It will disable all of the given target's currently bound Sh programs. Future calls to shUpdate for that target will do nothing. Future rendering calls corresponding to that target will not use programmable shaders. If programmable shaders are always necessary for a particular backend, the effect of shUnbind() is defined by that backend in particular (but is, in general, undefined).

If shUnbind is called without a target, every target which currently has a shader bound to it will be unbound.

10.2.4   Querying Binding State

By calling shIsBound with a string target, a user can determine if any Sh program is currently bound to a particular target. The shBound function, which also takes a string target, will return a pointer to the program object bound to a particular target. If no Sh program is currently bound to a given target, a NULL pointer will be returned.

The shBeginBound and shEndBound functions return iterators to pairs of strings and program objects, allowing access to all currently bound programs and the targets under which they are bound. Note that if shBind or shUnbind is called, previous values returned by these functions may no longer be valid and should be discarded.

10.3   Introspection

Sh program objects support introspection, allowing host applications to inspect them in various ways. This is particularly useful for host programs that provide some user interface layer on top of arbitrary Sh programs, such as the shrike application, which provides widgets to control uniform parameters and textures accessed by Sh programs. These introspection methods are also used internally by some of the built-in Sh functions, such as the "shader algebra" operators discussed in Section 10.4.

The compilation target assigned to the program at definition time is available by calling the target member function on **ShProgram** objects, which returns a string such as "gpu:vertex". This string may be empty, indicating that the program is generic. The generic compilation target is used for glue programs; programs with a generic target need a target assigned before they can be used.

Perhaps the most important introspection facilities for programs are accessors for scanning dependencies: the lists of uniforms, inputs, outputs, textures, streams, and temporary variables used by every program object. All of these lists are accessible using STL (standard template library) iterators. These iterators can be dereferenced, incremented, and compared to one another. The available iterator accessors are given in Table 10.1.

Several functions are also available to make setting up program objects more convenient. These *descriptor* functions return human-readable strings describing some aspect of an **ShProgram**. For instance, rather than trying to figure out the results of the rules for binding a vertex shader to the vertex attributes in OpenGL, you can just ask the shader to describe the binding it requires, and it will generate a report that states which OpenGL vertex attributes will get bound to which vertex shader inputs. The descriptor functions are listed in Table 10.2.

Programs, like most other Sh objects, also have all the metadata provided by the **ShMeta** class, as explained in Section 7.7. This is also true for the variables made available through the iterators listed in Table 10.1. The describers access

```
typedef std::list<ShVariableNodePtr> VarList;
  Variable node container
typedef std::list<ShTextureNodePtr> TextureList;
  Texture node container
typedef std::list<ShChannelNodePtr> ChannelList;
  Channel node container
```

```
VarList::iterator begin_inputs()
  SH_INPUT variable nodes
VarList::iterator end_inputs()
  SH_INPUT variable nodes
VarList::iterator begin_outputs()
  SH_OUTPUT variable nodes
VarList::iterator end_outputs()
  SH_OUTPUT variable nodes
VarList::iterator begin_parameters()
  Uniform parameter nodes
VarList::iterator end_parameters()
  Uniform parameter nodes
VarList::iterator begin_temps()
  Local (internal) variable nodes
VarList::iterator end_temps()
  Local (internal) variable nodes
TextureList::iterator begin_textures()
  Texture nodes accessed in program
TextureList::iterator end_textures()
  Texture nodes accessed in program
ChannelList::iterator begin_channels()
  Stream channel nodes accessed in program
ChannelList::iterator end_channels()
  Stream channel nodes accessed in program
```

Table 10.1. Accessor iterators for **ShProgram** objects.

```
describe_bindings()
  human-readable binding description under current backend
describe_bindings(std::string target)
  human-readable binding description for target
describe_interface()
  human-readable description of inputs and outputs
```

Table 10.2. Describer member functions for **ShProgram** objects. All these functions return std::strings.

this metadata to make a report. A describer function is really querying the metadata of the objects on which the program depends. Note that you have to actually provide this data, such as names and titles, for the describers to be useful.

10.4   Algebra

As shaders and stream program objects become larger and more complex the ability to reuse and encapsulate code and data becomes more important. The Sh toolkit, due to its close integration with C++, can support many standard forms of modularity such as functions, overloaded operators, classes, namespaces, and separate compilation.

However, additional forms of modularity are possible. A dataflow model, for instance, is very natural for both shaders and stream programs. In a dataflow language, modules are connected by pipes, and data flows from one end of the network to another. We use the term dataflow loosely to mean any form of modularity that supports this network structure; both data-driven and event-driven, synchronous and asynchronous dataflow models have been developed. Visual dataflow languages are often used for end-user programming in modelling, image processing, signal processing, numerical, and animation applications, such as Houdini, Maya, LabView, and Khoros. Visual dataflow languages, in turn, are related to functional languages, where higher-order functions provide useful forms of modularity not supported directly by C++, such as currying.

An algebra consists of a set of operators and a set of objects which is closed under application of those operators. To support dataflow and functional forms of modularity, Sh supports an algebra over program objects [91]. Using the operators in this algebra, we can manipulate and specialize program objects without having to modify (or even have access to) the source code of the original shaders.

It should be emphasized that the operators in the algebra do not simply build a multipass network. Shader algebra operations are compiled, not interpreted. They actually operate on the internal representation of program objects to build a completely new program object, which is ultimately run through the full suite of optimizations and virtualizations supported by the Sh backend. The resulting implementations are as efficient as if the programs had been built from scratch or with the use of library functions. Even if a multipass implementation is eventually executed after virtualization, the components of the multipass implementation need not have any particular relationship to the components used in a shader algebra expression.

Two operators are defined: connection, which is defined as functional composition or application, and combination, which is equivalent in the case of Sh to concatenation of source code. These operators are defined over shader objects, in which case they create new shader objects. These operators in effect create a functional language, in which program objects are treated as functions that take an ordered sequence of n inputs and map them to an ordered sequence of m outputs.

10.4.1   Connection

Suppose we have a shader object q1 with n inputs and k outputs and another shader object p1 with k inputs and m outputs. The *connection* operator creates a new shader object with n inputs and m outputs by taking the outputs of q1 and feeding them in the same order to the inputs of p1. In other words, it performs functional composition.

We denote this operator in Sh using the "<<" operator, with inputs on the right and outputs on the left. For instance, the k outputs of q1 can connected to the k inputs of p1 using "p1 << q1".

The outputs of q1 must match the inputs of p1 in number, size, and type (both storage and semantic). These are checked dynamically at C++ runtime.

The connection operator can also be used to apply a program to tuple or stream data, and to convert an attribute input to a parameter input. An inverse ">>" is also supported to convert parameters to inputs. This is discussed in more detail in Section 10.8.

10.4.2   Combination

Suppose we are given two shader objects p2 and q2. Let p2 have n inputs and m outputs, and let q2 have k inputs and ℓ outputs. We define the *combination* of p2 and q2 to have $n+k$ inputs and $m+\ell$ outputs, with the inputs and outputs of p2 appearing first, followed by the inputs and outputs of q2. The computations of p2 and q2 are both performed, with the local variables of each in different scopes.

We denote the combination operator in Sh using "&", the combination of p2 and q2 is denoted by "p2 & q2". Note that "&" binds more loosely than "<<".

Because of the way Sh is defined, the combination operator is, in fact, equivalent to the concatenation of the source code of the input shaders, using two separate scopes. Such a concatenation would ensure that the inputs and outputs of p2 are declared before q2, and so would give the same result as defined above.

For vertex and fragment shaders, a special ***ShPosition*** semantic type is defined which is semantically equivalent to an ***ShPoint*** but binds to the special position input and output of these shader units on GPUs. The last definition always dominates, so if a position is computed in two shaders that are combined, only the position in the second shader will be used, and the first position will be converted to a point. This is important when combining two shaders each of which have an ***ShPosition*** declaration.

The combination operator can also be used to combine channels of data into streams for use in the implementation of Sh's stream processing model. This is discussed in more detail in Section 10.8.

10.5   Nibbles

Connecting and combining existing programs using the algebra operators can result in redundant computation. The optimizer can only do so much, especially if redundant inputs or outputs are present, or the same computation is expressed in different ways.

Fortunately, the "<<" operator, in conjunction with the optimizer in the Sh compiler (particularly dead code removal), and the definition of some simple "glue" programs, can be used to specialize program objects and eliminate redundant computation.

For instance, suppose we combine two program objects and the resulting program computes the same value twice (in two different ways, so we cannot discover this fact automatically). We can define a simple program that copies its inputs to its outputs *except* for one of the redundant results. This "discard" program can be connected to the output of the combined shader and the Sh dead code eliminator will remove the redundant computation.

Nibbles are functions that build and return small ***ShPrograms*** that support primitive, but useful, operations. These primitives can be used to glue together other program objects, or even to generate new programs from scratch. You can combine nibbles using the shader algebra operators to generate many useful programs. The shader algebra operators provide a functional language, and the nibbles are the basic functions from which other functions can be built.

10.5.1   Interface Adaptation and Specialization

The supported interface manipulation nibbles include the following:

keep<T>(int n = 1):
    Generates a program that copies n channels of type T from its input to its output. The names of the channels are retained if they are set.

`keep<T>(const std::string & name):`
> Generates a program that passes through one input of type `T` with the given name on both input and output.

`lose<T>(int n = 1):`
> Generates a program that reads n channels of type `T` from its input and discards them (no outputs).

`lose<T>(const std::string & name):`
> Generates a program that reads one channel of type `T` from its input with the given name (this is really just a sanity check) and discards it.

`dup<T>(int n=2, const std::string & name = ""):`
> Generates a program that reads one input channel of the given type `T` and creates n duplicates on its output. An optional name can be given that is checked against the input. However, the outputs are unnamed (since they would be ambiguous if they all had the same name).

Combinations of `keep`, `lose`, and `dup` with "`&`" can be used to describe mappings that retain or make copies of a subset of outputs.

Sh also provides manipulator versions of this functionality, described in Section 10.6. To distinguish the two, these particular nibbles use a lower-case naming convention like that of the standard library rather than the `sh` prefix convention used by other nibbles. You should use the manipulator versions if you want to avoid specifying type information. Also, manipulators are available for specifying general swizzles, extractions, and insertions.

10.5.2   Passthrough

The `shOutputPass` nibble function generates a passthrough program that copies the outputs of a given **ShProgram** and keeps all the names. This is like the `keep` nibble, but it uses a program as an argument and can generate a glue program with different types on different channels. The `shInputPass` function does the same thing for the inputs of a given **ShProgram**. This is useful in cases where vertex shader outputs need to be duplicated before being passed to the fragment shader.

```
ShProgram shOutputPass (
  const ShProgram & p
);
ShProgram shInputPass (
  const ShProgram & p
);
```

10.5.3 Texture Access

The shAccess nibble generates an *ShProgram* that takes a texture coordinate as input and performs a texture lookup. The return type of the lookup is the storage type of the texture. The shAccess nibble is overloaded on all built-in texture types, as shown in Listing 10.1.

```
template<typename T>
ShProgram shAccess (
    const ShBaseTexture1D<T> &tex,
    const std::string & output_name = "result"
    const std::string & input_name = "u"      // ShTexCoord1f
);
template<typename T>
ShProgram shAccess (
    const ShBaseTexture2D<T> &tex,
    const std::string & output_name = "result",
    const std::string & input_name = "u"      // ShTexCoord2f
);
template<typename T>
ShProgram shAccess (
    const ShBaseTextureRect<T> &tex,
    const std::string & output_name = "result",
    const std::string & input_name = "u"      // ShTexCoord2f
);
template<typename T>
ShProgram shAccess (
    const ShBaseTexture3D<T> &tex,
    const std::string & output_name = "result",
    const std::string & input_name = "u"      // ShTexCoord3f
);
template<typename T>
ShProgram shAccess (
    const ShBaseTextureCube<T> &tex,
    const std::string & output_name = "result",
    const std::string & input_name = "u"      // ShVector3f
);
```

Listing 10.1. Access nibbles.

10.5.4 Type and Size Conversion

The casting nibble shCast generates a program that casts an input of tuple type T to type T2. If the number of elements of T is less than the number of elements of T2, this nibble pads the result tuple with 0 components at the end.

If the opposite is true, it truncates the result tuple. In other words, it has the same behavior as the `cast` library function.

```
template<typename T, typename T2>
ShProgram shCast(
  const std::string & output_name = "result",
  const std::string & input_name = "x"
);
```

The fill-casting nibble `shFillcast` casts from tuple type T to type T2, with the same semantics as the `fillcast` library function. If the number of elements in T is less than the number of elements in T2, the generated program pads with copies of the last component at the end.

```
template<typename T, typename T2>
ShProgram shFillcast (
  const std::string & output_name = "result",
  const std::string & input_name = "x"
);
```

10.5.5 Transformations

The transformation nibble `shTransform` creates an *ShProgram* that transforms a variable of type T2 by a matrix of type *ShMatrix*<Rows, Cols, Binding, T>.

```
template<typename T2, int Rows, int Cols,
        ShBindingType Binding, typename T>
ShProgram shTransform (
  const ShMatrix<Rows, Cols, Binding, T> &M,
  const std::string & output_name = "result",
  const std::string & input_name = "x"
);
```

10.5.6 Basis Conversion

The basis conversion nibble function `shChangeBasis` generates a program that takes three vectors defining an orthonormal basis and projects the fourth vector onto them, returning the coordinates of the vector in the new basis.

```
ShProgram shChangeBasis (
    const std::string & output_name="result",
```

```
    const std::string & input_name0="v0",
    const std::string & input_name1="v1",
    const std::string & input_name2="v2"
);
```

10.5.7   Primitive Computations

There are also nibbles corresponding to all unary library functions and operators. These nibbles all have one input and one output. By default the input
is named "x" and the output is named "result" (although both can be configured). For example, nibbles for shAbs, shCos, shAcos, shSin, shAsin,
shFrac, shSqrt, shNeg (negate), shNormalize, and shPos all exist. All the
unary nibbles have similar interfaces. We only give one:

```
template<typename T> ShProgram shAbs (
  const std::string & output_name = "result",
  const std::string & input_name = "x"
);
```

Nibbles are also defined for all of the binary library functions and operators. These nibbles all have two inputs and one output. By default the first
input is named "x, " the second input is named "y, " and the output is named
"result" (although all three can be configured). For example, shAdd, shSub,
shMul, shDiv, shDot, shPow, shSlt, shSle, shSgt, shSge, shSeq, shSne,
shFmod, shMin, and shMax are all defined. Note in particular the names of
the Boolean functions (set less-than, set less-than-or-equal, etc.). All the binary
nibbles have similar interfaces. We only give one:

```
template<typename T> ShProgram shAdd (
  const std::string & output_name = "result",
  const std::string & input_name0 = "x",
  const std::string & input_name1 = "y"
);
```

Lastly, ternary functions also have corresponding nibbles, in particular
shLerp and shCond. The shLerp nibble has two type parameters, the type of
the interpolation parameter and the type of the value to be interpolated. If only
one type is given, these are assumed to be the same.

```
template<typename T1, typename T2 = T1> ShProgram shLerp (
  const std::string & output_name = "result",
  const std::string & input_name0 = "t",
```

```
  const std::string & input_name1 = "x",
  const std::string & input_name2 = "y"
);
```

The function shCond takes two type parameters: the type of the conditional and the type of the two values to choose from. Again, these are assumed to be the same by default.

```
template<typename T1, typename T2 = T1> ShProgram shCond (
  const std::string & output_name = "result",
  const std::string & input_name0 = "t",
  const std::string & input_name1 = "x",
  const std::string & input_name2 = "y"
);
```

10.6 Manipulators

Unfortunately, to satisfy the type rules for connecting program objects using the shader algebra operators, we need to define compatible interfaces in advance. This is annoying if all we want to do is rearrange the inputs and outputs of a shader. We would like to be able to specify simple rearrangements inline, within an expression, and have the system figure out the details. For example, if we just want to eliminate an output to specialize a shader, it would be nice if we didn't have to fully specify the type of the output we are trying to eliminate.

Sh provides some shortcuts, similar to manipulators in the C++ iostream library, for manipulating the input and output channels of shaders. These manipulators are really functions that return instances of special manipulator classes. Manipulator classes store information about the particular manipulation required. When connected to a program object in an expression, the appropriate glue program is automatically generated, using introspection over the programs it is connected with, to perform the desired manipulation. This mechanism automatically resolves type issues. Manipulators can also be combined with each other using shader algebra operators to create more complex manipulations. However, manipulators are limited to interface adaptation. For more complex operations, ordinary program objects are necessary.

There are two kinds of manipulators: those that operate on a fixed number of channels (which we call atomic), and expandable manipulators that "grow" to consume all channels available. Atomic (fixed) manipulators can be combined with each other and with program objects using both the "&" and "<<" operators to create more complex manipulations. Expandable manipulators can only be combined with programs and other manipulators using the "<<" operator.

10.6.1 Fixed Manipulators

Fixed manipulators include the following:

shKeep(int n = 1): Represents an operation that copies n channels of any type. The names are retained if they are set.

shKeep(const std::string & name): Represents an operation that copies one channel (which must have the given name).

shLose(int n = 1): Represents an operation that reads n channels and discards them (no outputs).

shLose(const std::string & name): Represents an operation that reads one channel and discards it (no outputs). The input is checked against the name if it is provided (as a sanity check).

shDup(int n = 2, const std::string & name = ""): Represents an operation that duplicates one channel n times. An optional name can be given that is checked against the channel. However, the outputs are unnamed.

Combinations of the manipulator objects returned by shKeep, shLose, and shDup with "&" can be used to describe mappings that retain and optionally create duplicates of an arbitrary subset of outputs.

Sh also provides nibble versions of this functionality, described in Section 10.5. To distinguish the two, the nibbles use a lower-case naming convention like that of the standard library: keep, lose, and dup. You should use the nibble versions if you *want* type checking.

10.6.2 Expandable Manipulators

Expandable manipulators include the following:

shExtract(T i): Moves the referenced channel to the beginning of the attribute list, rearranging the other channels to close the gap.

shInsert(T i): Moves the first channel to the referenced channel, rearranging the other channels as necessary.

shDrop(T i): Discards the referenced channel and rearranges the other channels to close the gap.

shSwizzle(T i0, T i1, ...): Performs a swizzle of the given indices. The channels are rearranged into the order given by the arguments. Note that duplication and deletion of channels is also possible. This manipulator accepts between 1 and 10 indices.

shRange(T i0)(T i1, T i2): Takes an arbitrary sequence of (T i) (to identify a single channel) or (T i1, T i2) (to identify a channel range) postfixes. This manipulator is an alternative form for specifying a swizzle.

These manipulators all need to identify the channels on which they act. To identify channels by position an integer is used for T. Negative numbers may be used to specify the position of a channel counted from the end of the attribute list, with -1 identifying the last channel. Channels can also be identified by name, using **const char** * for T.

Note that names are not automatically assigned to Sh variables, since C++ has no standard way to find out the names of its own variables. A name method is therefore provided on most Sh types to provide string names for such identification purposes; see Section 7.7. (Other string metadata can also be attached for introspection purposes.)

The shInsert manipulator is useful when combined with currying, described later, to replace a named attribute with a parameter, or when you just want to refer to inputs by name rather than position. The shExtract manipulator is handy if you want to reference the outputs of a program by name rather than position. The shSwizzle (not to be confused with the swizzle operator on tuples) and shRange manipulators are generally useful when "adapting" the interface of some program objects to others, or to the order in which data is presented.

These manipulators cannot handle all possible cases. In particular, types are retained, and sometimes extra computation (such as normalization of vectors) is required. Manipulators are just a convenience; more complex adaptation of the input and output of shaders, including type casts and any additional computation required, can be accomplished by using either nibbles or defining suitable "glue" programs.

All manipulators can be attached (using the << operator) to either the outputs (on the left-hand side) or the inputs (on the right-hand side) of a program. Note that standard C++ precedence for << is left-to-right, and hence parentheses may be needed to achieve the desired effect.

10.7   Kernels

The Sh library includes implementations of some standard program kernels; these are functions to generate parameterized shader objects. Kernel programs are designed to be used immediately, specialized, or combined with other kernels to build useful custom shaders using shader algebra operations.

Several design decisions were made in an attempt to keep the kernel library easy to use:

- Commonly curried inputs are placed at the beginning of the input list to reduce the need for manipulators.

- All inputs and outputs are named (have name metadata attached) which allows manipulation and selection by name.

- Names for inputs and outputs that should be joined together on connection have the same name and type and are usually in the same order. This allows these kernels to be connected by position or by name without complex manipulator expressions.

In the following subsections, we will describe the available kernel generators. For each, we will give a list of input and output attributes together with their string names and positional ordering. Negative positions denote position from the end (-1 means last attribute, -2 means second last, etc.). Note that negative positions are accepted by manipulators.

> The interface to some of the more complicated kernels described here may change in the future. Since the Shader Algebra is a fairly new addition to Sh, these kernels are still being developed and may not yet have the ideal interface.

10.7.1 Universal Vertex Shader Kernel

The shVsh kernel function is a generalized vertex program generator. It creates a "universal" vertex shader that can generate many common attributes required by fragment shaders. There are some construction parameters, but you can also just generate a shader with this function and then specialize it, for instance, to discard the half vector or tangents if you don't need them. Its definition is given as follows:

```
template<ShBindingType B, typename T>
ShProgram shVsh (
    const ShMatrix<4, 4, B, T> &MV,      // MCS to VCS transformation
    const ShMatrix<4, 4, B, T> &VM,      // VCS to MCS transformation
    const ShMatrix<4, 4, B, T> &MD,      // MCS to DCS transformation
    const ShMatrix<3, 3, B, T> &T,       // texture transformation
```

```
    int num_tangents = 0,
    int num_lights = 1,
    int use_scs = 0,
    int provide_scs_frame = 0,
);
```

This function generates a program with the following inputs and outputs, which are given these precise names:

Inputs: 0: ***ShTexCoord2f*** u; surface texture coordinate.

  1: ***ShNormal3f*** nm; normal vector (MCS).

  2: ***ShVector3f*** tm; primary tangent (MCS);
        only included if num_tangents > 0.

  *: ***ShVector3f*** sm; secondary tangent (MCS);
        only included if num_tangents > 1.

  *: ***ShPoint3f*** lpvi; light position (VCS);
        for $i = 0 \ldots$ num_lights $- 1$.

  -1: ***ShPosition4f*** pm; vertex position (MCS).

Outputs: 0: ***ShTexCoord2f*** u; transformed surface texture coordinate.

  1: ***ShPoint3f*** pv; vertex position (VCS).

  2: ***ShPoint4f*** pm; vertex position (MCS).

  3: ***ShNormal3f*** nv; normal vector (VCS).

  4: ***ShVector3f*** tv; primary tangent (VCS);
        only included if num_tangents > 0.

  *: ***ShVector3f*** sv; secondary tangent (VCS);
        only included if num_tangents > 0.

  *: ***ShVector3f*** vv; view vector (VCS).

  *: ***ShVector3f*** hv; half vector (VCS);
        equals hv0.

  *: ***ShVector3f*** hv$i$; half vector (VCS),
        for $i = 0 \ldots$ num_lights $- 1$.

  *: ***ShVector3f*** lwv; light vector (VCS);
        equals lwv0.

  *: ***ShVector3f*** lwv$i$; light vector (VCS),
        for $i = 0 \ldots$ num_lights $- 1$.

  *: ***ShVector3f*** lpv; light position (VCS);
        equals lpv0.

  *: ***ShPoint3f*** lpv$i$; light position (VCS),
        for $i = 0 \ldots$ num_lights $- 1$.

  *: ***ShNormal3f*** ns; normal vector (SCS).

  *: ***ShVector3f*** vs; view vector (SCS).

     *: ***ShVector3f*** hs; half vector (SCS);
             equals hs0.

     *: ***ShVector3f*** hs$i$; half vector (SCS),
             for $i = 0 \ldots$ num_lights $- 1$.

     *: ***ShVector3f*** lws; light vector (SCS);
             equals lws0.

     *: ***ShVector3f*** lws$i$; light vector (SCS),
           for $i = 0 \ldots$ num_lights $- 1$.

    -1: ***ShPosition4f*** pd; position (HDCS).

If num_tangents is 0, then tv and sv are not included in the inputs. In this case, no surface coordinate frame outputs will be included either. If num_tangents is 1, then only one tangent is given an input. In this case, sv is computed from the normal nv and the single tv. All surface coordinate outputs are valid. If num_tangent is greater than or equal to 2, then the first two tangents on the input are taken to define a surface coordinate frame; the rest are just transformed.

All other kernels in this section generate fragment shaders designed, generally, to interact with this particular vertex shader.

10.7.2 Surface Shader Kernels

These kernels implement various basic lighting models at the fragment level. These lighting models are actually defined in a coordinate-free manner and so, as long as all vectors are consistent, vectors in the VCS, MCS, or SCS can be used. To make it easier to plug shaders together, we drop the coordinate system suffix from names when the coordinate system does not matter.

Diffuse. The shDiffuse kernel function generates a fragment program for diffuse lighting. This does not do much; it just passes through the interpolated diffuse color given it on its input, after multiplying it by the irradiance color from the light source.

```
template<typename T>
ShProgram shDiffuse();
```

It creates an ***ShProgram*** with the following interface:

Inputs: 0: T *kd*; diffuse coefficient.
           1: T irrad; irradiance from the light source.
           2: ***ShNormal3f*** n; normal.

3: *ShVector3f* `lw`; light direction vector.

4: *ShPosition4f* `pd`; position (HDCS).

Outputs: 0: `T` `c`; result color.

The `specular` kernel is coordinate-system independent, so n, h, and lw can be in any space (as long as it is the same space for all three vectors).

Specular. The `shBlinnPhongSpecular` kernel function generates a fragment program that computes a Blinn-Phong highlight.

```
template<typename T>
ShProgram specular();
```

It creates an *ShProgram* with the following interface:

Inputs: 0: `T` `ks`; specular coefficient.

1: *ShAttrib1f* `spec_exp`; specular exponent.

2: `T` `irrad`; irradiance from the light source.

3: *ShNormal3f* `n`; normal.

4: *ShVector3f* `h`; half vector.

5: *ShVector3f* `lw`; light vector.

6: *ShPosition4f* `pd`; position (HDCS).

Outputs: 0: `T` `c`; result color.

The `specular` kernel is coordinate-system independent, so n, h, and lw can be in any space (as long as it is the same space for all three vectors).

Blinn-Phong. The `shBlinnPhong` kernel function generates a fragment program that combines the effects of the `shDiffuse` and `shBlinnPhong` kernels.

```
template<typename T>
ShProgram shBlinnPhong();
```

It creates an *ShProgram* with the following interface:

Inputs: 0: `T` `kd`; diffuse coefficient.

1: `T` `ks`; specular coefficient.

2: *ShAttrib1f* `spec_exp`; specular exponent.

3: `T` `irrad`; irradiance from the light source.

4: *ShNormal3f* `n`; normal.

5: *ShVector3f* `h`; half vector.

6: *ShVector3f* `lw`; light vector.

7: *ShPosition4f* `pd`; position (HDCS).

Outputs: 0: `T` `c`; result color.

The phong kernel is coordinate-system independent, so n, h, and lw can be in any space (as long as it is the same space for all three vectors).

Gooch. The shGooch kernel function generate a fragment program that computes Gooch illustrative shading [49].

```
template<typename T>
ShProgram shGooch();
```

It creates an *ShProgram* with the following interface:

Inputs: 0: T kd; diffuse coefficient.
             1: T cool; cool multiplier,
                   when $l \mid n = -1$.
             2: T warm; warm multiplier,
                   when $l \mid n = 1$.
             3: T irrad; irradiance from the light source.
             4: *ShNormal3f* n; normal.
             5: *ShVector3f* lw; light vector.
             6: *ShPosition4f* pd; position (HDCS).
Outputs: 0: T c; result color.

The shGooch kernel is coordinate-system independent, so n and lw can be in any space (as long as it is the same space for both).

Identity. The shIdentity kernel generates a surface shader that does nothing, just copies its irradiance to its output.

```
template<typename T>
ShProgram shIdentity();
```

It creates an *ShProgram* with the following interface:

Inputs: 0: T irrad; irradiance from the light source.
             1: *ShPosition4f* pd; position (HDCS).
Outputs: 0: T c; result (copy of irrad).

10.7.3   Light Shader Kernels

Light kernels are designed to be connected to the vertex shader outputs from a universal vertex shader. Each outputs one irrad output representing the irradiance at a surface of type T (usually *ShColor3f*).

Point Light Kernel. The shPointLight kernel builds a shader that represents a point source.

```
template<typename T>
ShProgram shPointLight();
```

It generates an *ShProgram* with the following interface:

Inputs: 0: T lc; color and power of source.
Inputs: 0: T lp; position of source.
Outputs: 0: T irrad; irradiance.

Spot Light Kernel. The shSpotLight kernel builds a shader that has a linear falloff from the light vector in the same direction as the given direction vector to zero at the falloff angle.

```
template<typename T>
ShProgram shSpotLight();
```

It generates an *ShProgram* with the following interface:

Inputs: 0: T lc; color and power of source.
            1: *ShAttrib1f* falloff; angle in radians
                    where spotlight intensity begins to decrease.
            2: *ShAttrib1f* angle; angle in radians
                    where spotlight intensity equals 0.
            3: *ShVector3f* direction; direction light faces.
            4: *ShPoint3f* lp; light position.
            5: *ShPoint3f* p; surface point position.
Outputs: 0: T irrad; irradiance.

Projector Light Kernel. This light source projects a texture onto a surface like a slide projector (except it does not itself handle shadows). This kernel is really a spotlight with a texture instead of a fixed falloff function.

```
template<typename T>
ShProgram shProjectorLight(const ShBaseTexture2D<T> &tex);
```

It generates an *ShProgram* with the following interface:

Inputs: 0: *ShAttrib1f* scale; scaling on the texture (tiles).
            1: *ShAttrib1f* angle; angle in radians
                    for field of view of light.
            2: *ShVector3f* direction; direction light faces.

3: **ShVector3f** up; up direction of light,
     must be orthogonal to direction.
4: **ShPoint3f** lp; light position.
5: **ShPoint3f** p; surface point position.

Outputs: 0: T irrad; irradiance.

10.7.4 Surface Map Kernels

These kernels modify some surface property.

SCS Bump Map Kernel. This takes a two-dimensional gradient vector (usually acquired from a texture lookup, where the texture value in turn was obtained by differencing values in a height field) and the base normal represented relative to the surface coordinate space. It computes a perturbed normal represented relative to the surface coordinate space. Note that we do not use the space suffix to make it easier to hook this up to other shaders, but that it will only work with normals expressed relative to the SCS.

ShProgram shBumpMapSCS();

It generates an **ShProgram** with the following interface:

Input: 0: **ShAttrib2f** gradient; gradient
            1: **ShNormal3f** n; normalized normal vector (SCS).
Output: 0: **ShNormal3f** n; perturbed normal (SCS).

Bump Map Kernel. This does the same thing as SCS bump mapping, but in an arbitrary space (such as view space). It needs an explicit surface frame, because what it really has to do is transform the perturbed normal from the surface coordinate frame back out to the given coordinate frame. It computes the perturbed normal in the SCS then uses those coordinates to create a linear combination of the vectors in the given surface frame.

ShProgram shBumpMap();

It generates an **ShProgram** with the following interface:

Input: 0: **ShVector2f** gradient; gradient vector
            1: **ShVector3f** t; normalized tangent vector.
            2: **ShVector3f** s; normalized secondary tangent.
            3: **ShNormal3f** n; normalized normal vector.
Output: 0: **ShNormal3f** n; perturbed normal.

All vectors should be in the same space.

10.7.5   Postprocessing Kernels

These are postprocessing kernels, which modify the output color in some way, creating a new output color. Several postprocessing kernels can be connected together to create a more complicated postprocessing kernel.

Simple postprocessing kernels take an input of type T and return one output of type T named `result`. More complex postprocessing kernels might require extra information, such as the texture coordinates of each surface point, or the position.

Halftoning Kernel. The `halftone` function generates a kernel that performs halftoning/hatching independently in each color channel. A texture provided as an argument is tiled and used as a threshold image, indexed by texture coordinates passed as inputs. A value of 1 is output if the input is larger than the corresponding component in the texture; otherwise, 0 is output. Intermediate values will also be output for halftoning. (The threshold is actually a smooth step.)

```
template<typename T>
ShProgram shHalftone(const ShBaseTexture2D<T> &tex);
```

It generates an **ShProgram** with the following interface:

Inputs: 0: T c; output from previous set of shaders.
     1: **ShTexCoord2f** tc; texture coordinate for lookup.
Outputs: 0: T c; result

Noise-Adding Kernel. The `shNoisify` kernel function generates a shader that adds noise to some attribute, such as a rendered image.

```
template<typename T, int N>
ShProgram shNoisify();
```

It generates an **ShProgram** with the following interface:

Inputs: 0: **ShAttrib1f** noise_scale; scaling on cell noise.
     1: T c; value to be perturbed.
     2: **ShAttrib**<N> tc; coordinate used for noise.
Outputs: 0: T c; result

10.8   Streams

Stream objects, which hold sequences of data to be operated upon by programs compiled to a "cpu:stream" or "gpu:stream" compilation target, are represented in Sh using the ***ShChannel*** template class and ***ShStream*** class.

A channel is a sequence of elements of the type given as its template argument. Channels are an abstraction and the channel data representation is opaque, but channel data can be used as a vertex array input. The Sh runtime attempts to use the most efficient operations and representations available for managing buffers. Updates to data are timestamped to avoid data transfers whenever possible.

Streams are containers for several channels of data, and are specified by combining channels (or other streams) with the "&" operator. Streams only *refer* to channels, they do not create copies. However, streams may not refer to themselves as components. A channel can still be referenced as a separate object and can also be referenced by more than one stream at once. For convenience, an ***ShChannel*** of any type can also be used directly as a single-channel stream.

Sh uses a reference-counting garbage collection scheme; most Sh types are in fact smart pointers to separate data items. Even if a channel is destroyed (explicitly or implicitly), if a stream refers to this data the memory will not be released.

In addition to being viewed as a sequence of channels, a stream can also be seen as a sequence of homogeneous records, each record being a sequence of elements from each component channel. Stream programs conceptually map an input record type to an output record type. If an ***ShProgram*** is compiled using a "stream" compilation target, it can be applied to streams. Stream programs are applied in parallel (conceptually) to all records in the stream.

The *connect* operator is overloaded to permit the application of stream programs to streams. For instance, a stream program p can be applied to an input stream a and its output directed to an output stream b as follows:

```
b = p << a;
```

When specified, the above stream operation will execute immediately and will return when it is complete. (Later on, we plan to add a retained mode to permit greater optimization.) At the point of execution, Sh will check (dynamically) that the input and output types of the program match the types of the input and output streams.

Use of "p << a" alone creates an unevaluated program kernel, which is given the type ***ShProgram*** (and can be assigned to a variable of this type, if the user does not want execution to happen immediately). Internally, input attributes are replaced with fetch operators in the intermediate language representation of the program. These fetch operators are initialized to refer to the given stream's channels. Such program objects can also be interpreted as a "procedural stream." Only when this unevaluated procedural stream is assigned to an output stream is the kernel executed.

The implementation of the << operator permits currying. If a program object is applied to a stream with an insufficient number of channels, an unevaluated program with fewer inputs is returned. This program requires the remainder of its inputs before it can execute.

In a functional language, currying is usually implemented with deferred execution. Since, in a pure functional language, values in variables cannot be changed after they are set, this is equivalent to using the value in effect at the point of the curry. However, in an imperative language, we are free to modify the value provided to the curried expression. We *could* copy the value at the point of the curry, but this would be expensive for stream data. Instead, we use deferred read semantics: later execution of the program will use the value of the stream in effect at the point of actual execution, *not* the value in effect at the point of the currying. This is useful in practice, as we can create (and optimize) a network of kernels and streams in advance and then execute them iteratively.

The "<<" operator can also be used to apply programs to Sh tuples. A mixture of tuple and stream inputs may be used. In this case, the tuple is interpreted as a stream, all of whose elements are the same value. The same by-reference semantics are applied for consistency. In effect, what happens is that an input "varying" attribute is converted into a "uniform" parameter—a useful operation.

Since we provide an operator for turning a varying attribute into a uniform parameter, we also provide an inverse operator for turning a parameter into an attribute. Given program object p and parameter object x, the following removes the dependence of p on x, creating a new program object q:

```
ShProgram q = p >> x;
```

The parameter is replaced by a new attribute of the same type, pushed onto the *end* of the input attribute list.

The "&" operator can also be applied to streams, channels, or tuples on the left-hand side of an assignment. This can be used to split apart the output of a kernel. For instance, let a, b, and c be channels or streams, and let x, y, and z be streams, channels, or tuples. Then the following binds a program p to inputs, executes it, and extracts the individual channels of the output:

```
(a & b & c) = p << x << y << z;
```

This syntax also permits Sh programs to be used as subroutines (let all of a, b, c, x, y, and z be tuples).

Chapter 11

Control Constructs

C++ control constructs can be used to manipulate Sh programs. These control constructs are not seen or processed by the Sh compiler, which only sees the operation sequences generated by them. However, C++ if statements can be used to selectively include variations in an Sh program, and C++ for, while, and do/until constructs can be used to repeat parts of Sh shaders.

C++ control constructs can only depend on compile-time (C++ run-time) values, not values computed in a shader itself. In this manner, C++ is effectively a macro language for Sh.

To express data-dependent control constructs, Sh supports a set of C++ macros that can encode control construct keywords into the operation stream processed by Sh. These keywords act semantically much like C++ keywords, but have a syntax more in line with that of Algol. In particular, there are special keywords to mark the end of each different kind of control construct. There are also a few other minor differences having to do with the need to encode these keywords as macros. There can be no space between an Sh keyword and its arguments, and the arguments to Sh keywords with multiple arguments, such as *SH_FOR*, must be separated by commas, not semicolons.

Each statement subsequence inside an Sh control construct is automatically given a new scope, as if it were wrapped in "{}" braces. Additional braces are not necessary; they are already included in the macros. Because of this, Sh control constructs must be properly nested with C++ control constructs. The basic nesting properties of the Sh control constructs will also be checked at C++ compile time. However, detailed syntax checking will not take place until C++ run-time when the shader definition code is actually executed, the shader is built, and Sh runs a recursive-descent parser over the operation sequence to reconstruct the parse tree of the Sh program.

> You should include the braces around bodies of Sh control constructs. This is useful partly for ease of reading but also as a hint to code editors to indent the contained lines appropriately. Similarily, putting a semicolon after the **SH_END*** keywords will avoid confusion on the part of the syntax highlighter.

The arguments to Sh control construct keywords can be arbitrary expressions, including C++ functions, which can themselves invoke arbitrary sequences of Sh control constructs.

We plan to support data-dependent control constructs for as many compilation targets as possible, but for some compilation targets it may not be feasible, or may be inefficient. For instance, for GeForceFX and ATI Radeon 9700 GPUs, we have demonstrated that it is possible to support true data-dependent control flow using multiple passes, even though data-dependent branches are not supported in the machine language. Our implementation provides true conditional execution, not just SIMD-style conditional assignment; computation is actually avoided, as necessary for proper implementation of general iteration. However, our approach is still highly experimental at this point and can only be supported in stream programs and not shaders. This latter restriction is due to the way Sh interacts with the graphics API. (Sh cannot at present invoke multiple renderings with the same geometry.)

11.1   Selection

Sh supports two styles of conditional execution, indicated by the **SH_IF** and **SH_WHEN** keyword sets. Both sets of keywords support the same semantics but have different execution models. The implementation of **SH_IF** tries to actually avoid the execution of the computation specified in the sequence of statements it guards. The implementation of **SH_WHEN** executes *all* operation sequences and then discards unneeded results. The first execution model results in multipass execution or branches and may have additional overhead, but should be used if the cost of executing the body is large or possibly non-terminating. The **SH_WHEN** construct should be used when the cost of the body is low.

> Only **SH_IF** is currently implemented. We are planning to add support for **SH_WHEN** soon, but in the meantime you can make use of the cond() library function to perform conditional assignment.

The compiler will take the use of either conditional control construct as a (strong) hint only and may choose to use the alternative execution model in some circumstances. For instance, if **SH_IF** is used around a very short body and the compiler determines that conditional assignment will always be cheaper than multipass execution, then conditional assignment will be used. On the other hand, if the body of an **SH_WHEN** includes a loop that cannot be unrolled (for which termination in a finite number of steps cannot be guaranteed) then it may be necessary to use true conditional execution. Sh will not use the conditional assignment model for operation sequences it cannot prove will terminate, even if **SH_WHEN** is specified. However, in all cases Sh will preserve the semantics of the program specified by the user.

> Sh does not currently support a `switch` statement. Sh compilation targets operate primarily on floating-point values, where equality comparisons are not reliable and integer clamping is expensive, so a `switch` statement does not make much sense. One could imagine a `switch`-like statement with a set of intervals instead of exact values given, but this would not give much syntactic convenience over a list of **SH_ELSEIF**s, and would be unlikely to provide additional efficiency. However, an **SH_SWITCH**/**SH_CASE** keyword is reserved and may be provided in the future when/if integer support improves.

11.1.1   IF

True conditional execution is controlled by the **SH_IF**, **SH_ELSE**, **SH_ELSEIF**, and **SH_ENDIF** keywords. These keywords are used as in Listing 11.1. The **SH_ELSE** and **SH_ELSEIF** parts are optional. There can be as many **SH_ELSEIF** parts as necessary.

```
SH_IF(a) {
    // body1: executed only if (a > 0)
} SH_ELSEIF(b) {
    // body2: executed only if (a ≤ 0) and (b > 0)
} SH_ELSEIF(c) {
    // body3: executed only if (a ≤ 0) and (b ≤ 0) and (c > 0)
} SH_ELSE {
    // body4: executed only if (a ≤ 0) and (b ≤ 0) and (c ≤ 0)
} SH_ENDIF;
```

Listing 11.1. The **SH_IF** control construct.

The value of the test argument is interpreted relative to the Sh rules for logical values: true corresponds to positive, non-zero values, false is anything zero or negative. This value must be a scalar. When doing comparisons on tuples, use the `any` or `all` library functions to collapse tuples of logical values to a single scalar.

11.1.2 WHEN

The *SH_WHEN* construct has identical semantics and syntax to the *SH_IF* construct. However, its execution model is different: it uses conditional assignment, whereas *SH_IF* is implemented by true conditional execution using multipass execution or branching, depending on the compilation target. Normally, all branches of a *SH_WHEN* construct are actually executed, but only one set of variable updates is ultimately performed, and the results of the other set of computations are discarded. This is more compatible with the SIMD mode of execution used by some GPUs, so it can be executed in a single pass. For short conditional computations, it may actually be more efficient. However, care should be taken that the computations invoked by the bodies of *SH_WHEN* control constructs are small. The interpretation of the control value is the same as *SH_IF*. Conditional assignment can also be expressed using the `cond` library function.

An example is given in Listing 11.2. The *SH_OTHERWISEWHEN* and *SH_OTHERWISE* parts are optional.

```
SH_WHEN(a) {
    // body1: assignments taken only if (a > 0)
} SH_OTHERWISEWHEN(b) {
    // body2: assignments taken only if (a ≤ 0) and (b > 0)
} SH_OTHERWISEWHEN(c) {
    // body3: assignments taken only if (a ≤ 0) and (b ≤ 0) and (c > 0)
} SH_OTHERWISE {
    // body4: assignments taken only if (a ≤ 0) and (b ≤ 0) and (c ≤ 0)
} SH_ENDWHEN;
```

Listing 11.2. The *SH_WHEN* control construct.

11.2 Iteration

Sh supports three iterative control constructs: *SH_FOR*, *SH_WHILE*, and the pair *SH_DO* and *SH_UNTIL*. For compatible compilation targets, Sh supports data-dependent loop continuation conditions. It is our intention to attempt to support this feature on all compilation targets eventually, but it may require extraordinary efforts on some platforms involving transformation to a multipass implementation. This is a significant research problem. However, Sh may, in some circumstances, unroll these loops into statically repeated code if the control expressions evaluate to Sh-compile-time constants.

It is possible to write loops that will not terminate. It is the programmer's responsibility to avoid this. Sh cannot, in general, detect non-terminating loops at compile time, and the runtime engine does not include any timeouts to allow Sh to support long-running scientific applications. Attempts to execute Sh programs with non-terminating loops may therefore, on some compilation targets, fail to return to the host application.

Sh also does not currently support any specialized control constructs such as RenderMan's `illuminance`. Such constructs are, however, easy to simulate with the use of the provided control constructs and a suitable set of conventions.

11.2.1 FOR

For loops are used when it is necessary to loop while maintaining an index. The syntax of **SH_FOR** loops is shown in Listing 11.3. Note that the multiple arguments to the **SH_FOR** control constructs are separated by commas, not semicolons. If you want to use the comma to encode multiple expressions in the argument to **SH_FOR**, enclose these expressions in an additional set of parentheses.

The arguments to the **SH_FOR** control construct consist of an initializer, a test, and an update expression. The initializer is run before the loop starts. This expression may include a declaration. In this case, the scope of the declaration is limited to the loop body, and the value of the variable will not be available after the matching **SH_ENDFOR** keyword. The test is interpreted using the same rules as other logical expressions in Sh: negative or zero values are false. The test expression c must evaluate to a scalar; it is evaluated at the top of the loop. If the test fails the first time, that is, if $(c > 0)$ is false, *no* iterations are executed. The last expression can be any expression and is run at the end of the loop, after the body.

```
SH_FOR(initialization, c, update) {
    // body: repeated only while (c > 0)
} SH_ENDFOR;
```

Listing 11.3. The **SH_FOR** control construct.

11.2.2   WHILE

While loops are used when it is necessary to check a condition at the start of a loop. The syntax of **SH_WHILE** loops is shown in Listing 11.4.

The argument to the **SH_WHILE** control construct consists of a test. The interpretation of the test value uses the same rules as other logical expressions in Sh: negative or zero values are false. This expression must evaluate to a scalar, and is evaluated at the top of the loop. If the test fails (is zero or less than zero) the first time it is evaluated, *no* iterations are executed. The body of the loop should update variables used in the test or use **SH_BREAK** to exit the loop.

```
SH_WHILE(c) {
    // body: repeated only while (c > 0)
} SH_ENDWHILE;
```

Listing 11.4. The **SH_WHILE** control construct.

11.2.3   DO/UNTIL

Do/until loops are used when it is necessary to check a condition at the end of a loop. The syntax of **SH_DO/SH_UNTIL** loops is shown in Listing 11.5.

The argument to the **SH_UNTIL** keyword consists of a test. The interpretation of the test value uses the same rules as other logical expressions in Sh: negative or zero values are false. This expression must evaluate to a scalar and is evaluated at the bottom of the loop. At least one iteration is always executed. The loop is exited if the condition evaluates to true, which is interpreted in Sh as a positive value greater than zero. Normally, the body of the loop should update variables used in the test, or **SH_BREAK** should be used to exit the loop.

```
SH_DO {
    // body: repeated only until (c > 0)
} SH_UNTIL(c);
```

Listing 11.5. The **SH_DO/SH_UNTIL** control construct.

11.2.4   BREAK/CONTINUE

The statements **SH_BREAK** and **SH_CONTINUE** are valid within the bodies of all Sh loop constructs. These statements allow early termination of a particular iteration of a loop. They are analogous to their C++ counterparts break and continue. However, unlike the case with C++, **SH_BREAK** and **SH_CONTINUE** are conditional and take a scalar value as an argument. They execute the break or continue if the condition is true (which in Sh, means strictly greater than zero).

The **SH_BREAK** statement with a true argument causes control flow to leave the innermost loop body containing it immediately and continue at the end of the current containing loop body (after the next **SH_ENDWHILE**, **SH_ENDFOR** or **SH_UNTIL** statement).

When **SH_CONTINUE** is invoked with a true argument, it causes control flow to leave the innermost loop body, but continues with the next iteration if the loop condition is still fulfilled.

Chapter 12

Backends

Sh has a strong separation between the frontend, which the user interfaces with directly, and its backends, which generate code for a particular GPU or CPU.

To maximise this separation, there is no direct function call interface to the backends themselves. By enforcing this, we allow the backends to be changed and updated frequently without breaking existing programs.

Sometimes one wishes to write some backend specific code, however, and control it through Sh. This might be necessary to make use of functionality offered by a particular backend, but not exposed by the Sh API. This can be done by setting metadata in the form of arbitrary name-value pairs on Sh objects. A backend can check for metadata, but metadata interpretation is entirely up to and specific to each particular backend. See Section 7.7 for details on metadata in general.

An application must provide at least one choice of backend to Sh. The simplest way to do this is to call the shSetBackend(std::string) function, which takes a string consisting of the backend's name. This will cause any future interactions with the backend to use only that backend. If the specified backend is unavailable, an ShBackendException error will be signalled.

It may be useful to specify a list of possible backends and use the most appropriate one for a particular program. This can be done using the shUseBackend(std::string) function. Each call to this function will add the given backend to the end of a list of potential backends. The first appropriate backend in the list for a particular *ShProgram* will then be chosen. To clear the list of backends, call shClearBackends(). A call to shSetBackend also clears the list of backends before adding the given backend as the only item.

To check if a particular backend is available, call the shHaveBackend function with a std::string argument specifying the backend's name. This function returns an integer indicating the version of the given backend which is available. If the backend is unavailable, it returns zero.

12.1   OpenGL Backends

OpenGL defines a standard API for three-dimensional rendering. In recent years, much of the effort related to OpenGL has been toward making the rendering pipeline more programmable. Sh aims to target these recent advances in programmability with a set of backends.

There are multiple OpenGL-related backends which share various subsystems. At the time of writing, the most complete OpenGL-like backend is the `arb` backend, which compiles to `ARB_fragment_program` and `ARB_vertex_program` assembly code.

Other backends in progress include the `nv` backend targeting the `NV_fragment_program` and `NV_vertex_program` assembly interfaces, as well as a `glsl` backend aiming to produce high-level code in the OpenGL 2.0 Shading Language. The `glsl` backend will probably become the most commonly used OpenGL backend in Sh, but at the time of writing the driver support for GLSL is still lacking.

12.1.1   Input and Output Binding

At both the vertex and fragment stage, OpenGL provides several named inputs and outputs, corresponding to their purpose in the traditional fixed-function pipeline. The `arb` backend allows inputs and outputs in Sh programs to be mapped to these special tuples in a fairly intuitive manner. The alternative is to ignore any sort of special semantic meaning and only allocate attributes by their order, ignoring the type completely. The `arb` backend also allows this mode of mapping Sh variables to OpenGL attributes.

The default method of assigning variables to attributes is the semantic approach. Here, the mapping happens in two stages. In the first stage, any variables with types in the third column of Table 12.1 are assigned to the matching slots in order. In the second pass, any remaining variables are assigned to available slots marked as generic in the order they appear in the table.

The semantic method of binding is useful, in particular, when interacting with older applications, as it allows fairly straightforward interactions. However, especially when writing a new application, it may be simpler to ignore the semantic types and simply pass all data in order. To this end, the `arb` backend provides a generic attribute binding mode. In order to use this mode, you must set the `opengl:matching` metadata on your programs to `generic` by calling the `meta()` member function. Other values are reserved; you can enforce the semantic matching mode by setting the value to `semantic`.

Note that there is one semantic type which even under the generic mode has special meaning; that is `SH_POSITION`. The last **ShPosition** will always

OpenGL attribute	Count	Sh Semantic Type	Generic?
Vertex inputs			
`vertex.position`	1	SH_POSITION	no
`vertex.normal`	1	SH_NORMAL	no
`vertex.color`	1	SH_COLOR	no
`vertex.texcoord`	8	SH_TEXCOORD	yes
`vertex.fogcoord`	1	SH_ATTRIB	yes
Vertex outputs			
`result.position`	1	SH_POSITION	no
`result.color`	1	SH_COLOR	no
`result.texcoord`	8	SH_TEXCOORD	yes
`result.fogcoord`	1	SH_ATTRIB	yes
`result.pointsize`	1	SH_ATTRIB	yes
Fragment inputs			
`fragment.position`	1	SH_POSITION	no
`fragment.color`	1	SH_COLOR	no
`fragment.texcoord`	8	SH_TEXCOORD	yes
`fragment.fogcoord`	1	SH_ATTRIB	yes
Fragment outputs			
`result.color`	1	SH_COLOR	yes
`result.depth`	1	SH_ATTRIB	no

Table 12.1. Binding specifications for the `arb` backend.

be mapped to `vertex.attrib[0]`, as that is where GL places the vertex and fragment positions by convention.

Table 12.2 gives an example of what a sequence of Sh types would be mapped to for a vertex program under the two mappings.

Sh Variable	Semantic	Generic
ShInputNormal3f	`vertex.normal`	`vertex.attrib[1]`
ShInputVector3f	`vertex.texcoord[1]`	`vertex.attrib[2]`
ShInputVector3f	`vertex.texcoord[2]`	`vertex.attrib[3]`
ShInputTexCoord2f	`vertex.texcoord[0]`	`vertex.attrib[4]`
ShInputPosition4f	`vertex.position`	`vertex.attrib[0]`

Table 12.2. Example of binding under the `arb` backend for a vertex program.

12.1.2 Texture Bindings

By default, Sh and the OpenGL backends will manage textures completely automatically, taking care of allocating texture units, uploading texture data (as needed), etc.

Sometimes it can be useful, however, to set up textures outside of Sh. This may be because you are adapting a legacy application, or because you want to use an extension or texture format which Sh does not (yet) support. For this reason, the `arb` backend supports a few metadata settings on textures and programs.

First, the `opengl:reservetex` metadata can be set on **ShProgram**s with a string representation of an integer texture unit to indicate that Sh should not use that texture unit to store any of its textures. This can be useful if you have some textures set up outside of Sh (e.g., using the fixed-function pipeline) and don't want Sh to clobber them.

Another option is to set the `opengl:preset` property on a texture itself to a particular texture unit. This will cause texture data allocated to that texture to be ignored by the `arb` backend, and instead have it assume that the texture is already set up appropriately in the given texture unit.

12.1.3   Parameter Bindings

OpenGL defines a fairly large number of parameters corresponding to state, mostly originating from the older fixed-function model. It is possible to access this state in Sh shaders by setting the appropriate metainformation on uniform parameters and accessing them as usual. This allows you to both change this state from Sh and access it from shaders.

By setting the `opengl:state` metadata to the name of an OpenGL state variable (following the same conventions as in the `ARB_vertex_program` specification), the corresponding OpenGL state will be set to the uniform parameter's value when a program using it is bound or `shUpdate()` is called. The value will be used directly when the parameter appears in a program.

In addition to setting the `opengl:state` information on a parameter, it is possible to define `opengl:readonly` as `true`. If this metadata is set, the `arb` backend will never write that variable's data to the OpenGL state. This is particularily useful if you are still using traditional OpenGL calls to set up the OpenGL state. You should set the `opengl:readonly` property *before* setting the `opengl:state` to be sure that no OpenGL data will be overwritten accidentally.

12.2   CPU Backends

Sh can be used to generate programs for the CPU. At the time of writing this is supported by the `gcc` backend, which can execute stream programs by compiling them into C code which is passed on to the GCC compiler and linked into the program dynamically. The backend is particularily useful if you intend to run a stream program that uses features not supported by any GPU backends, e.g., data-dependent conditional control flow.

> While the GCC backend is the only available CPU backend at the time of writing, we are considering implementing several other CPU backends, including an interpreter, a dynamic code generation backend for x86 CPUs and a libtcc (Tiny C Compiler library [13]) backend.

To use the GCC backend exclusively, simply run shSetBackend("gcc"). This will set the GCC backend as the only backend. Alternatively, you can use a gcc:stream or cpu:stream target in your program declaration, which will cause the program to execute on the GCC backend (or, in the latter case, any CPU backend) regardless of what backend is set as the default. The GCC backend does not consider any particular metadata at this time.

12.3   The Sm Backend

Sm is a software GPU simulator written at the University of Waterloo. It implements a software version of a programmable GPU pipeline based on a packet stream architecture. It is geared particularly toward scalable parallelization in the context of a distributed memory system. It is modular and designed to allow the selective replacement of modules with hardware simulations or limited hardware implementations.

Sm has a C function call interface similar to OpenGL, but with more generic vertex attribute management. It supports assembly shader programs with a per-instruction function call interface. Shader programs are currently implemented with a machine language interpreter. The sm backend makes calls to this interface to set up shader programs. It can also construct equivalent C++ code, and we plan to replace the interpreted shader programs with custom-compiled Sm modules for higher performance in the near future. Attributes in Sm are bound to shader input by order alone and have no special semantic meaning. Therefore, they are simply set up in Sm in the order they appear in Sh programs. Originally, Sm and Sh were two halves of one system, and the attribute management systems, in particular, are designed to be compatible.

Part III

Engineering

Chapter 13

Engineering Overview

This part of the book discusses the existing Sh implementation. While the previous chapters are written as a specification and in some places require the implementation to catch up to them, the following chapters specifically discuss the workings of the current implementation. Sh is open source and is intended to be both a useful GPU programming language for commercial applications and a research tool. In both cases, it may be necessary to understand and modify the implementation; in the former to provide backend-specific hooks or tune performance and in the latter to modify Sh to implement and test new GPU compiler and runtime algorithms. We have therefore made some attempts to keep the internals of Sh modular and have documented its structure here.

Chapter 14 discusses the Sh Intermediate Representation. To some extent the IR is the heart of the current implementation. Programs are just graphs of IR statements in Sh's view, and internally all operations (e.g., the shader algebra program manipulation operations) act on the IR.

Chapter 15 explains how streams and textures are represented internally in Sh and how memory for these objects is managed.

Chapter 16 presents the current and potential future state of the Sh optimizer and discusses why particular optimizations are important for stream and shader programs.

Finally, Chapter 17 provides an overview of the interface between the Sh frontend and the processor-specific backends, and discusses issues relevant to implementing a backend.

Each chapter discusses the current state of the Sh implementation, as well as future work that could be done to improve the implementation. Please check the website for the status of any item mentioned under "future work" here.

13.1 Code Organization and Build System

The current Sh implementation has the following directory structure:

sh: Root directory; contains some documentation and build system files.

sh/config: M4 support files for build system.

sh/src: C++ source files for Sh frontend.

sh/backends: C++ source files for standard backends; each backend is in a separate subdirectory.

sh/util: C++ source files of extensions and experimental functions.

sh/test: Small test programs.

sh/doc: Destination for Doxygen documentation.

sh/win32: Microsoft Visual Studio .NET project files.

We will provide a quick tour of the build system as of the time of writing. You should consult the website and the documentation delivered with Sh for the most up-to-date instructions.

On POSIX systems, such as GNU/Linux, the GNU `automake` and `autoconf` tools are used to maintain the Sh build system. These tools parse some files located primarily in the root `sh` directory. They generate a shell script called `configure` which, in turn, generates `Makefiles` for the project based on the compilation environment.

If you obtain Sh directly from its subversion repository, you will need to run `bootstrap` before doing anything else:

```
$ cd sh
$ ./bootstrap
```

This will call `automake` and `autoconf` to generate the appropriate files. If you downloaded a release of Sh from the website, this is not necessary, and you can continue directly to the next step, which is to run `configure` itself, compile and install the library:

```
$ ./configure --prefix=/usr/local \
              --enable-arb-backend --disable-sm-backend
$ make
$ make install
```

The arguments given to `configure` here are just an example. You can run `./configure --help` to obtain a list of possible options. The most important argument is probably `prefix`, which specifies where Sh will be installed. You need to have write permissions to this directory.

Doxygen is a tool used to generate HTML and other forms of documentation directly from source code comments. Sh is set up to provide Doxygen comments of the API, which can be useful to get an overview of the source or quickly look up particular functions in the library. If Doxygen is installed, documentation will automatically be generated in the `doc` directory in HTML form. The Doxygen documentation for the most recent release is also always available on the Sh website.

If you are using Microsoft Visual Studio .NET under Windows to build Sh, you should load the project file located in the `win32` directory and build it as you would any other Visual Studio project.

13.2   Template Instantiation

Sh uses templates to make its code more compact. Note that Sh does not generally use advanced template techniques such as template metaprogramming, which can often make C++ code hard to port and slow to compile. This is not because we don't like these techniques, but simply because Sh doesn't need them.

Nonetheless, there are many template classes and functions in Sh. For instance, all Sh tuple types such as *ShAttrib* and *ShVector* are templated on several of their properties, including size and binding type. Similarly, library functions such as `pow` return different types depending on their argument types, and hence are templated also.

We try to avoid placing too much C++ code into template functions, as such code will be instantiated many times and potentially slow down compiles or increase the object size. C++ offers the option of either implicitly instantiating template types and functions when they are first used in a compilation unit, or explicitly instantiating those templates in a separate unit. We attempted to explicitly instantiate types for some time, but this caused too much object code bloat, as there were too many different versions of types, and complicated Sh usage slightly. Instead, we have now made almost all template classes and functions into thin wrappers around non-template equivalents, and moved most of the code out of templates into separate functions.

Chapter 14

Intermediate Representation

Internally Sh stores programs using the Sh Intermediate Representation, or IR for short. The IR encapsulates both the statements and the control-flow contained by a program. This chapter details the IR and related concepts.

We first provide an overview of the reference-counting mechanism used by Sh. Next, we explain the way basic blocks are stored, and then present the Control-Flow Graph structure holding information about branches and loops. We also explain how frontend statements are parsed into this structure.

14.1 Reference Counting

Many types in Sh are actually *reference-counted*. This means that for each object declared of such a type, a count is kept of how many pointer variables refer to it. If this count goes to zero, the object is destroyed, and the memory it occupies is released.

For the most part this reference-counting is hidden from the user — after all, its intent is to make the user's life easier by removing the burden of worrying about memory management and making the Sh syntax more useable. However, it can be useful to know a bit about how Sh does reference counting, since occasionally a reference-counted pointer surfaces.

Every class in Sh that should be reference counted (almost all internal classes fall into this category) inherits from the ***ShRefCountable*** class. Such classes can be contained in ***ShPointer*** objects, which are reference-counted pointers. Often you will see types ending in ***Ptr***, e.g., ***ShMemoryPtr***. By convention, these are **typedef**s of ***ShPointer***<T>.

Many other reference-counting pointer systems do not require the pointee type to hold the reference count and are, hence, *non-intrusive*. However, this requires an additional indirection with every pointer operation that needs to access the reference count, and does not allow the pointer to be safely cast between a regular pointer and a reference-counting pointer. In implementing Sh, we control all types, and hence it was easy to use the more efficient but intrusive method from the ground up.

ShPointers act very similarly to normal C++ pointers. They can be dereferenced in the same way, using * or ->. You can copy pointers, assign null values to them, check if they are null, etc. Furthermore you can get a true pointer to the referenced object by calling the object() member function, but this is usually not necessary.

Several template functions are provided if you need to cast between different types for which you are holding a reference-counted pointer. These are shref_dynamic_cast<T>(), shref_static_cast<T>(), and shref_const_cast<T>(). They each take a pointer of type **ShPointer**<T2> and cast it to a pointer of type **ShPointer**<T> as appropriate, with the same rules as their C++ counterparts.

Many of the externally visible Sh types are *not* reference counted objects, e.g., **ShAttrib** or **ShTexture2D**<T>. Instead, they are usually thin wrappers containing a pointer to a reference-counted object representing the actual entity. This way they can contain additional information and have more convenient syntax in certain situations.

Note that there is a difference between a **const ShPointer**<T> and a **ShPointer**<const T>. The former is a constant pointer to a non-constant object, and the latter a non-constant pointer to a constant object. In Sh, **CPtr** types are conventionally provided for reference-countable types; these types specify non-constant pointers to constant objects.

14.2   Basic Blocks

Basic blocks are sequences of statements that do not contain any data-dependent control flow. In other words, the statements listed in a basic block always execute in the same linear order. Basic blocks are represented in Sh by the **ShBasicBlock** class. While basic blocks may not contain branches, conditional assignments are allowed. Note, however, that in the case of a conditional assignment, both possible values are always computed, even if one of them is thrown away.

Each statement in a basic block is represented by an **ShStatement** object. This class consists of an operation, a destination variable, and three source variables, some of which may be NULL.

Operations are simply represented as an enumerated type, **ShOperation**. The possible operations are listed in Tables 14.1 through 14.6.

Name	Arity	Meaning
ASN	1	assignment
ADD	2	addition
CBRT	1	cube root
CMUL	1	product of components
CSUM	1	sum of components
DIV	2	division
EXP	1	natural exponent
EXP2	1	base-2 exponent
EXP10	1	base-10 exponent
LOG	1	natural logarithm
LOG2	1	base-2 logarithm
LOG10	1	base-10 logarithm
LRP	3	linear interpolation
MAD	3	multiply and add
MUL	2	multiplication
POW	2	power
RCP	1	componentwise reciprocal
RSQ	1	reciprocal square root
SQRT	1	square root

Table 14.1. General mathematical IR operations.

Name	Arity	Meaning
SLT	2	set less than
SLE	2	set less than or equal
SGT	2	set greater than
SGE	2	set greater than or equal
SEQ	2	set equal
SNE	2	set not equal
COND	3	conditional assignment

Table 14.2. Boolean IR operations.

Name	Arity	Meaning
ABS	1	absolute value
CEIL	1	ceiling
FLR	1	floor
FMOD	2	float modulus
FRAC	1	fractional part
MAX	2	componentwise maximum
MIN	2	componentwise minimum
RND	1	nearest integer
SGN	1	sign

Table 14.3. Clamp-like IR operations.

Name	Arity	Meaning
DOT	2	dot product
DST	2	distance
LEN	1	length
NORM	1	normalize vector
XPD	2	cross product

Table 14.4. Geometric IR operations.

Name	Arity	Meaning
ACOS	1	arccosine
ACOSH	1	hyperbolic arccosine
ASIN	1	arcsine
ASINH	1	hyperbolic arcsine
ATAN	1	arctangent
ATAN2	2	arctangent of src[1]/src[0]
ATANH	1	hyperbolic arctangent
COS	1	cosine
COSH	1	hyperbolic cosine
SIN	1	sine
SINH	1	hyperbolic sine
TAN	1	tangent
TANH	1	hyperbolic tangent

Table 14.5. Trigonometric IR operations.

Name	Arity	Meaning
DX	1	screen-space derivative in x
DY	1	screen-space derivative in y
FETCH	1	stream fetch
HASH	1	hash function
KIL	1	conditional fragment kill
LIT	3	compute lighting coefficient
OPTBRA	1	reserved for optimizer
NOISE	1	noise function
TEX	2	texture lookup
TEXI	2	indexed texture lookup

Table 14.6. Miscellaneous IR operations.

More information about operations is kept in the shOpInfo array, which contains elements of type *ShOperationInfo*. This array provides a textual name for each operation and an integer specifying the operation's arity (which ranges from 1 to 3).

Variables in statements are represented by the *ShVariable* type. This type is a base class of all templated tuple types in Sh, such as *ShAttrib* and *ShVector*. It consists of a reference-counted pointer to an *ShVariableNode* as well as a swizzle and negation bit.

The *ShVariableNode* object of a variable represents the *actual* variable being referred to in the statement. It is unique but may have one or more *ShVariable* objects referring to it at any time. This allows the same variable to appear in multiple statements with different swizzles or negation bits. It also ensures that uniform parameters (which are represented in the same manner) are kept alive even if they go out of scope, as long as at least one program refers to them. Thus one should consider an *ShVariable* as a *mention* of a variable, and an *ShVariableNode* as the variable itself. An *ShVariable*'s node may be accessed through the node() member function.

Swizzling is represented by the *ShSwizzle* class, which stores a list of swizzle indices. It also keeps track of the original element size of the variable it is swizzling, in order to be able to tell whether a swizzle is an identity swizzle (which is particularily useful during optimization) and raise an error if an out-of-bound swizzle is constructed. The swizzle of a variable may be accessed using the *ShVariable*::swizzle() member function.

Negation is simply a Boolean flag. By default, it is set to **false**, but when a variable is negated (using the prefix **operator-**()), the returned variable has this flag toggled. The reason we keep this information in the variable itself (rather than using, for example, a NEG instruction) is that most GPUs allow negation of source registers at minimal or no cost in the instruction set itself. The negation flag of a variable may be obtained from the **ShVariable**::neg() member function.

14.2.1 Special Statements

Most Sh operations are arithmetic or logic in nature. There are, however, a few operations which do something different. In particular, the TEX, TEXI, KIL, OPTBRA and FETCH instructions are special.

The KIL operation differs from other operations in that it has no destination. It only makes sense in fragment or stream programs, and its semantics are to conditionally discard a fragment or stream element. In other words, if the condition of a KIL instruction is met, the program will not write any outputs. This can be useful in many cases. One could consider the KIL instruction as a control-flow instruction, since it affects whether or not later statements will be executed. However, it is simpler to leave it as a basic statement and is usually not complicated to treat as a special case, e.g., in optimizations.

The TEX and TEXI instructions represent texture fetches. They expect the texture node and texture coordinates as their source arguments. The texture coordinates are simply passed using a regular **ShVariable**, and the two instructions differ only in how they map the texture coordinates to the stored texels. The TEX instruction maps $[0, 1]$ to the entire range of the texture, whereas TEXI is similar to an array lookup and maps the range $[0, w] \times [0, h] \times [0, d]$ (in the case of a three-dimensional texture) to the whole texture.

The other argument to the texture instructions—the texture itself—is of more interest. Since **ShStatement**s keep only **ShVariable**s as their source arguments, we must somehow place a texture reference into an **ShVariable**. This is done using the **ShTextureNode** type, which is derived from **ShVariableNode**. It contains information about the texture such as the buffer it is bound to (see Chapter 15), the dimensions of the texture, and the interpolation modes used to access it. The **ShVariableNode** includes an enumerated type specifying what kind of "variable" it represents called the *binding type*. This is stored as an enumerated type **ShBindingType** which includes values such as **SH_INPUT**, **SH_TEMP**, **SH_CONST**, and **SH_TEXTURE**.

The texture used by a texture access instruction is then simply stored as an **ShVariable** pointing at an **ShTextureNode**. The swizzle and negation parts of the variable are simply ignored. When a texture is constructed using a user-visible type such as **ShArray2D**, an **ShTextureNode** is created internally and is referenced whenever the user performs a texture lookup.

A similar instruction is the FETCH instruction. This instruction is used for Sh's stream programming capabilities. The fetch instruction represents an element fetch from a stream channel. Stream channels are very similar to textures. They are externally (to the user) represented using the templated *ShChannel* type, but internally referenced using an *ShChannelNode* which is reference counted. They differ from textures in that no coordinates are passed to the FETCH instruction. Instead a program is assumed to have a unique current element for each channel, which is fetched using this instruction. How this is done is up to the backend. The PBufferStreams implementation used in the OpenGL backend replaces FETCH instructions with texture fetches using computed texture coordinates, for example.

Perhaps the strangest instruction is the OPTBRA instruction. This is not actually an instruction at all, but merely a hint to the optimizer. The optimizer inserts an OPTBRA instruction for each conditional branch, which is useful in dead-code elimination. It can be ignored outside of the optimizer and, in fact, should never appear in an externally visible program. More details on this instruction and why it is required are given in Chapter 16.

14.3 The Control-Flow Graph

Sh programs can include more than just basic blocks: they can contain arbitrary data-dependent control flow. In less technical terms, Sh programs are allowed to contain branches and loops that depend on values calculated inside of the program.

Storing these instructions requires more than just a basic block representation. One way to store these branches would be to label all the basic blocks and then insert "jump" statements which divert control flow to another block if a particular condition is met. This is how branches are represented in many intermediate representations.

Instead, we decided to use a different representation. The previously mentioned method is useful if the intermediate representation is inherently textual, but because of the unique way in which Sh programs are parsed, this is not the case. Thus we opted to store these control constructs directly in a form called the Control-Flow Graph.

The Control-Flow Graph (or CFG for short—not to be confused with a Context-Free Grammar) is a graph whose nodes contain basic blocks (as discussed in the previous section) and whose edges represent branches. In the Sh implementation, the Control-Flow Graph is represented by the *ShCtrlGraph* class. Each *ShProgram* contains a single *ShCtrlGraph* instance. Nodes in the graph are represented by objects of type *ShCtrlGraphNode*. Edges are contained by the nodes themselves, with each node storing the edges leaving it.

There are two special nodes in each graph: *entry* and *exit*. These are accessed by calling the `entry()` and `exit()` member functions of *ShCtrlGraph*, respectively. All nodes in the graph have an edge towards them except for the entry node. Furthermore, all nodes except for the exit node in the graph have at least one leaving node called the *follower*. The follower is an unconditional branch. Nodes may also have zero or more conditional branches called *successors*. Each conditional branch has an associated variable. If any of that variable's elements are greater than zero, the branch is taken. Successors are stored in an ordered list, and the conditions are assumed to be evaluated in order, taking the first branch with a true condition. If no conditional branches are followed (because all conditions are false or no such branches exist), the follower is taken.

14.4   Parsing

We will now explain how Sh statements are parsed into basic blocks and Control-Flow Graphs.

14.4.1   Basic Blocks

Library functions are implemented on top of IR statements. For each IR operation, a function is declared in `ShInstructions.hpp` and defined in the `ShInstructions.cpp` file. For example, the

---

shADD(*ShVariable*& dest, **const** *ShVariable*& a, **const** *ShVariable*& b)

---

function represents an addition. If this function is called outside of a shader definition, it computes the actual componentwise addition of a and b, which are asserted to be uniform variables or constants, and places the result in dest, which must also be a uniform variable.

We determine whether or not we are inside of a shader program by considering the *ShEnvironment*::shader variable. When *SH_BEGIN_PROGRAM* is invoked, a new *ShProgramNode* is created and *ShEnvironment*::shader is assigned this node. When *SH_END* is then called, i.e., the program definition is complete, the *ShEnvironment*::shader variable is set to NULL again.

If a library function is called inside of a shader definition, a different operation takes place. Returning to our addition example, rather than calculating the result, we create an *ShStatement* containing ADD, dest, a, and b. This statement is then added to the end of the current basic block of the shader program currently being defined.

The partial program contains an **ShTokenizer** object, which contains a list of blocks stored as an **ShBlockList**. When a statement is to be added, the current basic block is obtained from the program's **ShBlockList**. If there is no current basic block, a new one is created containing only the newly added statement; otherwise the statement is pushed onto the end of the current basic block.

It is important to note that this is all the work that needs to be done to parse basic blocks. Unlike traditional compilers, Sh does not need to do any tokenizing or construct a parse tree for expressions. This is because C++ already does the parsing for us, by calling our library functions and overloaded operators in exactly the same order as we would parse them ourselves. This significantly simplifies the work we need to do and is one of the nice benefits of implementing Sh in this manner.

14.4.2   Control Constructs

Since Sh includes control constructs such as **SH_IF** and **SH_FOR**, we need to convert these to our Control-Flow Graph form somehow.

This is done in two passes. As control constructs are encountered, they are stored as tokens in the half-parsed program's **ShBlockList**. In addition to basic blocks, this list stores **ShToken**s, which represent one of the possible control construct keywords in Sh, such as **SH_FOR**, **SH_ENDIF**, or **SH_BREAK**.

During this tokenization phase, basic blocks and tokens are interleaved in the **ShBlockList** of the program. But arguments for tokens need to be stored also, for instance the three arguments to **SH_FOR**. All arguments represent some computation. Thus they are stored in turn as an **ShBlockList** specifying the computation and an **ShVariable** specifying the variable in which the computation is stored. A basic block (rather than a list of blocks and tokens) is not sufficient, since the argument itself might contain a function call which uses a control construct. These arguments are stored within the **ShToken** as **ShTokenArgument** objects.

In order to store the arguments, we need to keep a stack of **ShBlockList**s. This requires executing the arguments of a control construct such as **SH_FOR** in a specific order. To do so, we make use of the fact that the && operator in C++ requires its arguments to be evaluated strictly from left to right. We then define macros for **SH_FOR**, etc., in the following manner:

```
#define SH_PUSH_ARG_QUEUE \
  ::SH::ShEnvironment::shader->tokenizer.pushArgQueue()
#define SH_PUSH_ARG \
  ::SH::ShEnvironment::shader->tokenizer.pushArg()
#define SH_PROCESS_ARG(arg) \
  ::SH::ShEnvironment::shader->tokenizer.processArg(arg)

// ...

#define SH_FOR(init,cond,inc) \
  shFor(SH_PUSH_ARG_QUEUE && \
        SH_PUSH_ARG && SH_PROCESS_ARG(init) && \
        SH_PUSH_ARG && SH_PROCESS_ARG(cond) && \
        SH_PUSH_ARG && SH_PROCESS_ARG(inc));

// ...

void shFor(bool)
{
  ShRefCount<ShToken> token = new ShToken(SH_TOKEN_FOR);

  for (int i = 0; i < 3; i++) {
    token->arguments.
      push_back(ShEnvironment::shader->tokenizer.getArgument());
  }
  ShEnvironment::shader->tokenizer.popArgQueue();

  ShEnvironment::shader->tokenizer.blockList()->addBlock(token);
}
```

Thus, we first push a new argument queue into the tokenizer. Then we push each argument, and process it. Note that the expression passed into SH_PROCESS_ARG is evaluated after the call to pushArg(), but before the call to processArg. Pushing simply pushes a new block list onto the current tokenizer, and process pops it off, places it in a **ShTokenArgument**, and sets the argument's result variable to be whatever was passed in. Finally, the call to shFor() makes the actual token, fetches the arguments from the tokenizer, and pops the current argument queue.

Note that each of the push, pop and process functions return a Boolean that is completely ignored. Actually, they all return **true**. The only reason to do this is to cause the entire && expression to be evaluated, thus causing the functions to be called in the required order. Had we just made these arguments to shFor, they could have been called in arbitrary order, as C++ makes no guarantees about the order of evaluation of arguments.

Once this process is complete, we have the entire program in block-list form. At this point all expressions are parsed, the arguments to control structures are somewhat parsed, but the overall structure of the program is still linear.

To parse the program into a control-flow graph, we employ a simple recursive-descent parser implemented by the ***ShParser*** class. Since the parsing itself is quite simple, we parse directly into a Control-Flow Graph, without going through an intermediate layer such as a parse tree.

The only public function in ***ShParser*** is the `parse` member function. It takes an ***ShBlockList*** and returns a parsed control graph by passing back the head and tail (i.e., entry and exit node of the control graph). Internally, several functions are defined: one for generic blocks and another for each kind of control structure. The generic function `parseStmts` only parses basic blocks (by simply setting both the head and tail to be a single control graph node containing the basic block) and then calls itself recursively to parse the rest of the blocks. If it encounters a token, it calls the appropriate parsing function instead, which puts together a control graph fragment based on the arguments and body of the control construct, calling `parseStmts` recursively to parse the blocklists involved and checking the semantics of the program. This process repeats until no blocks are left to parse, and a completed Control-Flow Graph is constructed, or a parse error occurs.

Chapter 15

Streams and Textures

15.1 Stream Representation

Streams are represented in the Sh API by two classes, **ShStream** and **ShChannel**. Internally, these classes are really thin wrappers around **ShChannelNode** pointers.

ShChannel is a templated type which creates a single **ShChannelNode** on construction and holds it. The non-templated **ShStream** type contains any number of channel nodes. Streams and channels can be combined in any way to yield larger streams. Note that a stream may refer to the same channel node as another channel or stream.

Each **ShChannelNode** object contains only two data items. It holds a reference-counted pointer to an **ShMemory** object representing the actual stream data, as well as a count. These two properties can be obtained and set using the memory() and count() member functions of **ShChannel** and **ShChannelNode**.

Channels have an **operator**() that may be called to obtain the "current" stream element. As there can only be a current stream element in the execution of a stream program, this operation only makes sense inside a program definition. It results in an SH_OP_FETCH instruction, as explained in Section 14.2.1.

These stream fetch instructions are then translated by the appropriate backend when the stream program is prepared for execution. For example, the PBufferStreams implementation, which is part of the OpenGL backend, generates texture nodes for each stream node used in a program and replaces fetch instructions with texture reads, passing in the appropriate texture coordinates.

15.2   Texture Representation

Textures are represented by Sh in a very similar way to streams. Externally, they are presented as a variety of types, such as *ShArray2D* or *ShTable3D*, specifying interpolation and filtering modes as well as the texture layout. Internally, these are simply thin wrappers around reference-counted pointers to *ShTextureNode* objects.

Each *ShTextureNode* consists of some layout information (such as the width, height and depth of a texture), a reference-counted pointer to one or more memory objects, and an *ShTextureTraits* object. The *ShTextureTraits* object contains trait information such as filtering, wrapping, and interpolation modes. Note that multiple texture nodes can share the same memory object but can have different traits or even different layouts.

Most texture nodes have only one memory object, but cube maps can have a different memory object for each of the six faces. For this reason, the `memory()` member function takes an optional argument specifying which memory object is to be specified or retrieved.

It is useful to allow texture sizes to change after construction. However, under some circumstances, we need to insert code for particular backends to transform between indexed texture accesses and [0, 1]-based texture accesses. This translation involves a scaling by the size of the texture. In order to allow texture sizes to change dynamically, we use a uniform variable (rather than a constant) in the scaling and keep this variable with the texture node. Whenever the texture node's size is changed, the value of this variable changes with it. Other dynamic mode changes, however, are intentionally not supported at the level of the user API, since generally they would expose platform dependencies.

15.3   Stream and Texture Memory

Since Sh supports texture and stream objects that can contain large amounts of data, it is important to manage these objects efficiently. This section explains Sh's internal model of data for these types.

Most of the classes described here are intended to be internal to Sh and are generally hidden from the average user.

15.3.1   Memory and Storage Objects

The key component of the stream and texture memory management system is the *ShMemory* class. It represents memory abstractly. Rather than corresponding to a particular chunk of physical memory, it represents some amount of *information* that may be stored in more than one place. All memory-related code not specific to any backend may be found in the `ShMemory.hpp` and `ShMemory.cpp` files.

Not only can information be stored in several places at once, it can also be in different states in these places. Each location is represented by an ***ShStorage*** object which provides a concrete representation of the memory. Examples of potential storage classes include host storage in RAM, texture memory on a GPU, persistent storage on a hard drive, or even networked storage on a remote server. Each ***ShStorage*** object contains a time stamp, and each storage class provides a name identifying it. Each storage corresponds to exactly one ***ShMemory***, but as was already mentioned, a memory object may refer to one or more storage objects.

The time stamps on storages are used to identify how up-to-date each storage is. Each memory object has a time stamp that is always defined to be the largest time stamp of all its storages. If a storage has a time stamp lower than its memory's time stamp, it is considered to be out-of-date.

Before a storage is accessed for a read operation, the `sync()` member function should be called. This does nothing if the storage is up-to-date. If not, it attempts to transfer data from an appropriate more up-to-date storage and updates the storage's time stamp.

If a storage is about to be written to, its `dirty()` member function should be called. This first `sync`s the storage, then increments its time stamp by one, and sets the memory's time stamp appropriately.

Sometimes it is possible to avoid synchronising a storage before marking a write, e.g., if the storage is going to be replaced entirely by the write. In that case, you can call the `override()` member function of a storage. This moves the storage's time stamp up to the memory's current time plus one, but as opposed to `dirty()`, does not call `sync()`.

The type of a storage is obtained by calling the `id()` member function, and its time stamp is fetched by calling the `timestamp()` function. ***ShMemory*** also has a `timestamp()` function which returns the most up-to-date time stamp.

By convention, some storage type identifiers contain a colon to provide a namespace separation, much like Sh program targets. For example, OpenGL textures are identified by `opengl:texture`.

Memory objects store reference-counted pointers to their storages. This ensures that as long as the memory is alive and referenced from somewhere, its storages will not be accidentally deallocated. Sometimes it is useful to unlink a storage from its memory. This can be done by calling the `removeStorage()` member function on the memory object with the appropriate storage.

15.3.2   Finding Storages

In order to access a storage attached to a particular memory, the findStorage member function, which takes an std::string as its sole argument, is available in **ShMemory**. This attempts to find a storage of the given identifier. Another version of findStorage is available; it takes a template functor. This functor is called for every storage of the given type. The first storage for which this functor returns **true** is then returned.

15.3.3   Transfer Operators

When sync() is called on an **ShStorage** which is not up to date, the storage needs to be updated from somewhere else. By definition, there is always a storage which is up-to-date for a particular memory object, and therefore a potential candidate from which to update.

We call such a copy a *transfer*, and a transfer between two particular types of storage is represented by the **ShTransfer** class in Sh. In order to implement a new transfer, one simply subclasses **ShTransfer**, provides the source and destination type identifiers to the constructor, and instantiates a singleton copy of the new transfer. By adding transfers in this manner, they are kept separate from the actual storage types, and new transfer objects can be made without having to modify the storages themselves.

The only two operations an **ShTransfer** supplies are the transfer() and cost() member functions. The function transfer() takes two **ShStorage** pointers as arguments and attempts to perform the transfer. Note that it need not worry about updating time stamps; if the transfer succeeds, sync() will do so automatically.

The **ShTransfer**::cost() member function takes two storages and returns an integer. This integer represents the relative cost of performing that transfer. The definition of "relative cost" is fairly arbitrary, but should be chosen to roughly reflect how long it would take to transfer a storage between those two types, by looking at other transfer costs. For example, a transfer between two host memory storages should generally cost less than a transfer between the host and a texture unit on a graphics card of the same size. Therefore, a smaller host-to-host transfer cost should be chosen than a host-to-GPU transfer.

15.3.4   Existing Implementations

Sh and its backends provide several concrete subclasses of the **ShTransfer** and **ShStorage** types, which we discuss here.

The Sh frontend currently provides only one storage type, **ShHostStorage**, identified by the string `host`. Every host storage has a length (in bytes) and pointer to some memory on the host. This memory can either be allocated manually by the user or allocated and managed by the storage itself. The method of allocation is determined by which constructor of **ShHostStorage** is called.

Together with **ShHostStorage**, an **ShHostMemory** class is provided. This class is intended to represent some memory which originates on the host. It keeps a reference-counted pointer to the host storage that it creates. It is provided purely for convenience.

The OpenGL backends provide storages of type `opengl:texture`. These storages represent texture data stored in a particular texture unit of a GPU. Functions to transfer from and to `host` storages are provided.

15.4   Future Work

This section discusses future work to be done to improve streams and the memory abstraction.

The stream interface present in Sh at the time of writing is very basic, as it has only been introduced relatively recently. There are many ways in which it can be improved to allow more flexible general-purpose programming. We will discuss some of the planned improvements here. We also discuss improvements to make the buffer management scheme more efficient and general.

15.4.1   Stream Interface Improvements

Sometimes it is useful to have several streams using the same memory, but accessing different parts of it. Two properties of a stream need to be added for this: strides and offsets. The stride of a stream specifies how many tuple sizes the beginning of two adjacent tuples are away from one another. Currently Sh always assumes a stride of one, i.e., adjacent tuples. A stream offset would simply specify how many tuples to skip at the start of the stream. Thus, the ith element of a stream s with stride t and offset o would be looked up as $s[o + t * i]$.

It may be useful to have negative offsets. For instance, in a cloth simulation or in image processing algorithms, it can be useful to access forward and backward neighbors. This could be implemented by providing three streams: the original stream with offset zero, a forward stream with offset one, and a backward stream with offset -1. These streams would all share the same memory. Around the edges, however, a special case arises. Since there is no "-1th" element, some other value would have to be substituted instead. This could be worked around by computing the edge cases as special cases, or Sh could allow specification of a default value or wrapping mode for streams.

Similarly, a negative stride might be used to specify a stream whose elements are to be aligned in backward order. This may be useful for certain algorithms or to rearrange data that is out of order.

15.4.2   Index Streams

It is often useful to pass in a stream of indices, i.e., a sequence of integers. This is certainly currently possible, by creating a stream of the appropriate size and filling it with the index data. However, it is both convenient and possibly more efficient to provide a special type for these kinds of streams. This would allow us to dynamically generate them, for instance, by using the rasterizer as an address generator. Since indices probably have to be computed by the backend anyway in the final executable version of a stream program, there is no reason not to reuse these. Suitable index stream types (and index stream generators) should thus be added to Sh.

15.4.3   Reductions

Stream operations currently map an N-tuple stream to an N-tuple stream. It is often desirable to map an N-tuple stream to a single tuple by *reducing* the data in some way.

Reductions may be specified as stream programs that "fold" a function that takes two inputs and reduces them to a single output in some manner (e.g., by adding them together). By recursively or iteratively applying a reduction operator to a long stream it can then be reduced into shorter streams and, eventually, to a single tuple.

We have not yet decided on an interface for reductions in Sh. Most likely it will be a program which takes two sets of (equally typed) inputs and returns another set of outputs with the same types. This program will then, along with a stream of input data matching the signature of the program, be passed on to the backend to be reduced in a way appropriate to the program, data, and backend.

15.4.4   Stream Ordering

Sh's current stream execution model assumes that the result of a computation must be aligned with the inputs, i.e., that stream execution preserves order. In some cases, such as a simple particle system, this is not necessary. It may be possible to improve performance if this is taken into account. In particular, if stream computation including data-dependent control flow is virtualized, it is useful to be able to scramble the order of stream data, and not doing so may involve additional computation. For instance, iteration often involves some stream records requiring more iterations than others. Rather than blocking the short iterations while they wait for a long one to complete, we would like to just write out the short iterations when they are complete.

To take advantage of this, we intend to add a type such as **ShSet**, which specifies that its channels need not preserve order when assigned to. Of course, channels within both sets and streams must still be aligned with one another.

15.4.5 Memory Abstraction Improvements

While the memory abstractions provided by Sh are a good start, there are some features which will need to be added in the future. The primary reason for these features, and in fact the primary reason for having these abstractions to begin with, is efficiency. Downloading data between the host program and the processor running the Sh kernel can be a very expensive operation. Thus, we should minimize the amount of data transferred.

Currently the transfer operators overwrite an entire piece of storage at once. Often only part of some memory will be overwritten, and it may be possible to more efficiently propagate such changes by only transferring part of a buffer. This would require information about memory layout (e.g., the width and height of an image) and subregions to be attached to memory objects, which is not currently available.

We have tried to keep the memory abstraction as simple and abstract as possible. In the future we may make it slightly more concrete by attaching more detailed information to storages, such as what basic type or with what tuple size (i.e., how many elements per tuple) the data is stored. This may allow more complicated transfer operations that involve some data conversion to happen automatically.

We are also planning to add new storage types to the system. An obvious example is persistent hard-drive storage, which may be useful for caching purposes. Another possibility is the addition of networked storage to the system, which becomes particularly interesting when clusters of machines are considered as targets for Sh stream programs.

Another possible addition to the memory abstraction is freezing and thawing. It can be useful to *freeze* a memory object at a certain time stamp. This will cause future calls to sync to transfer from that time stamp instead of the newest available time stamp. Some storage might then be written to, causing its time stamp to increment, but not affecting other storages. At a later point the memory could be thawed again, causing it to behave as usual. An example where this is useful is stream execution with output virtualization. If a stream kernel uses more than one output, it may be virtualized by executing it once for each output. If at the same time any of the outputs are also used as inputs, the state of the input at the start of the execution may need to be conserved for later use. Freezing the memory when the multi-pass execution starts, then thawing it later, would achieve the desired semantics.

Chapter 16

Optimization

This chapter documents the Sh optimizer. The optimizer is currently fairly bare-bones, and there is much functionality missing. We intend to improve the optimizer significantly by the end of 2004, and some possibilities are discussed in Section 16.4.

The Sh optimizer is based on the Sh Intermediate Representation we discussed in Chapter 14. In the following, we will first discuss the optimizations conceptually, then give more detail on how they are implemented.

In general, all of the code related to optimization is kept in ShOptimizer.cpp in the Sh compiler source.

16.1   Copy Propagation and Forward Substitution

Two optimizations, copy propagation and forward substitution, are performed on basic blocks.

Copy propagation finds copies (i.e., straightforward assignment statements, represented by ASN instructions) in basic blocks and replaces future references of the destination of the copy with the copied variable. The goal here is to eliminate redundant copies, and hence potentially remove the need for an unused temporary.

For example, consider the following IR code:

```
s := a DOT b
t := s
u := t MUL a
v := t MUL b
o := u MUL v
```

The copy propagator would change this code to the following:

```
s := a DOT b
t := s
u := s MUL a
v := s MUL b
o := u ADD v
```

In this case, t is no longer used. If it is a temporary variable, we can get rid of the assignment and discard t entirely. The dead code eliminator will perform this optimization.

One of the primary reasons copy propagation is useful in the case of Sh is due to copy constructors being called in C++ as part of the implementation of our "parser" and when Sh types are passed around in C++ functions. When a function returns an Sh tuple type, say an **ShAttrib3f**, a redundant copy of the return value will be made due to the way objects are returned in C++.

For example, the statement x = a + b; will cause the following IR code to be generated:

```
t := a ADD b
x := t
```

If we can replace future references of x with t directly, we should be able to get rid of the assignment to x.

It would be nice to avoid the problem of copy constructors altogether. C++ does in fact allow copy constructor calls to be *elided*, i.e., skipped, in certain situations. Unfortunately this can actually cause invalid code to be generated in certain cases, in particular, when initializing a new tuple from a swizzle of another tuple. For this reason, we take special care to force the constructor to be called by making the type of a swizzled tuple different from a regular one.

One case in which copy propagation would not be sufficient is if, in the preceding example, x were an output variable. In this case, we would not be able to get rid of it, since the assignment is semantically meaningful. Instead, we would like to directly assign the addition to x and get rid of t instead of x.

We implemented a fairly naïve method to reduce the amount of copying called *forward substitution*. In this case, we look for assignment statements and replace assignments with a repetition of the right-hand side's last computation. This is only done if the arguments to that computation have not since changed.

As an example, consider the following IR code:

```
...
s := t MUL a
t := a ADD b
```

```
o := t
p := s
```

Forward substitution would replace this by:

```
...
s := t MUL a
t := a ADD b
o := a ADD b
p := s
```

The assignment t should then be eliminated by the dead code remover.

This "optimization" is slightly arguable, as it may in fact introduce additional computation. In practice, however, it does tend to work fairly well on typical code. It might be improved by narrowing the scope of the transformation to a smaller set of cases. What's really needed is another step of common subexpression elimination, which in some ways is the inverse of forward substitution. In that case, duplicate expressions would be found and replaced by a single evaluation of the expression. We will discuss this further in Section 16.4.

16.2   Dead Code Removal

A very important optimization for shader programs is *dead code removal*. We have already discussed copy propagation and forward substitution, both of which rely on dead code removal. The shader algebra operators connect and combine are also cases which can potentially lead to dead code, and the implementation of specialization using shader algebra depends on its existence in the compiler.

Dead code is defined as any code which does not contribute to the final result in any way, i.e., Sh IR statements which could be safely removed and would not cause the result of the overall computation to change under any circumstances.

In the following example, dead and live code is indicated by comments. The variable o1 is taken to be an output variable.

```
t1 := a ADD b    // (1) Live (due to (3))
t2 := b ADD c    // (2) Dead
t3 := a ADD t1   // (3) Live (due to (6))
t4 := a DIV c    // (4) Dead
o1 := b MUL t2   // (5) Dead (overwritten)
o1 := a MUL t3   // (6) Live (outputs value)
```

Dead code removal begins by first finding some statements which are obviously live, e.g., all statements which assign to an output variable and are not overwritten at a later point. Then one repeatedly marks all statements contributing to live statements as live also, until there are no more statements left to mark. The last step is to remove all functions not marked as live.

Determining which statements can contribute to which other statements is fairly easy for a simple basic block, but it becomes complicated when control-flow is allowed. Thus, we must first build data structures which contain this information. We use *use-def chains* to hold the information, storing a link between each use of a variable to all statements than can possibly define it (and vice versa).

16.2.1   Block Predecessors

The first piece of information we need is the predecessors for each block, i.e., all blocks which have the current block as a follower or successor. This is done by iterating through all nodes in the graph using a depth-first search and adding each node to its followers' and successors' predecessor list.

16.2.2   Reaching Definitions

The next step is to solve the *reaching definitions* problem. Here we are trying to enumerate which definitions (i.e., IR statements) reach a particular block. In other words, we are trying to find the set `rchIn(B)` for each block B such that each definition in `rchIn(B)` contributes to the value of its destination at the start of B, no matter what path the program has taken to get to B.

We use an iterative method, storing definitions in bitsets. Because of write-masking, we consider a definition to be overwritten only if the overwriting definition's destination is not writemasked at all. This gives a more pessimistic solution to the problem than the optimal one, and we plan to improve this in the future.

16.2.3   Use-Def Chains

Once we have solved the reaching definitions problem, we are ready to construct the use-def chains. These are stored inside **ShStatement** as `std::set-<`**ShStatement***`>`s (with one ud set for each source and a du set for the statement's destination).

For each block, we keep track of the set of statements defining each variable by initially considering the reaching definitions information. We then iterate through each statement in the block.

Using the set of possible definitions, we attach use-def information to each source variable in the statement. Every time we add a definition to the use-def chain of a source variable, we also add the source variable to the definition's def-use chain.

Once we have processed all source variables of a statement, we consider its destination. If the destination is writemasked, we add the current statement to the destination's set of definitions. If there is no write mask, we replace the destination's entire set of definitions with only the current statement.

When all statements in all blocks have been processed in this manner, we have the complete use-def and def-use information for the program.

16.2.4   Live and Dead Code

Actually removing dead code then becomes fairly straightforward. We first iterate over all blocks and mark all the live code. This includes all assignments to outputs, all fragment kill instructions, and special OPTBRA instructions. The OPTBRA instructions are inserted at the end of every block for every conditional branch, with their only source argument being the variable on which the branch depends. Their only purpose is to keep assignments to those variables alive, and they are removed once dead-code removal is done.

While we are marking each initial live statement, we also add it to a queue called the *work list*. Once we are done marking initial statements, we then repeatedly remove statements from the work list and mark all statements in their use-def chains as live, also adding these new statements to the work list. This repeats until no statements are left on the work list.

As a last step, we then simply consider all blocks and remove all statements which are not marked.

16.3   Graph Straightening

Graph straightening is a very simple optimization. Unlike the previous optimizations, this optimization happens at the level of the control graph rather than the level of blocks.

Sometimes a program can have two separate basic blocks that are connected by a single edge, with the destination of the edge having no other sources and the source of the edge having no other destinations. In this case, there is no reason that the two blocks should be separated, and we can merge them into a single basic block. This may allow some additional basic-block optimizations to be performed and more efficient code to be generated.

Performing this change is known as graph straightening. We visit each block, check whether it can be merged with the next block, and if so perform the merge.

One situation in which graphs that need to be straightened arise is in the implementation of the shader algebra connect operation, where graphs from two separate programs are connected by plugging together inputs and outputs.

16.4   Future Work

In the preceding sections, we have discussed the optimizations which Sh performs. There are however many more optimizations which we consider important, and many ways in which the existing optimizations can be improved.

In this section, we discuss what we believe are the most important optimizations that should be added to Sh, and in what ways one might improve the existing optimizer. This discussion is by no means complete, leaving out many other optimizations that could be performed. However, the optimizations discussed here are the ones that we plan to implement next.

16.4.1   Eliminating Redundancies

Both *common subexpression elimination* and *value numbering* are important optimizations with similar goals. They both attempt to eliminate redundant computations by storing the result of computation in a temporary variable and reusing that temporary variable the second time the computation is needed.

Value numbering involves computing hashes for statements in such a way that two statements with the same effect will have the same hash. This way a hash table mapping previous computations to destinations can be consulted, and the previous value can be copied instead of recomputed if it is found.

Common subexpression elimination searches for two equal statements in a program and replaces duplicates by copies if the operand values have not changed between the two statements. This is very similar to value numbering, but both approaches have cases in which they yield better results than the other.

These optimizations are important in shader and stream programs for several reasons. A simple reason is that many lighting expressions (which are frequent in shaders) involve the same computation multiple times, e.g., the dot product of two vectors. It is tedious to store this in a temporary variable manually, and if library functions are involved, it is hard to remove these and other redundancies (such as the normalization of input vectors) without breaking modularity. The common subexpression and value numbering optimizations would be able to find such duplicate expressions and generate the additional temporary automatically.

Lastly, the forward substitution optimization described earlier may sometimes lead to code containing redundant expression evaluations. Thus, a pass of subexpression elimination or value numbering should be performed (after running the dead code remover) to collect these expressions back into one evaluation.

16.4.2 Constant Folding and Uniform Lifting

It is common to write code in a stream or shader program that only depends on values which are either uniform or constant. In such cases, the computation need not happen every time the program is executed. It can be performed once and reused on many invocations of the program. This sort of optimization is often done manually with other shading languages, but with the close integration of Sh with the host application, we have the opportunity to automatically and transparently lift such computations to the host.

In the case of constants, the computation can simply be done once and for all when the program is compiled and the result stored as a constant in the program. Doing this computation during the optimization phase is known as *constant folding*.

In the case of computations depending on uniforms, the value of the operands may change after the program has been compiled. We cannot simply use the values of the uniforms at definition time and store the result in the program directly. We need to add a new uniform to the program, but this uniform must be changed every time its operands (the other uniforms it was computed from) change. Doing this multiple times can lead to a chain of dependencies between uniforms. Moving such uniform computations from the shader or stream program to the host is called *uniform lifting*.

To perform uniform lifting, we need to keep track of dependencies between uniforms, and define how and when uniforms are computed. The simplest way to do this is to optionally attach a list of Sh IR statements (i.e., an **ShProgram**) to a uniform, as well as registering it with other uniforms as a dependent. We then would execute the program defined for the uniform every time one of the values it depends on changes. We call such a computed uniform value a *dependent uniform*.

The code used to update a dependent uniform is essentially the same code we would need to perform constant folding. It is also equivalent to interpreting an Sh program. Thus, dependent uniform computation, constant folding, and an interpreting backend could all share the same code to evaluate the expressions.

It may also be useful to find common computations in the current set of dependent uniforms. If two programs compute the inverse of the same matrix, for instance, there is no need to perform the inverse computation twice. This problem is similar to that of eliminating redundancies explained in the previous section.

Both of these optimizations require knowing whether a computation depends only on constants or uniforms. To determine this, we must perform two additional optimizations.

Constant propagation is an optimization where assignments from constants to variables are found and later references of such variables replaced with the appropriate constants. We define *uniform propagation* in the same manner for uniform assignments.

16.4.3   Algebraic Simplification

Algebraic simplification is a set of optimizations that aims to find expressions which can be simplified due to some algebraic property. For example, an addition of zero to a number can be removed completely, as it will have no effect.

A very common case for algebraic simplification is repeated normalization. When writing library routines, one often requires some of the inputs to be normalized. This could be documented in source code comments, or the function could simply call `normalize` on its inputs before using them. However, the normalization may be unnecessary if the input was normalized already. Since normalization is a fairly expensive operation and can increase numerical error, one would normally not want the second normalization to take place. On the other hand, without an optimizer to get rid of these, we have to break modularity or make library functions harder to use (by requiring normalized inputs, for instance, when necessary). We are trying to build a GPU programming language with both an easy-to-use standard library and strong support for modularity. Thus, it is important that the optimizer remove such redundant statements.

There are other similar *domain-specific* optimizations that could be implemented in Sh. For instance, if certain properties for matrices hold (e.g., that the matrix represents an Euclidean transformation), certain computations involving such matrices (such as the inverse or normal transformation) can be simplified.

One possible implementation of some of these simplifications would be to eliminate the calls entirely as the IR statements are constructed. For example, we could keep a flag with each variable storing whether it is normalized or not, and then do nothing when `normalize` is called on a variable with that flag set. This works for basic blocks (and we actually implemented it at one point), but breaks down in the case of control constructs. In that case, the order in which operations are added to the IR does not necessarily match the order in which they will be called when the program is executed. We could clear the normalized flag at every basic block boundary, but this would be a suboptimal solution. Given the added complexity of tracking and changing these flags in many operations, we chose to defer this optimization until the analysis phase, when we can obtain better information about where a variable was last defined using techniques such as use-def chains.

This "later-is-better" philosophy applies to other optimizations and transformations too, such as constant and uniform propagation. In general we have decided to defer any such optimizations in order to keep the front-end implementation simple and the Sh API as stable as possible.

16.4.4   Conditional Assignment

While Sh provides the ability to include arbitrary conditional selection using the *SH_IF* control construct, it may sometimes be more efficient to simply use conditional assignment instead of conditional evaluation. In conditional assignment, which corresponds to the `cond` library function and the COND IR statement, a variable is assigned to one of two values depending on a condition. As opposed to conditional execution, both possible values are computed.

There are cases in which conditional assignment may be faster than conditional execution. This is especially true when the two computations are very simple, e.g., simple assignments. Furthermore, some of Sh's targets, in particular some of the GPU targets, may support conditional assignment but not conditional execution.

For these reasons, it may be worthwhile to add replacement of branches with conditional assignments under certain circumstances. This is essentially the same work as implementing the *SH_WHEN* construct.

16.4.5   Static Single Assignment and Other Forms

In addition to providing new optimizations, the optimizations already implemented could be significantly improved. We describe some of the possibilities for improvement in this section.

Tuple variables are the casue of a major difference between the Sh IR and conventional intermediate representations. In most languages, IR operations operate primarily on scalars, i.e., single elements of data. We use tuple types as our primitive types, and most statements in Sh operate on more than one element of data at a time. This would not be a significant difference were it not possible to writemask a statement's destination.

Many of the commonly used optimization techniques make use of a form called *static single assignment*, or SSA for short. Cytron et al. describe in detail what SSA is and how to convert an IR program to SSA form [28]. The most important property of SSA is that every variable is assigned to only once. In other words, there is a unique definition for every variable, and the information provided by use-def chains described earlier is trivially available. A program is transformed into SSA form by relabelling uses of the same variable in different assignments. At points in the control flow graph, where several definitions of a variable merge, a so-called ϕ-function is inserted which selects among all possible definitions.

SSA, however, assumes that every assignment to a variable completely overwrites that variable's value. Because of writemasking, this may not be true for an entire tuple variable in the Sh IR. The challenge is then to find a suitable modification to SSA that takes into account individual tuple elements, with the hopes of implementing optimization algorithms based on SSA. One such algorithm is Wegman and Zadeck's sparse conditional constant propagation algorithm [149], which is a classical example of an SSA-based algorithm.

Even if we do not adopt SSA, there are improvements to the existing algorithms that can be made. Our reaching-definitions solver currently deals very pessimistically with the case of writemasking. If a destination is masked, it simply assumes that any previous definition of the variable is still valid. It is relatively simple to extend the implementation by widening the bitvector entries used to keep track of whether definitions are killed or preserved to the width of each variable. This way we would be able to determine much more information about variables, such as being able to perform copy propagation on subparts of a variable. These changes are particularly important to improve the optimizer's results for code that involves a lot of manual packing of variables. It would also be possible to pack multiple variables into single registers automatically, and making these simple improvements to the optimizer would make this more worthwhile.

An alternative route to modifying traditional compiler algorithms is to first convert the Sh IR into something that matches what traditional algorithms expect. This can be done by splitting each tuple into its elements and scalarizing all instructions. Then SSA's assumption of completely overwriting variables would always hold. On the other hand, this is not a satisfactory approach unless the scalar version of the program can be revectorized after the optimizations take place. Unfortunately, this is no trivial task, as the optimized version may move, replace, or delete single-element instructions that were previously part of a larger vector instruction. This may lead to less efficient code than one had to begin with if vectorization is not done carefully. However, this method has a lot of potential if it can be implemented reasonably, as a vectorizer may be able to find better uses of the vectorized instruction set than the programmer had. It might even be possible to have the compiler implement both approaches and then always pick the better result.

Chapter 17

Backend

17.1 The Backend Interface

Every Sh backend needs to implement the **ShBackend** interface, found in the ShBackend.hpp file. This interface has a few virtual functions which need to be implemented, which are listed in Table 17.1.

```
std::string name() const;
   unique backend name
ShBackendCodePtr generateCode(std::string target,
const ShProgram& p);
   generate backend code
void execute(const ShProgram& p, ShStream& dest);
   execute stream program
```

Table 17.1. *ShBackend* virtual interface.

The name() member function returns a unique name string for the backend. Examples of this include arb, sm, and gcc. This name will be used by users to identify the backend.

Two member functions deal with programs. The execute() member function specifically executes stream programs, placing the result of the computation in the given stream. The backend should verify that the outputs of the program match the signature of the destination stream and that the program is a valid stream program.

Finally the generateCode member function is used for non-stream (i.e., shader) programs. This function returns a reference-counted pointer to a **ShBackendCode** object, representing the compiled code corresponding to the given program. **ShBackendCode** is another virtual class from which each

261

backend should derive a concrete implementation. Its list of virtual functions is
shown in Table 17.2.

```
void upload();
  upload code to processor
void bind();
  bind uploaded code, set up uniforms and textures
void updateUniform(const ShVariableNodePtr&);
  update value of uniform after a change
std::ostream& print(std::ostream& out);
  print string representation of code
std::string describe_bindings();
  return human-readable variable bindings

bool allocateRegister(const ShVariableNodePtr& var);
void freeRegister(const ShVariableNodePtr& var);
  used by the linear register allocator.
```

Table 17.2. *ShBackendCode* virtual interface.

The *ShBackendCode* class represents compiled code for a particular backend. The upload function is used to send this compiled code to the appropriate processor. The bind function is then used to activate the chosen program
so that it will be used in subsequent rendering passes, until another program is
bound. At this point, the backend should also upload any required resources,
such as textures.

The updateUniform() member function is called on a bound program if
a particular uniform variable changes. If the backend code uses the given uniform, it should ensure that the target processor has the most up-to-date value.

Calling the print() member function outputs the generated code (as far
as that is possible) to the given output stream. Some backends, such as the Sm
backend, do not have a direct string representation. In the Sm backend's case,
the program is specified by a sequence of C++ function calls. The print()
function then simply prints the corresponding C++ code.

The describe_bindings() function is used by the *ShProgram* member
function of the same name. It is intended as a documentation tool for developers to determine how variables are bound by the program. This function is
particularly useful when long tuples are used with backends that do not support them directly, i.e., break them into smaller tuples.

Two more member functions, allocateRegister and freeRegister,
will be explained in the following section.

Every *ShProgram* object keeps track of backend code generated for it. The
ShBackend class keeps track of all instantiated backends automatically.

It supports looking up backends by name using the static `lookup` member functions.

17.2   Linear Register Allocation

Backends which do not support control constructs, and, therefore, only operate on single basic blocks, need not have a very complicated register allocator. Linear register allocation is perfectly adequate in this case. To avoid having to repeatedly write register allocation code, Sh provides a utility class called **ShLinearAllocator** which does exactly that.

In order to use the linear allocator, a backend's code class needs to implement the `allocateRegister` and `freeRegister` functions. To perform the allocation, the backend creates a **ShLinearAllocator** object and repeatedly calls the `mark()` member function on it for each variable used in each statement. This constructs a list of *live ranges*, one for each variable. Once all variable ranges have been marked, the backend can call the `allocate()` function. This consults the live range information and repeatedly calls the `allocateRegister` and `freeRegister` functions on the backend code. These keep track of a pool of free registers, assigning free registers to variables when `allocateRegister` is called and placing registers back into the pool when `freeRegister` is called.

17.3   Transformers

Sh supports many operations that may not be directly available in a particular backend. Some of these operations are implemented on top of more basic statements, but some are represented directly by IR statements. Furthermore, Sh supports some features which may not map directly to target architectures. Some of these features include arbitrary length tuples, arbitrary texture modes (e.g., [0, 1]-indexed bilinearly interpolated filtered rectangular floating-point unclamped textures, which many GPUs do not directly support currently), reading from outputs, and writing to inputs.

One approach to some of these problems would be to make use of metaprogramming at definition time. As the program is being defined, we could ask the backend whether it supports a particular feature and insert appropriate code to make up for unhandled features as necessary. This is actually a useful idiom, especially when it comes to adding user-defined types. However, this method has several disadvantages. By rewriting the statements at definition time, we need to redefine the program if we ever want to compile it under another backend. We may also be unable to deal with all problems that may come up when future backends are added to the system.

A more useful approach is transforming the program in the backend before compiling it. If all platform-dependent transformations are done this way, then we can also retarget a program to a new platform without the need to redefine it—unless the user himself uses platform-dependent metaprogrammed code generation. We therefore recommend that user metaprogramming *not* be used to adapt a program to a particular platform, other than scaling complexity to meet a performance target. Instead, an appropriate backend should be written along with any necessary transformers. To maximise reuse, the Sh library includes several useful transformations for backends. All of these are located in the **ShTransformer** class.

Each transformer operates on a copied version of the program to be transformed. In general, most transformers involve finding a particular sequence of statements or uses of variables with certain properties, then replacing those statements with a new sequence of statements.

17.3.1   Splitting Long Tuples

The `splitTuples()` transformation is used to split long tuples into shorter ones for backends that do not support arbitrary-length tuples. It takes two arguments. The first is an integer specifying the maximum tuple length supported by the backend. Tuples of length greater than this will be broken into smaller pieces up to that size. The second argument is a `VarSplitMap`, which is defined to be a `std::map` from **ShVariableNode** pointers to `std::vectors` of other **ShVariableNode** pointers. Any long tuples that are split will be placed in this map, pointing at the variables into which they have been split.

Most IR statements involve the same amount of work to split, as almost all Sh statements operate componentwise (with one of the components possibly being a scalar). Statements which do not operate in this way, such as `DOT`, are handled as special cases.

Currently only temporary, input, and output variables are split. Uniform parameters could be split by adding temporary variables which are assigned to the appropriate subparts of the uniform at the start of the program. Alternatively, if uniform dependencies were tracked as explained in Section 16.4.2, dependent uniforms could be split from the original uniform. This would be more efficient than using temporaries, but requires dependent uniform computation. Splitting textures of long tuples is a more complicated problem and is not (currently) handled by Sh, but we plan support for it in the near future.

17.3.2   Input and Output Conversion

Sh allows programs to read from outputs and write to inputs. This may not necessarily seem like a very useful feature, at first, but consider the following code:

```
ShInputNormal3f normal;
ShInputVector3f light[N];   // N light sources
// ...
ShOutputColor3f col;

for (int i = 0; i < N; i++) {
  col += dot(normal, light[i]) * lightcol[i] * diffuse;
}
```

The above situation often arises very naturally when accumulating reflection models. Note that the += operation needs to read its left-hand operand.

Writing to inputs is useful when some input needs to be transformed or processed before it can be used:

```
ShInputNormal3f n;
n = normalize(n);   // make sure normal is unit length
```

Some compilation targets, unfortunately, do not permit writing to input registers or reading from output registers. In both cases, it is possible to add an intermediate temporary variable to circumvent this problem. Adding this temporary automatically is a simple transformation, and so we can save programmers the hassle of doing so manually. This also cleans up the code considerably; if these temporaries would have to be declared in the source program, the programmer would have to come up with a name similar to, but different from, the original variable.

Sh also provides *InOut* types. These are a convenient shorthand notation for inputs which are transformed and then assigned to similar outputs at the very end of the program. They are particularly useful in vertex programs (where variables are often transformed fairly simply, perhaps even just copied) and stream programs (which often perform an "update" computation). However, most backends do not support such types directly.

The convertInputOutput transformer performs three related conversions. First, *InOut* variables are converted to input and output variables. Inputs which are written to are then converted to temporaries initially assigned from an input. Finally, outputs which are read from are converted into temporaries that are finally assigned to an output. This conversion is fairly straightforward. In a first pass, all variables that need to be converted are collected in a map, with the appropriate substitutions. References to those variables are then replaced throughout the program, and assignment code is inserted at the beginning or end of the control graph.

17.3.3   Texture Indexing Conversion

Sh allows textures to be indexed in two ways. Textures are indexed by coordinates in the range $[0, 1]$ in all dimensions, or they are indexed by integral coordinates in the range $[0, w - 1] \times [0, h - 1] \times \cdots$ depending on the dimensions of the texture. Both notations are convenient in different situations. If the texture is treated as a decal to be applied to a surface, the $[0, 1]$ representation is usually more convenient. If the texture represents a data structure, the indexed representation is often the more convenient choice.

In most GPUs however, only one of these modes is usually supported for each texture type. It is common that $[0, 1]$-based access is used for all types except rectangular (non-power-of-two) textures, where only index-based access is available. Thus, we provide a transformer which changes arbitrary texture accesses into the appropriate accesses, possibly inserting extra code to scale the texture coordinates.

17.4   Future Work

17.4.1   New Backends

Currently Sh includes a relatively small number of backends. We hope to increase this number over the next few months. In particular, we hope that, by the time this book reaches publication, backends for the DirectX High-Level Shading Language (HLSL) and the OpenGL 2.0 Shading Language (GLSL) will be part of the system. These backends should be fairly simple to implement, as they will be translating high-level code to other high-level code with similar semantics, and we can share the existing transformers with the ARB backend.

We also plan to add a backend for NVIDIA's Cg shading language. This will allow Sh to take advantage of the backends Cg provides and allow us to directly compare our optimizer to Cg's (as well making use of the Cg optimizer in the short term). We may also add support for the NV_fragment_program and related vertex program extensions, as these expose some interfaces which the ARB extensions do not, such as derivatives, but are otherwise very similar to the ARB backend.

More CPU backends are also on our agenda. Currently we provide the gcc backend, which generates C code and uses the GCC compiler to compile and

link this code into the running application. We would like to add support for
the TCC (TinyCC) compiler, which has a library version that allows this runtime compilation directly. In addition we would like to target SIMD-within-a-
register CPU instructions, as are provided by the SSE2 or AltiVec vector processing extensions. We may target these either by generating suitably vectorizable
code for the Intel C++ compiler (for example), or by emitting the appropriate
vector intrinsics ourselves.

17.4.2   Better Transformations

The transformers described above, while reusable, are fairly specific and written in an ad-hoc manner. Furthermore, the code is not trivial to understand,
and touches the IR directly. In some cases this is inevitable, but we could, in
particular, specify the texture index rescaling as a simple program.

We intend to implement a more generic mechanism for program transformation and to replace of IR statements with sequences of other statements.
These transformations should be pluggable and be registered with particular
strings, so that backends can identify which transformations they do or do not
require. Each transformation would consist of a function which recognizes
transformable statements, as well as an Sh program (which could be written
simply using the high-level functions already provided by Sh) which would
replace the given statements.

We may go as far as to add an EXT statement to the IR. This statement would
contain a string and would be intended as a general-purpose extendable statement. Transformations would have to be provided for particular EXT statements to transform them to more basic statements if the current backend does
not support them directly. This would allow us to add experimental statements
to the language as add-on libraries without breaking backwards compatibility.
Because we would not necessarily have to implement these new functions on
top of existing statements, this would allow us to introduce new functionality
that relies on particular backends without having to change the entire Sh library.

Most users will not need to use these statements to add library functionality
to the language. They can simply use metaprogramming to define their own
types or functions on top of the existing library. While these new statement
types add a powerful mechanism to extend the language, they should be used
only when necessary.

17.4.3   Better Reuse

A lot of code is common to more than one backend. Placing reusable algorithms, such as the linear register allocator and the transformers, in the Sh

library core itself is a good step towards reuse. There are many more examples of code that could be shared. In particular, much of the stream execution code could be common among backends. This includes code to verify that the stream destination is aligned with the program outputs, that all source channel sizes match, etc.

17.4.4   Instruction Count Virtualization

Many backends, in particular older GPU backends, set a limit on the number of instructions which can be executed in a single pass. There may also be different restrictions on certain types of instructions, such as dependent or direct texture fetches and arithmetic instructions.

It is possible to virtualize arbitrary-length basic block programs to run on a GPU in multiple passes. Chan et al. propose a method to do so [23] which could be implemented in Sh. Implementing this kind of virtualization for fragment programs would require Sh to interface with the graphics API or provide some sort of callback interface to run the appropriate fragment programs at the appropriate time. Ideally, this would happen through a rendering interface provided by Sh, which is planned but only in the long term. Stream programs, however, may be virtualized in this manner without requiring a rendering interface.

Chan's algorithm makes a few assumptions which could potentially be relaxed. For example, it assumes that only one output is available in the fragment unit. This is true for some, but not all, GPUs. By making use of multiple outputs available in some GPUs, a virtualization algorithm may yield virtualizations which run in fewer passes. This is one possible extension that could be made to the algorithm, but it may come at an increased partitioning cost and higher complexity.

The only form of virtualization performed on stream programs at the moment is mapping multiple stream outputs to GPUs with only one fragment output. This is done using the shader algebra, by simply ignoring all but one output on each pass and relying on dead code elimination in the optimizer to clean up each program. If multiple outputs were supported, we would try to maximize the overlap of computation between outputs by packing them together, thus avoiding redundant calculations in multiple passes.

17.4.5   Data-Dependent Control Flow Virtualization

Another form of virtualization is replacing data-dependent loops and branches with a multipass scheduler. We have done some research into doing this, and a graduate student at the University of Waterloo, Tiberiu S. Popa, has implemented a working prototype in Sh already, so it is likely that this virtualization will move into the main Sh implementation relatively soon.

Most GPUs do not, at the time of writing, support data-dependent branches and loops in the fragment program, although new GPUs have been announced that do. The closest widely implemented feature is conditional assignment, which can be considered semantically equivalent to branches, but not to loops. Also, conditional assignment always incurs the cost of both possible computations.

It is possible to break up a stream or fragment program into basic blocks, then run each basic block in a separate rendering pass. Each block has a stream of data attached to its inputs. A scheduler decides which blocks run on each pass, primarily based on the amount of data waiting for each block.

When a conditional occurs, a stream is split into two. These streams will initially be interleaved according to the result of the conditional. By packing these two streams into two contiguous blocks of data, it is possible to efficiently execute computations on only those elements of data which are appropriate. This packing algorithm can theoretically be implemented completely on the GPU, although it may take a number of passes to complete.

By scheduling and packing effectively, we believe it is possible to implement data-dependent control constructs relatively efficiently even on GPUs or traditional SIMD processors which do not inherently support them. We intend to add this type of virtualization into Sh itself, so that any backend can make use of it. Alternative strategies are also possible, for instance, making use of occlusion culling hardware to avoid doing work on "masked out" pixels. However that approach would require vertex buffer feedback to pass data back through the vertex unit since the occlusion culling unit is between the vertex unit and the fragment unit. This would also reduce the computational overhead, but not the bandwidth overhead, of multipass implementation. It would be nice if GPUs supported some form of pack-on-write, so that output fragment streams could be conditionally written to a packed sequence. This would take a relatively small amount of hardware, but is not supported on any current GPU. Recently released GPUs seem to have taken a MIMD approach to the problem of data-dependent control flow instead.

Bibliography

[1] 3DLabs. *OpenGL 2.0 Shading Language White Paper*, 1.1 edition, December 2001.

[2] Gregory D. Abram and Turner Whitted. "Building Block shaders." *Computer Graphics (Proc. SIGGRAPH)*, 24(4): 283–288, 1990.

[3] A. V. Aho, R. Sethi, and J. D. Ullman. *Compilers: Principles, Techniques, Tools*. Reading, MA: Addison-Wesley, 1986.

[4] Kurt Akeley. "Realityengine Graphics." In *Proceedings of SIGGRAPH 93, Computer Graphics Proceedings, Annual Conference Series*, edited by James T. Kajiya, pp. 109–116. New York: ACM Press, 1993.

[5] Kurt Akeley and Tom Jermoluk. "High-Performance Polygon Rendering." *Computer Graphics (Proc. SIGGRAPH)*, 22(4): 239–246, 1988.

[6] Tomas Akenine-Möller and Eric Haines. *Real-Time Rendering*, Second edition. Wellesley, MA: A K Peters, Ltd., 2002.

[7] R. Alverson, D. Callahan, D. Cummings, B. Koblenz, A. Porterfield, and B. Smith. "The Tera Computer System." In *Proc. Supercomputing*, pp. 1–6. New York: ACM Press, 1990.

[8] John Amanatides. "Algorithms for the Detection and Elimination of Specular Aliasing." In *Proc. Graphics Interface*, pp. 86–93. Wellesley, MA: A K Peters, 1992.

[9] Phil Amburn, Eric Grant, and Turner Whitted. "Managing Geometric Complexity with Enhanced Procedural Models." *Computer Graphics (Proc. SIGGRAPH)*, 20(4): 189–195, 1986.

[10] Anthony A. Apodaca and Larry Gritz. *Advanced RenderMan: Creating CGI for Motion Pictures*. San Francisco: Morgan Kaufmann, 2000.

[11] Andrew W. Appel. *Modern Compiler Implementation in C: Basic Techniques*. Cambridge, UK: Cambridge University Press, 1997.

[12] ATI. *Pixel Shader Extension*, 2000. Specification document. Available from `http://www.ati.com/online/sdk`.

[13] Fabrice Bellard. "Tiny C Compiler – C Scripting Everywhere." Available from `http://fabrice.bellard.free.fr/tcc/`, 2004.

[14] James F. Blinn. "Models of Light Reflection for Computer Synthesized Pictures." *Computer Graphics (Proc. SIGGRAPH)*, 11(2), 192–198, 1977.

[15] Jim Blinn. *Jim Blinn's Corner: Dirty Pixels*. San Francisco: Morgan Kaufmann, 1996.

[16] David Blythe, Brad Grantham, and Mark J. Kilgard. "Lighting and Shading Techniques for Interactive Applications." In *SIGGRAPH Course Notes*. New York: ACM Press, 1999.

[17] David Blythe, Brad Grantham, Mark J. Kilgard, Tom McReynolds, and Scott R. Nelson. "Advanced Graphics Programming Techniques using OpenGL." In *SIGGRAPH Course Notes*. New York: ACM Press, 1999.

[18] Jeff Bolz, Ian Farmer, Eitan Grinspun, and Peter Schröder. "Sparse Matrix Solvers on the GPU: Conjugate Gradients and Multigrid." *ACM Trans. on Graphics*, 22(3): 917–924, 2003.

[19] David E. Breen, Donald H. House, and P. Getto. "A Physically-Based Particle Model of Cloth." *The Visual Computer*, 8: 264–277, 1992.

[20] David E. Breen, Donald H. House, and Michael J. Wozny. "Predicting the Drape of Woven Cloth using Interacting Particles." In *Proceedings of SIGGRAPH 94, Computer Graphics Proceedings, Annual Conference Series*, edited by Andrew Glassner. pp. 365–372, New York: ACM Press, 1994.

[21] Ian Buck. "BrookGPU Project." Available from `http://graphics.stanford.edu/projects/brookgpu/`, 2003.

[22] Ian Buck, Tim Foley, Daniel Horn, Jeremy Sugerman, Kayvon Fatahalian, Mike Houston, and Pat Hanrahan. "Brook for GPUs: Stream Computing on Graphics Hardware." *ACM Trans. on Graphics*, 23(3): 2004.

[23] Eric Chan, R. Ng, Pradeep Sen, Kekoa Proudfoot, and Pat Hanrahan. "Efficient Partitioning of Fragment Shaders for Multipass Rendering." In *Proc. Graphics Hardware*, pp. 69–78, Aire-la-Ville, Switzerland: Eurographics Assoc., 2002.

[24] Robert L. Cook. "Shade Trees." *Computer Graphics (Proc. SIGGRAPH)*, 18(3): 223–231, 1984.

[25] Robert L. Cook and Kenneth E. Torrance. "A Reflectance Model for Computer Graphics." *Computer Graphics (Proc. SIGGRAPH)*, 15(3): 307–316, 1981.

[26] Robert L. Cook and Kenneth E. Torrance. "A Reflectance Model for Computer Graphics." *ACM Trans. on Graphics*, 1(1): 7–24, 1982.

[27] Franklin C. Crow. "A More Flexible Image Generation Environment." *Computer Graphics (Proc. SIGGRAPH)*, 16(3): 9–18, 1982.

[28] Ron Cytron, Jeanne Ferrante, Barry K. Rosen, Mark N. Wegman, and F. Kenneth Zadeck. "Efficiently Computing Static Single Assignment Form and the Control Dependence Graph." *ACM Transactions on Programming Languages and Systems*, 13(4): 451–490, 1991.

[29] Krzysztof Czarnecki, John O'Donnell, Jörg Striegnitz, and Walid Taha. "DSL Implementation in MetaOCaml, Template Haskell, and C++." In *DSPG*, Lecture Notes in Computer Science 3016, pp. 50–71, Berlin: Springer Verlag, 2004.

[30] W. J. Dally, Pat Hanrahan, M. Erez, T. J. Knight, F. Labont, J.-H. Ahn, N. Jayasena, U. J. Kapasi, A. Das, J. Gummaraju, and Ian Buck. "Merrimac: Supercomputing with Streams." In *Proc. Supercomputing*, pp. 35–42, New York: ACM Press, 2003.

[31] B. Dawes and D. Abrahams. Boost++ Web Site. *http://www.boost.org*, 2003.

[32] P. Diefenbach. "Pipeline Rendering: Interaction and Realism through Hardware-Based Multi-pass Rendering." PhD thesis, Department of Computer and Information Science, University of Pennsylvania, 1996.

[33] P. Diefenbach and N. Badler. "Pipeline Rendering: Interactive Refractions, Reflections and Shadows." *Displays (Special Issue on Interactive Computer Graphics)*, 15(3): 173–180, 1994.

[34] P. Diefenbach and N. Badler. "Multi-Pass Pipeline Rendering: Realism for Dynamic Environments." In *ACM Symposium on Interactive 3D Graphics*, pp. 59–70, New York: ACM Press, 1997.

[35] David Dobkin, Leonidas Guibas, John Hershberger, and Jack Snoeyink. "An Efficient Algorithm for Finding the CSG Representation of a Simple Polygon." *Computer Graphics (Proc. SIGGRAPH)*, 22(4): 31–40, 1988.

[36] Scott Draves. "Compiler Generation for Interactive Graphics using Intermediate Code." In *Dagstuhl Seminar on Partial Evaluation*, pp. 95–114, Berlin: Springer, 1996.

[37] Tom Duff. "Interval Arithmetic and Recursive Subdivision for Implicit Functions and Constructive Solid Geometry." *Computer Graphics (Proc. SIGGRAPH)*, 26(2): 131–138, 1992.

[38] David S. Ebert, F. Kenton Musgrave, Darwyn Peachey, Ken Perlin, and Steven Worley. *Texturing and Modeling: A Procedural Approach*, Second edition. San Diego, CA: Academic Press, 1998.

[39] Matthew Eldridge, Homan Igehy, and Patrick M. Hanrahan. "Pomegranate: A Fully Scalable Graphics Architecture." In *Proceedings of SIGGRAPH 2000, Computer Graphics Proceedings, Annual Conference Series*, edited by Kurt Akeley, pp. 443–454, Reading, MA: Addison-Wesley, 2000.

[40] Conal Elliott, Sigbjørn Finne, and Oege de Moor. "Compiling Embedded Languages." In *SAIG/PLI*, Lecture Notes in Computer Science 1924, pp. 9–27, Berlin: Springer, 2000.

[41] Nick England. "A Graphics System Architecture for Interactive Application-Specific Display Functions." *IEEE CG&A*, 6(1): 60–70, 1986.

[42] Dawson R. Engler. "VCODE: A Retargetable, Extensible, Very Fast Dynamic Code Generation System." In *Proc. ACM SIGPLAN*, pp. 160–170, New York: ACM Press, 1996.

[43] Randima Fernando and Mark Kilgard. *The Cg Tutorial: The Definitive Guide to Programmable Real-Time Graphics*. Reading, MA: Addison-Wesley, 2003.

[44] F. Fisher and A. Woo. "R.E versus N.H Specular Highlights." In *Graphics Gems V*, pp. 388–400, San Diego, CA: Academic Press, 1994.

[45] C. W. Fraser, D. R. Hanson, and T. A. Proebsting. "Engineering a Simple, Efficient Code Generator." *ACM Letters on Programming Languages and Systems*, 1(3): 213–226, 1992.

[46] Chris W. Fraser and David R. Hanson. *A Retargetable C Compiler: Design and Implementation*. San Francisco: Benjamin Cummings Pub. Co., 1995.

[47] H. Fuchs, J. Goldfeather, J. Hultquist, S. Spach, J. Austin, Jr. F. Brooks, J. Eyles, and J. Poulton. "Fast Spheres, Shadows, Textures, Transparencies, and Image Enhancements in Pixel-Planes." *Computer Graphics (Proc. SIGGRAPH)*, 19: 111–120, 1985.

[48] Henry Fuchs, John Poulton, John Eyles, Trey Greer, Jack Goldfeather, David Ellsworth, Steve Molnar, Greg Turk, Brice Tebbs, and Laura Israel. "Pixel-planes 5: A Heterogeneous Multiprocessor Graphics System using Processor-Enhanced Memories." *Computer Graphics (Proc. SIGGRAPH)*, 23(3): 79–88, 1989.

[49] Amy Gooch, Bruce Gooch, Peter S. Shirley, and Elaine Cohen. "A Non-Photorealistic Lighting Model for Automatic Technical Illustration." In *Proceedings of SIGGRAPH 98, Computer Graphics Proceedings, Annual Conference Series*, edited by Michael Cohen, pp. 447–452, Reading, MA: Addison Wesley, 1998.

[50] L. Gritz and J. Hahn. "BMRT: A Global Illumination Implementation of the Renderman Standard." *Journal of Graphics Tools*, 1(3): 29–47, 1996.

[51] Larry Gritz, Tony Apodaca, Ronen Barzel, Doug Epps, Clint Hanson, and Scott Johnston. "Advanced RenderMan: Beyond the Companion." In *SIGGRAPH Course Notes*, New York: ACM Press, 1999.

[52] B. Guenter, T. Knoblock, and E. Ruf. "Specializing Shaders." In *Proceedings of SIGGRAPH 95, Computer Graphics Proceedings, Annual Conference Series*, edited by Robert Cook, pp. 343–350, Reading, MA: Addison Wesley, 1995.

[53] P. Haeberli. "ConMan: A Visual Programming Language for Interactive Graphics." *Computer Graphics (Proc. SIGGRAPH)*, 22(4): 103–111, 1988.

[54] Pat Hanrahan and Jim Lawson. "A Language for Shading and Lighting Calculations." *Computer Graphics (Proc. SIGGRAPH)*, 24(4): 289–298, 1990.

[55] Chandlee B. Harrell and Farhad Fouladi. "Graphics Rendering Architecture for High Performance Desktop Workstation." In *Proceedings of SIGGRAPH 93, Computer Graphics Proceedings, Annual Conference Series*, edited by James T. Kajiya, pp. 93–100, New York: ACM Press, 1993.

[56] John C. Hart, Nate Carr, Masaki Kameya, Stephen A. Tibbitts, and Terrance J. Coleman. "Antialiased Parameterized Solid Texturing Simplified for Consumer-Level Hardware Implementation." In *SIGGRAPH/Eurographics Workshop on Graphics Hardware*, pp. 45–53, New York: ACM Press, 1999.

[57] H. Hedelman. "A Data Flow Approach to Procedural Modeling." *IEEE CG&A*, 3(1): 16–26, 1984.

[58] Wolfgang Heidrich. "High-Quality Shading and Lighting for Hardware-Accelerated Rendering." PhD thesis, Universität Erlangen-Nürnberg, 1999.

[59] Wolfgang Heidrich and Hans-Peter Seidel. "View-Independent Environment Maps." In *Eurographics/SIGGRAPH Workshop on Graphics Hardware*, pp. 39–45, New York: ACM Press, 1998.

[60] Wolfgang Heidrich and Hans-Peter Seidel. Realistic, Hardware-Accelerated Shading and Lighting." In *Proceedings of SIGGRAPH 99, Computer Graphics Proceedings, Annual Conference Series*, edited by Alyn Rockwood, pp. 171–178, Reading, MA: Addison Wesley Longman, 1999.

[61] J. Herrington. *Code Generation in Action*. Greenwich, CT: Manning Publications, 2003.

[62] Karl E. Hillesland, Sergey Molinov, and Radek Grzeszczuk. "Nonlinear Optimization Framework for Image-Based Modeling on Programmable Graphics Hardware." *ACM Trans. on Graphics*, 22(3): 925–934, 2003.

[63] Kenneth Hoff, John Keyser, Ming Lin, Dinesh Manocha, and Tim Culver. "Fast Computation of Generalized Voronoi Diagrams using Graphics Hardware." In *Proceedings of SIGGRAPH 99, Computer Graphics Proceedings, Annual Conference Series*, edited by Alyn Rockwood, pp. 277–286, Reading, MA: Addison Wesley Longman, 1999.

[64] D. Ingalls et al. "Fabrik: A Visual Programming Environment." In *Proc. OOPSLA*, pp. 176–190, New York: ACM Press, 1988.

[65] Ujval Kapasi, William J. Dally, Scott Rixner, John D. Owens, and B. Khailany. "The Imagine Stream Processor." In *Proc. Intl. Conf. Computer Design*, pp. 282–288, Los Alamitos, IEEE Computer Soc., 2002.

[66] Ujval J. Kapasi, William J. Dally, Scott Rixner, Peter R. Mattson, John D. Owens, and Brucek Khailany. "Efficient Conditional Operations for Data-Parallel Architectures." In *Proc. IEEE/ACM Symposium on Microarchitecture*, pp. 159–170, New York: ACM Press, 2000.

[67] Michael Kass. "CONDOR: Constraint-Based Dataflow." *Computer Graphics (Proc. SIGGRAPH)*, 26(2): 321–330, 1992.

[68] Jan Kautz and Michael D. McCool. "Approximation of Glossy Reflection with Prefiltered Environment Maps." In *Proc. Graphics Interface*, pp. 119–126, Wellesley, MA: A K Peters, Ltd., 2000.

[69] Jan Kautz, Pere-Pau Vázquez, Wolfgang Heidrich, and Hans-Peter Seidel. "Unified Approach to Prefiltered Environment Maps." In *Rendering Techniques (Proc. Eurographics Workshop on Rendering)*, pp. 185–196, Berlin: Springer, 2000.

[70] Brian W. Kernighan. "Pic – A Language for Typesetting Graphics." *Software – Pract. and Exper. (GB)*, 12: 1–21, 1982.

[71] John Kessenich, Dave Baldwin, and Randi Rost. *OpenGL 2.0 Shading Language*, 1.051 edition, February 2003. Available at www.opengl.org.

[72] Brucek Khailany, William J. Dally, Scott Rixner, Ujval Kapasi, Peter Mattson, J. Namkoong, and John D. Owens. "Imagine: Media Processing with Streams." *IEEE Micro*, 21: 35–46, 2001.

[73] David Kirk and Douglas Voorhies. "The Rendering Architecture of the DN10000VS." *Computer Graphics (Proc. SIGGRAPH)*, 24(4): 299–308, 1990.

[74] Jens Krüger and Rüdiger Westermann. "Linear Algebra Operators for GPU Implementation of Numerical Algorithms." *ACM Trans. on Graphics (Proc. SIGGRAPH)*, 22(3): 908–916, 2003.

[75] E. Lafortune, S.-C. Foo, K. Torrance, and D. Greenberg. "Non-Linear Approximation of Reflectance Functions." In *Proceedings of SIGGRAPH 97, Computer Graphics Proceedings, Annual Conference Series*, edited by Turner Whitted, pp. 117–126, Reading, MA: Addison Wesley, 1997.

[76] E. Lafortune and Y. Willems. "Using the Modified Phong Reflectance Model for Physically Based Rendering." Technical Report CW197, Department of Computer Science, K.U. Leuven, 1994.

[77] Anselmo Lastra, Steven Molnar, Marc Olano, and Yulan Wang. "Real-Time Programmable Shading." In *Symposium on Interactive 3D Graphics*, pp. 59–66, New York: ACM SIGGRAPH, 1995.

[78] Peter Lee and Mark Leone. "Optimizing ML with Run-Time Code Generation." In *SIGPLAN Conference on Programming Language Design and Implementation*, pp. 137–148, New York: ACM Press, 1996.

[79] Jon Leech. "OpenGL Extensions and Restrictions for PixelFlow." Technical Report TR98-019, Department of Computer Science, University of North Carolina, 1998.

[80] John R. Levine, Tony Mason, and Doug Brown. *lex & yacc*, Second edition, Sebastopol, CA : O'Reilly & Associates, 1992.

[81] Erik Lindholm, Mark J. Kilgard, and Henry Moreton. "A User-Programmable Vertex Engine." In *Proceedings of SIGGRAPH 2001, Computer Graphics Proceedings, Annual Conference Series,* edited by E. Fiume, pp. 149–158, Reading, MA: Addison-Wesley, 2001.

[82] Vincent Ma and Michael McCool. "Low Latency Photon Mapping using Block Hashing." In *Proc. Graphics Hardware,* pp. 89–98, New York: ACM Press, 2002.

[83] William R. Mark, R. Steven Glanville, Kurt Akeley, and Mark J. Kilgard. "Cg: A System for Programming Graphics Hardware in a C-Like Language." *ACM Trans. on Graphics (Proc. SIGGRAPH),* 22(3): 896–907, 2003.

[84] William R. Mark and Kekoa Proudfoot. "Compiling to a VLIW Fragment Pipeline." In *Graphics Hardware 2001,* pp. 47–56, New York: ACM Press, 2001.

[85] William R. Mark and Kekoa Proudfoot. "The F-Buffer, A Rasterization-Order FIFO Buffer for Multi-Pass Rendering." In *Graphics Hardware 2001,* pp. 57–64, New York: ACM Press, 2001.

[86] Peter Mattson. "A Programming System for the Imagine Media Processor." PhD thesis, Stanford University, 2002.

[87] Michael McCool. "SMASH: A Next-Generation API for Programmable Graphics Accelerators." Technical Report CS-2000-14, University of Waterloo, April 2001. API Version 0.2. Presented at SIGGRAPH 2001 Course #25, *Real-Time Shading.*

[88] Michael McCool, Jason Ang, and Anis Ahmad. "Homomorphic Factorization of BRDFs for High-Performance Rendering." *ACM Trans. on Graphics (Proc. SIGGRAPH),* 22(3) : 171–178, 2001.

[89] Michael McCool and Wolfgang Heidrich. "Texture Shaders." In *Proc. Graphics Hardware,* pp. 117–126, New York: ACM Press, 1999.

[90] Michael McCool, Zheng Qin, and Tiberiu Popa. "Shader Metaprogramming." In *Proc. Graphics Hardware,* pp. 57–68, Aire-la-Ville, Switzerland: Eurographics Assoc., 2002.

[91] Michael McCool, Stefanus Du Toit, Tiberiu Popa, Bryan Chan, and Kevin Moule. "Shader Algebra." *ACM Trans. on Graphics (Proc. SIGGRAPH),* 23(3): 2004.

[92] T. McReynolds, D. Blythe, B. Grantham, and S. Nelson. "Advanced Graphics Programming Techniques using OpenGL." In *SIGGRAPH Course Notes,* New York: ACM Press, 1998.

[93] Microsoft. *DirectX Graphics Programmers Guide.* Microsoft Developers Network Library, Directx 8.1 edition, 2001.

[94] Microsoft. *DX9,* 2001. Microsoft Meltdown 2001 presentation. Available from http://www.microsoft.com/mscorp/corpevents/meltdown2001/ppt/-DXG9.ppt.

[95] Don P. Mitchell. "Robust Ray Intersection with Interval Arithmetic." In *Proc. Graphics Interface*, pp. 68–74, Wellesley, MA: A K Peters, Ltd., 1990.

[96] S. Molnar, J. Eyles, and J. Poulton. "PixelFlow: High-Speed Rendering using Image Composition." *Computer Graphics (Proc. SIGGRAPH)*, 26(2): 231–240, 1992.

[97] Steven Molnar. "Image-Composition Architectures for Real-Time Image Generation." PhD thesis, University of North Carolina, Chapel Hill, 1991.

[98] R. Morgan. *Building an Optimizing Compiler*. Burlington, MA: Digital Press, 1998.

[99] Steven S. Muchnick. *Advanced Compiler Design and Implementation*. San Francisco, Morgan Kaufmann, 2000.

[100] Tom Nadas and Alain Fournier. "GRAPE: An Environment to Build Display Processes." *Computer Graphics (Proc. SIGGRAPH)*, 21(4): 75–84, 1987.

[101] Martin Newell. "The Utilization of Procedural Models in Digital Image Synthesis." PhD thesis, University of Utah, 1975.

[102] NVIDIA. *NVIDIA OpenGL Extensions Specifications*, March 2001.

[103] Marc Olano. "A Programmable Pipeline for Graphics Hardware." PhD thesis, University of North Carolina at Chapel Hill, 1999.

[104] Marc Olano, John C. Hart, Wolfgang Heidrich, and Michael McCool. *Real-Time Shading*. Wellesley, MA: A K Peters, Ltd., 2002.

[105] Marc Olano and Anselmo Lastra. "A Shading Language on Graphics Hardware: The PixelFlow Shading System." In *Proceedings of SIGGRAPH 98, Computer Graphics Proceedings, Annual Conference Series*, edited by Michael Cohen, pp. 159–168, Reading, MA: Addison Wesley, 1998.

[106] Barrett O'Neill. *Elementary Differential Geometry*. San Diego, CA: Academic Press, 1966.

[107] John D. Owens. "Computer Graphics on a Stream Architecture." PhD thesis, Stanford University, 2002.

[108] John D. Owens, William J. Dally, Ujval J. Kapasi, Scott Rixner, Peter Mattson, and Ben Mowery. "Polygon Rendering on a Stream Architecture." In *Proc. Eurographics/SIGGRAPH Workshop on Graphics Hardware*, pp. 23–32, New York: ACM Press, 2000.

[109] John D. Owens, Brucek Khailany, Brian Towles, and William J. Dally. "Comparing Reyes and OpenGL on a Stream Architecture." In *Proc. Graphics Hardware*, pp. 47–56, Aire-la-Ville, Switzerland: Eurographics Assoc., 2002.

[110] D. Peachey. "Solid Texturing of Complex Surfaces." *Computer Graphics (Proc. SIGGRAPH)*, 19(3): 279–286, 1985.

[111] Craig Peeper and Jason L. Mitchell. "Introduction to the Directx 9 High Level Shading Language." In *ShaderX²: Introductions and Tutorials with DirectX 9*, edited by Wolfgang F. Engel, pp. 1–61. Plpano, TX: Worldware Publishing, 2003.

[112] Mark S. Peercy, Marc Olano, John Airey, and P. Jeffrey Ungar. "Interactive Multi-Pass Programmable Shading." In *Proceedings of SIGGRAPH 2000, Computer Graphics Proceedings, Annual Conference Series*, edited by Kurt Akeley, pp. 425–432, Reading, MA: Addison-Wesley, 2000.

[113] Ken Perlin. "An Image Synthesizer." *Computer Graphics (Proc. SIGGRAPH)*, 19(3): 287–296, 1985.

[114] Ken Perlin. "Improving Noise." *ACM Trans. on Graphics (Proc. SIGGRAPH)*, 22(3): 681–682, 2002.

[115] Bui Tuong Phong. "Illumination for Computer Generated Pictures." *Comm. ACM*, 18(6): 311–317, 1975.

[116] Pixar. *The RenderMan Interface, Version 3.2*, July 2000.

[117] Massimiliano Poletto, Wilson C. Hsieh, Dawson R. Engler, and M. Frans Kaashoek. "'C and tcc: A Language and Compiler for Dynamic Code Generation." *ACM Trans. on Programming Languages and Systems*, 21(2): 324–369, 1999.

[118] Michael Potmesil and Eric M. Hoffert. "FRAMES: Software Tools for Modeling, Rendering and Animation of 3D Scenes." *Computer Graphics (Proc. SIGGRAPH)*, 21(4): 85–93, 1987.

[119] Michael Potmesil and Eric M. Hoffert. "The Pixel Machine: A Parallel Image Computer." *Computer Graphics (Proc. SIGGRAPH)*, 23(3): 69–78, 1989.

[120] K. Proudfoot, W. R. Mark, P. Hanrahan, and S. Tzvetkov. "A Real-Time Procedural Shading System for Programmable Graphics Hardware." In *Proceedings of SIGGRAPH 2001, Computer Graphics Proceedings, Annual Conference Series*, edited by E. Fiume, pp. 159–170, Reading, MA: Addison-Wesley, 2001. .

[121] Timothy Purcell, Craig Donner, Mike Cammarano, Henrik Wann Jensen, and Pat Hanrahan. "Photon Mapping on Programmable Graphics Hardware." In *Proc. Graphics Hardware*, pp. 41–50, 132, Aire-la-Ville, Switzerland: Eurographics Assoc., 2003.

[122] Zheng Qin. "An Embedded Shading Language." Master's thesis, School of Computer Science, 2003.

[123] William T. Reeves. "Particle systems – A Technique for Modeling a Class of Fuzzy Objects." *ACM Trans. on Graphics*, 2(2): 91–108, 1983.

[124] William T. Reeves and Ricki Blau. "Approximate and Probabilistic Algorithms for Shading and Rendering Structured Particle Systems." *Computer Graphics (Proc. SIGGRAPH)*, 19(3): 313–322, 1985.

[125] Craig W. Reynolds. "Flocks, Herds, and Schools: A Distributed Behavioural Model." *Computer Graphics (Proc. SIGGRAPH)*, 21(4): 25–34, 1987.

[126] John Rhoades, Greg Turk, Andrew Bell, Andrei State, Ulrich Neumann, and Amitabh Varshney. "Real-Time Procedural Textures." In *ACM Symposium on Interactive 3D Graphics*, pp. 95–100, New York: ACM Press, 1992.

[127] Scott Rixner. *Stream Processor Architecture*. Norwell, MA: Kluwer Academic, 2001.

[128] Randi J. Rost. *OpenGL Shading Language*. Reading, MA: Addison-Wesley, 2004.

[129] Andreas Schilling, Günter Knittel, and Wolfgang Straßer. "Texram: A Smart Memory for Texturing." *IEEE CG&A*, 16(3): 32–41, 1996.

[130] C. Schlick. "A Customizable Reflectance Model for Everyday Rendering." In *Eurographics Workshop on Rendering*, pp. 73–84, Aire-la-Ville, Switzerland: Eurographics Assoc., 1993.

[131] Marc Segal, Carl Korobkin, Rolf van Widenfelt, Jim Foran, and Paul Haeberli. "Fast Shadow and Lighting Effects using Texture Mapping." *Computer Graphics (Proc. SIGGRAPH)*, 26(2): 249–252, 1992.

[132] Mark Segal and Kurt Akeley. *The OpenGL Graphics System: A Specification (Version 1.2.1)*, 1999.

[133] Mark Segal and Kurt Akeley. *The OpenGL Graphics System: A Specification (Version 1.5)*, 2003.

[134] Peter Shirley and R. Keith Morley. *Realistic Ray Tracing*, Second edition, Wellesley, NA: A K Peters, Ltd., 2003.

[135] Dave Shreiner, Mason Woo, Jackie Neider, and Tom Davis. *OpenGL Programming Guide, Fourth Edition, The Official Guide to Learning OpenGL, Version 1.4*. Reading, MA: Addison Wesley, 2003.

[136] D. Sima, T. Fountain, and P. Kacsuk. *Advanced Computer Architectures: A Design Space Approach*. Reading, MA: Addison-Wesley, 1997.

[137] Karl Sims. "Particle Animation and Rendering using Data Parallel Computation." *Computer Graphics (Proc. SIGGRAPH)*, 24(4): 405–413, 1990.

[138] P. Slusallek, M. Stamminger, W. Heidrich, J.-C. Popp, and H.-P. Seidel. "Composite Lighting Simulations with Lighting Networks." *IEEE CG&A*, 18(2): 22–31, 1998.

[139] John M. Snyder. "Interval Analysis for Computer Graphics." *Computer Graphics (Proc. SIGGRAPH)*, 26(2): 121–130, 1992.

[140] John M. Snyder and James T. Kajiya. "Generative Modeling: A Symbolic System for Geometric Modeling." *Computer Graphics (Proc. SIGGRAPH)*, 26(2): 369–378, 1992.

[141] D. Terzopoulos, J. Platt, and K. Fleischer. "From Gloop to Glop: Heating and Melting Deformable Objects." In *Proc. Graphics Interface*, pp. 219–226, Wellesley, MA: A K Peters, LTD., 1989.

[142] John G. Torborg. "A Parallel Processor Architecture for Graphics Arithmetic Operations." *Computer Graphics (Proc. SIGGRAPH)*, 21(4): 197–204, 1987.

[143] Chris Trendall and A. James Stewart. "General Calculations using Graphics Hardware, with Applications to Interactive Caustics." In *Rendering Techniques '00 (Proc. Eurographics Workshop on Rendering)*, pp. 287–298, Berlin: Springer, 2000.

[144] B. Trumbore, W. Lytle, and Donald P. Greenberg. "A Testbed for Image Synthesis." In *Proc. Eurographics*, pp. 467–480, Berlin: Springer, 1991.

[145] Ben Trumbore, Wayne Lyttle, and Donald P. Greenberg. "A Testbed for Image Synthesis." In *Developing Large-scale Graphics Software Toolkits*, SIGGRAPH Course Notes, New York: ACM Press, 1993.

[146] Dean M. Tullsen, Susan J. Eggers, , and Henry M. Levy. "Simultaneous Multithreading: Maximizing On-Chip Parallelism. In *Proc. Symposium on Computer Architecture*, pp. 392–403, New York: ACM Press, 1995.

[147] Steve Upstill. *The RenderMan Companion: A Programmer's Guide to Realistic Computer Graphics*. Reading, MA: Addison-Wesley, 1990.

[148] Todd L. Veldhuizen. "C++ Templates as Partial Evaluation." In *ACM SIGPLAN Workshop on Partial Evaluation and Semantics-Based Program Manipulation*, pp. 13–18, New York: ACM Press, 1999.

[149] Mark N. Wegman and F. Kenneth Zadeck. "Constant Propagation with Conditional Branches." *ACM Trans. Program. Lang. Syst.*, 13(2): 181–210, 1991.

[150] T. Whitted and D. M. Weimer. "A Software Testbed for the Development of 3D Raster Graphics Systems." *ACM Trans. on Graphics*, 1(1): 43–57, 1982.

[151] Steven Worley. "A Cellular Texture Basis Function." In *Proceedings of SIGGRAPH 96, Computer Graphics Proceedings, Annual Conference Series*, edited by Holly Rushmeier, pp. 291–294, Reading, MA: Addison Wesley, 1996.

[152] Geoff Wyvill and Tosiyasu L. Kunii. "A Functional Model for Constructive Solid Geometry." *The Visual Computer*, 1(1): 3–14, 1985.

Index

Printed and bound by CPI Group (UK) Ltd, Croydon, CR0 4YY

22/10/2024

01777636-0008